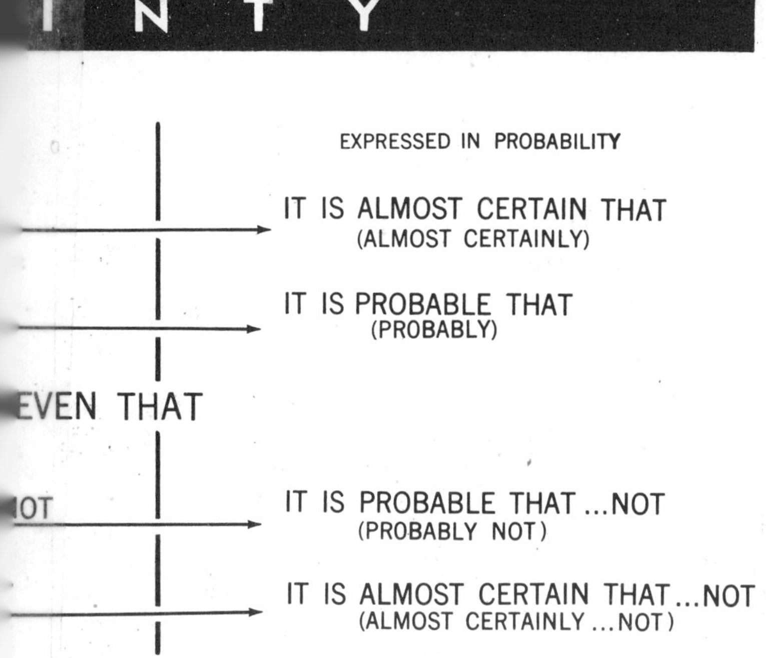
I N T Y
EXPRESSED IN PROBABILITY
IT IS ALMOST CERTAIN THAT
(ALMOST CERTAINLY)
IT IS PROBABLE THAT
(PROBABLY)
EVEN THAT
OT
IT IS PROBABLE THAT ...NOT
(PROBABLY NOT)
IT IS ALMOST CERTAIN THAT...NOT
(ALMOST CERTAINLY ...NOT)

B I L I T Y

STRATEGIC INTELLIGENCE PRODUCTION

STRATEGIC INTELLIGENCE PRODUCTION

BASIC PRINCIPLES

by

Washington Platt

Brigadier General USAR, (Ret.)

FREDERICK A. PRAEGER, Publishers

New York 22, N. Y.

Published in the United States of America in 1957 by
Frederick A. Praeger, Inc., 150 East 52 Street, New York 22.

Library of Congress Catalog Number 57-7073

Manufactured in the United States of America

DEDICATION

To those Intelligence Officers who are inspired with curiosity as to Principles and Methods:

TO SUCH MY ERRAND IS,
YET SOM THERE BE . . .

"Yet som there be that by due steps aspire
to lay their just hands on that Golden Key
That can unlock Uncertaintye:
To such my errand is, and but for such,
Found but too rarely in Intelligence,
I would not soil these pure Ambrosial weeds
With the rank vapours of this Sin-worn mould."

JOHN MILTON
(as revised by W.P.)

ACKNOWLEDGMENTS

Grateful acknowledgment is made to Dr. Dorothy Libby, who supplied most of the basic material and bibliography on National Character, and contributed many valuable suggestions; and to Dr. Churchill Eisenhart, who made helpful contributions to the preparation of the chapters on Probability, Certainty and Forecasting. Many other kind friends made useful suggestions based upon their long experience in intelligence production. No one but the present author is responsible for the final wording, statements or conclusions.

For Strategic Intelligence and the general field of intelligence production all workers, including certainly the present author, draw heavily on Kent's *Strategic Intelligence for American World Policy,* Princeton, 1949, which is a tower of strength.

Grateful acknowledgment is extended to the following for kind permission to quote from their publications as indicated in the Bibliography: Addison-Wesley Publishing Co.; American Association for the Advancement of Science; American Political Science Association; Appleton-Century-Crofts, Inc.; Cambridge University Press; Journal of Chemical Education; Columbia University Press; Creative Training Associates; André Deutsch, Ltd.; E. P. Dutton and Co.; General Motors Corp.; Harper and Bros.; Houghton Mifflin Co.; Association of the United States Army; Johns Hopkins Magazine; Alfred A. Knopf, Inc.; Longmans, Green & Co.; Macmillan Co.; McGraw-Hill Book Co.; Military Service Publishing Co.; New York Times; W. W. Norton and Co.; Penguin Books, Inc.; Princeton University Press; Henry Regnery Co.; Rutgers University Press; Charles Scribner's Sons; Journal of Social Psychology; Unicorn Publishers, Inc.; John Wiley and Sons.

CONTENTS

Page

PREFACE

IMPORTANCE OF STRATEGIC INTELLIGENCE

Of all the problems facing the civilized world today, certainly the most important is the prevention of a major war.

In the past, intelligence has been one of the key factors in the winning of wars. Under present conditions, however, the newly organized Strategic Intelligence is called upon to provide assistance in avoiding wars. With the enlarged responsibilities upon the United States for providing leadership in the post-war world, the preventive aspects of Strategic Intelligence have risen even higher. As Kent has well said, "Strategic Intelligence is the knowledge upon which our nation's foreign relations, in war and peace, must rest."

The intelligence worker, therefore, has the satisfaction of knowing that he has a part in what is literally one of the most important activities in the world.

If the intelligence worker has developed himself to the point where he brings to his work the touch of professional competence, he has the further satisfaction of knowing that he is one of relatively few, and that his services are greatly needed.

The Time Has Now Come!

The use of combat intelligence is as old as organized human combat. The production of Strategic Intelligence, however, on a comprehensive scale, and on a systematic basis in peace and war, extends back no farther than World War II.

That war and its turbulent aftermath required the immediate and constant production of high-grade Strategic Intelligence. Time was not then available for the development of a common doctrine, for the establishment of a sound intelligence organization, for training, and the improvement of methods. As a result we find in the Intelligence Community the same lack of any commonly accepted first principles, and the same misunderstandings that are usually found in any new organization carrying out activities without established precedents.

The time has now come to pause and take stock of the situation. The present book is intended as one step towards the development of first principles in the field of Strategic Intelligence Production. It was written as a result of nearly ten years' active experience in strategic and combat intelligence.

The book should be useful in conveying information about intelligence principles and the methods derived from them. Part of its value will probably consist in stimulating critical thought and fruitful discussion. The present author can say with Vannevar Bush, "Everything I say would be contested in some quarters." So great is the lack of a common doctrine of Strategic Intelligence.

Concentration on Fundamentals

In attempting to present a subject as new as Strategic Intelligence Production, it has seemed distinctly helpful to concentrate attention on some of the fundamentals. For this reason, in many chapters a few important points have been made to stand out boldly. We, thereby, follow the method already used with success in military science and in some of the related social sciences.

In this book, for example, we focus attention on: The Nine Principles of Intelligence, The Major Steps in the Scientific Method, The Four Stages in Creative Thinking, the Five Fundamental Factors in Forecasting, etc. In the present state of the art of Strategic Intelligence, we believe that this concentration on a few fundamentals may be helpful in intelligence training and production, and may be one step towards the development of an accepted basic doctrine.

Useful to Intelligence Officers, Social Scientists, and Executives

This book is intended primarily for the intelligence production officer and those who deal with him, including supervisors, editors and consultants.

The body of the present book points out how much intelligence production has to learn from the social sciences. On the other hand, social scientists could perhaps learn something in their turn from the point of view and methods of the humble intelligence worker as is set forth in these pages.

Business management may also find of interest some of the pioneering achievements of workers in Strategic Intelligence. Business executives and intelligence workers both have the problems of estimating what other human beings can and will do. Both face the necessity for "drawing important conclusions from inadequate premises" or information; in other words, for attacking the fundamental problem of intelligence production. The American businessman, who has already shown a genius for picking up ideas from psychology, engineering, economics and other disciplines when they will serve his purpose, will find here many problems similar to his own, together with some novel and helpful methods of solution.

PART I

Purpose and approach

One

INTRODUCTION

Scope : Purpose : Plan for Accomplishment
Strategic and Other Intelligence : Intelligence Production
Arkadia and Curtania : About Related Reading

SCOPE

The field of intelligence is vast and complex. It is certainly true that almost every branch of knowledge is to some degree pertinent directly or indirectly. All parts of the globe and all periods of history have some bearing. To make matters worse, little has been written on the principles of intelligence production. Where should one begin and where should one end?

Intelligence activities may be divided for convenience into field collection (overt and covert), production, and dissemination. Supporting these is administration and a wide variety of specialist techniques, such as photo interpretation, prisoner of war interrogation, etc.

Intelligence production on a given subject includes selecting and getting together the facts bearing on the problem (but not the field collection per se), their evaluation, selection and interpretation, then presenting them clearly and meaningfully as finished intelligence either oral or written. The reader will receive a broader understanding of intelligence production as the book proceeds.

This book is confined to a discussion of the principles of

Strategic Intelligence Production together with examples and methods which illustrate and apply these principles.

Because Strategic Intelligence is such a new field, staffs have been newly organized. Strategic Intelligence officers present a wide range of age, education, talents, and experience. The average of ability and dedication is high, but there is no uniformity in background, or doctrine, or methods. This wide variation in the points of view of intelligence workers adds to the difficulties of making contributions to the field.

The Table of Contents has purposely been prepared in considerable detail to show the prospective reader what to expect and where to find that part on which he seeks light. In such a new and unstandardized subject as Strategic Intelligence the reader will find it helpful to keep the outline constantly before him. The book assumes that the reader has curiosity regarding new ideas and a desire for progress, even at the expense of considerable mental effort.

PURPOSE

There is naturally very little general public understanding of intelligence activities. Persons considering intelligence as a career and those who have entered upon such a career, or who act as consultants, usually do so with only a limited knowledge of the intelligence point of view and of the principles of intelligence production. The purpose of this book is:

Primarily to present concepts pertaining to Strategic Intelligence Production which will be helpful to workers in this field. The emphasis is on the working level; namely, direct assistance to the analyst, research worker, author, or intelligence officer, as he may variously be called.

Second and indirectly, to assist those who supervise the analyst, or who work with him, such as editors and consultants.

Third, partly as a by-product of the above, to make a beginning towards the formulation of a basic doctrine for intelligence production and towards a common intelligence point of view.

More specifically the author hopes to assist intelligence officers in three ways:

First, *To point out solutions* to some intelligence problems when these solutions are already available from disciplines other than intelligence proper.

The intelligence officer has many problems involving first principles, meanings and methods which are new. But closely similar problems have often been solved by students of psychology, or the social sciences. Existing solutions and means for their applications to intelligence are therefore pointed out.

Second, *To point out promising intelligence tools.* We develop the intelligence applications of several methods, well known in military science and in the social sciences, but new to intelligence. We cannot afford to discard any that may help us.

The intelligence officer must accomplish much with limited facilities. The number of tested methods, concepts, tools at his disposal which have been developed specifically for his use by experience or research are few. It is essential that he should make full use of helpful concepts. As examples in intelligence production: What use should be made of probabilities? Or should we stick to near-certainties? Is there a place for "mere" opinion in an estimate? Is there such a thing as a national character, which can be used as a factor in an intelligence estimate much as a knowledge of personal character is used? Does history repeat itself? What are the tools for construction of a reliable forecast?

It is surprising how many valuable tools can be found.

Third, *To avoid common pitfalls.*

Unwarranted assumptions, untested methods and glib

statements, often lead to persuasive papers of doubtful reliability. Statements without clauses showing our degree of certainty often mislead the reader. Reasoning by analogy, for example, is easy, helpful and also dangerous.

However, we need not refuse to take full advantage of valuable terrain just because it contains pitfalls, if we know how to avoid them.

PLAN FOR ACCOMPLISHMENT

About Intelligence for Intelligence Workers

The plan for helping the worker in intelligence production assumes that such a worker comes to his intelligence career with a good foundation in some of the natural or social sciences; on in area, language or other pertinent specialties which he now expects to apply to intelligence. Specialties may include such diverse subjects as economics, meteorology, military science, or geographic area studies, for instance.

The book does not deal directly with these special fields. It deals only with activities which take on a special importance when applied to intelligence production, or which take on special modifications when used by an intelligence production officer.

Each idea here presented can be usefully pursued far beyond the limitations of the present volume. The text, therefore, presents many open doors through which the reader may glimpse interesting terrain that lies ready for intelligence exploitation. This book not only points to the open doors, but also may even guide him somewhat after he steps through them, by showing the intelligence applications of much that he will find in other fields of learning.

A Bird's-Eye View of the Field to be Explored

In the book as a whole the method of covering such an

undeveloped field as Strategic Intelligence Production is purposely discursive and unconventional.

In a field of this kind where there has been so little unity of background, or systematic development of basic principles, the discursiveness—this consideration of the same point from several different approaches—is necessary. In intelligence production—namely, getting the most useful meaning out of the facts available—understanding, judgment and perspective are essential for success. Perspective in intellectual processes, just like perspective in physical vision, requires the stereoscopic effect, i.e., the same object seen from more than one point of view. The author is convinced that this study of a principle from several angles is worthwhile even at the expense of occasional repetition and the sacrifice of conciseness.

Many of the answers are in the interesting "grey area," rather than all black or all white.[1] We do not dodge controversial questions, nor stick to "school solutions."

The book is divided into three parts.

In Part I we present a background of the whole field of intelligence. We recognize intelligence as one of the social sciences. After some definitions, we come to a discussion of the Basic Principles of Intelligence Production.

We find that the intelligence officer must have a point of view different from other human beings in his attitude toward *completeness, timeliness, pride of authorship* and other matters dear to the heart of the scholar. This part ends with the Nine Principles of Intelligence.

In Part II we examine "Intelligence Production as an Intellectual Process." We find that many methods useful in mathemetics, logic, the social sciences and the writing of history can be applied to intelligence production.

We help the intelligence worker to use many powerful tools derived from the scientific method, the requirements

[1] Trevelyan makes the interesting comment regarding history: "The truth is not grey, it is black and white in patches."

for creative thinking, the social sciences, and the theory of probability. This is in accordance with our specific aim to start the worker on his journey well equipped with the best intellectual tools available.

In Part III we look at the Characteristics of the Intelligence Profession in comparison with other learned professions. This has a practical purpose. We point out present shortcomings of the intelligence profession and suggest steps which each worker can take to improve himself professionally.

STRATEGIC AND OTHER INTELLIGENCE

Definition of Intelligence

Intelligence is a meaningful statement derived from information which has been selected, evaluated, interpreted, and finally expressed so that its significance to a current national policy problem is clear.

This definition brings out the distinction between raw information and finished intelligence, which distinction is a matter of so much professional pride in the Intelligence Community.

We are here concerned only with foreign intelligence, including intelligence of our foreign friends as well as that of our potential enemies.

Components of Strategic Intelligence

Strategic Intelligence is knowledge pertaining to the capabilities, vulnerabilities and probable courses of action of foreign nations. In the United States, it is directly or indirectly for the use of the National Security Council and other policy forming agencies of the Federal Government. It is intended principally for guiding the formulation and execution of national security measures in time of peace, and the conduct of military operations in time of war and for the development of strategic planning of the post war period.

It is always surprising to find how many aspects of foreign countries may affect our national interests directly or indirectly. Strategic Intelligence is usually considered to include eight or ten components. Each of these components is founded on one or more of the social or natural sciences. These components are given below arranged in the order of decreasing importance of natural science, and of increasing importance of human influence in the make-up of each of the components.

Components of Strategic Intelligence:

1. Scientific intelligence, including the natural sciences and health, scientific manpower, scientific capabilities to support industry, and to support scientific research and development (Scientific includes engineering.);
2. Geography, including weather, climate and oceanography;
3. Transportation, roads, telecommunications;
4. Economic intelligence including industry, finance, employment;
5. Military intelligence (excluding combat intelligence);
6. Sociological intelligence, including population, religion, education, national traditions, spirit of the people;
7. Political intelligence, including governments, political parties, foreign policy;
8. Biographical intelligence.

A Motto for Strategic Intelligence

"Total War" has made necessary "Total Intelligence" or in other words "Strategic Intelligence."

To sum up the wide-spread nature of Strategic Intelligence we can build onto the well-known motto from Terence: "Homo sum, humani nihil a me alienum puto," which may be translated: "I am a man: Nothing pertaining to human beings is outside of my interests." This may now be paraphrased: "I am a Strategic Intelligence man: Nothing pertaining to foreign human activities is outside of my interests."

To keep such a wide-spread and interesting field within useful and manageable limits much self-restraint, judgment, and concentration on critical problems is evidently necessary. In fact one of the great problems of Strategic Intelligence research is *to know where to stop* in carrying our studies backward in time or outward towards the periphery of our interests.

Combat Intelligence

Most of the general principles of intelligence production apply to combat intelligence as well as to Strategic Intelligence. We are not here concerned with considerations which pertain primarily to combat intelligence. Compared with Strategic Intelligence the point of view and problems of combat intelligence are delightfully simple. (Although to say they are simple, does not imply that they are easy.)

The Warp and the Woof

In any branch of Strategic Intelligence—economic intelligence, for example—the final intelligence is made up of sound economic methods (the warp) put together with sound intelligence methods (the woof). The combination yields a strong fabric of reliable economic intelligence The point is that the techniques of the economist must be interwoven with the skills of the professional intelligence officer for best results. There is a promising future for new combinations, weaving together the proven techniques of a social science with the techniques now developing in Strategic Intelligence to achieve an improvement in the present product.

INTELLIGENCE PRODUCTION

This book is concerned with intelligence *production.* It will now be well to discuss the meaning of this term. Perhaps it is easiest to start by stating what the term does *not* include.

First, it does *not* include that large, highly important and difficult activity known as field collection, whether overt or covert. This activity already has a voluminous and glamorous literature of its own pertaining to spies, covert operations, interviewing and such.

Intelligence production does *not* include the important activities connected with the procurement, indexing, translation, and distribution of books and documents—all that highly technical and useful activity connected with library science, punch cards, translations, and such.

It does *not* include cryptography or certain intelligence specialist techniques such as photo interpretation, prisoner of war interrogation. It does *not* include organization, supervision or administration of intelligence groups.

Intelligence production *does* include those activities which an analyst or intelligence officer himself carries out when he is directed to produce an intelligence paper on a certain subject. In short it includes the process by which a mass of raw information is transformed into finished intelligence for use at action or policy levels. It *does* include those activities connected with the planning, supervision, editing and coordination of intelligence production activities.

Intelligence Production in Action—An Example

General principles are usually neither clear nor useful unless considered in connection with some specific application.

The following simple example will make plain some of the fundamental procedures and problems of the worker in intelligence production to which the general principles discussed in the book may be applied.

Suppose you as an "analyst" in intelligence production are told to prepare a paper on the present status of meteorology in China. You are given terms of reference and a deadline. You are told the kind of paper it will be. You will naturally follow the general format of similar papers unless there is some good reason to the contrary.

It is fair to assume that you are already a meteorologist. You have probably written other intelligence papers on meteorology, so that you also have experience in meteorological intelligence.

Considering here only the high spots, what do you do?

First of all, you would certainly look the whole situation over in the broadest way. In any meteorological study what are the important factors to look for? What are the latest developments in meteorology which the Chinese may or may not have the knowledge of? Who has been there?

So you look the whole field over in a preliminary way to decide on a plan of action and *where* you will hunt for the information.

You review the deadline and terms of reference. If important changes are necessary, the analyst or his supervisor can often effect these changes if recommendations are made promptly.

You might well divide the project into parts. Then, taking one part at a time, you would go after information pertaining to that part; write the draft of the paper on that part, then go after the information for the next part. Or you might plan to get all the information at one time. Then sort it and do all the writing at one time.

You make a preliminary estimate of the time necessary to cover each part of the paper, with a liberal estimate for unexpected contingencies.

At this point estimates of information available, time, etc., are all preliminary. Adjustments will be made as work on the project develops.

A well balanced preliminary outline made at the very beginning to cover the high spots of your own activities, as the worker to carry out this project, is of the utmost practical value.

Your own judgment is best as to how long it will take *you* to carry out each of the steps in production. You should always be on the look-out for the limits that you can set to your studies on this project.

Nearly every project could logically be extended into a lifetime study if you consider everything that bears on it directly or indirectly. There is a temptation to wander too far afield. This temptation is greatest with those whose interest and knowledge pertaining to the subject is most comprehensive. In order to give adequate time to the key points, many interesting but non-essential side shows must be excluded at the very beginning. This is an important lesson which many analysts *never learn.*

Please note there are many advantages in an analyst's having a broad knowledge of his subject. In the present instance, you, as a meteorologist, should have acquired over past years and largely by professional reading on your own time, a broad view of meteorology and related sciences. As an intelligence officer you would probably have been collecting knowledge of Chinese intelligence, but *in the time allotted to this specific assignment,* you must limit yourself to the important points.

You next search your own files, the libraries and other sources by the usual methods for information, taking notes, evaluating the information obtained and classifying it as to subjects covered. This naturally leads to more search in some fields and less in others.

You now seek to evaluate and interpret the information before you, and to find its true significance as an indication of the status of Chinese meteorology. If the Chinese possess the latest improvements in weather forecasting, what would be the outward indications? Do these indications exist? Can they be found?

It is here that the real competence of a *meteorological intelligence officer* becomes evident as distinguished from a man who is a meteorologist, but has had no intelligence experience. It is here that high professional competence and *continuity of effort* in a given field of intelligence pay off. It is here that the worker in intelligence production can experience the thrills of high class professional accomplishment.

Finally you draw up your report, having the reader always in mind, striving to give him what he needs, in words that he can understand, making the outstanding points stand out, and properly labeling statements which are subject to considerable doubt.

Such is a general statement of the problems and procedures that are encountered in the production of intelligence, and which are discussed in more detail in this book.

Production Is the Pay-Off

In the United States, the Intelligence Community exists for the benefit of those in the Federal Government outside of the Intelligence Community who utilize intelligence as assistance in guiding action or forming policy. Examples of such customers are the Armed Forces, the State Department in formulating foreign policy, and the National Security Council at the top.

The means by which any part of the Intelligence Community makes its influence felt in action or policy is through intelligence production, oral or written. In the Intelligence Community, therefore, *production is the pay-off*. This is the "cash crop" which goes out to other agencies of the government, and which justifies the efforts expended by the intelligence organizations. No amount of information beautifully indexed and filed is of any value until the worker in intelligence production finds out the meaning of this mass of material, puts it together, and communicates it to other agencies in such a form that the significance is clear.

Some workers in intelligence production are by nature accumulators. They take great pride in accumulating great masses of pertinent information on their subject. This is good; but they are not production-minded, which is a serious shortcoming.

The intelligence producer stands in a key position, requiring long experience and deep understanding of many factors. Unless he performs his crucial task with initiative, skill and judgment, all the field collection and other efforts are wasted.

A Constant Challenge

Intelligence production activities are a constant challenge to the intelligence worker or analyst: What can he find? What shall he believe? What meaning can he extract from a mass of facts? How can the story be presented so as to be clear and interesting? So as to be as helpful as possible to the reader and to avoid misleading implications?

The intelligence worker has all the joys of overcoming natural difficulties inherent in a given situation that exist for the historian, the explorer, or the scientific research worker. He often has the stimulus of an intellectual contest with the nation which is endeavoring to prevent him from learning what he is seeking. Finally he has the stimulating problem of catching the attention of his readers and conveying ideas, correctly and with the proper emphasis and degree of certainty.

ARKADIA AND CURTANIA

In this book "Arkadia" will be used as the name of a fictitious nation, not behind an iron curtain and presumably friendly, when a typical example is to be cited.

"Curtania" will be used as the name of a fictitious nation behind the iron curtain, where facts are in general difficult to obtain. Curtania is a near neighbor of Kent's Great Frusina.

ABOUT RELATED READING

For each chapter, there is a selected bibliography on a few of the publications found helpful for those who wish to pursue further some of the subjects of the chapter.

These bibliographies, which appear in the back of the book, have no pretensions to completeness. Their mission is merely to introduce the reader to one or two good sources, with a word of description about each. Such sources in turn refer the reader to other sources so that he is then launched on an interesting and profitable quest.

Each source has been marked with a number in parentheses, to facilitate identification of references in the text (although not all sources are directly quoted or referred to in the text).

The trouble with Strategic Intelligence Production is that the world is literally its province. It is hard to think of any natural or social science which does not bear directly or indirectly upon some aspect of Strategic Intelligence. We must also include among helpful disciplines mathematics, logic, military science, and others not always included in the natural or social sciences.

Publications on any of the recognized disciplines as such will not be included in the bibliography. It is only when their application to intelligence production is quite direct that they are included. But a few exceptions are made.

Intelligence production is a human activity. It depends upon human understandings and points of view.

For a stimulating, readable and rewarding text, with many general applications to intelligence if you look for them, we suggest:

(1) Whitehead, Alfred North, *The Aims of Education,* New York, Macmillan, 1929. Published also as a Mentor Book by New American Library of World Literature, 1949.

Another book having wide-spread, general applications to intelligence including questions of Interpretations, National Character and Forecasting is:

(2) Gottschalk, Louis, *Understanding History, A Primer of Historical Method,* New York, Knopf, 1954. Specific principles of intelligence production can be gained by substituting "intelligence" for "history" in this text. One of the most helpful and readable books.

A splendid critical bibliography covering methodology in the social sciences, of which strategic intelligence may claim to be one, is a 26-page article:

(3) Driscoll, J. M. and Hyneman, C. S., *Methodology for Political Scientists: Perspective for Study.* Amer. Political Science Review *49* (1955), pp. 192-217.

In spite of the title more than half of the Driscoll and Hyneman bibliography pertains to the foundations and methods of social science in general.

Two

BASIC PRINCIPLES OF INTELLIGENCE PRODUCTION

PROFESSIONAL POINTS OF VIEW

Intelligence activities are superficially much like scholarly activities in some other professions. An analyst producing an intelligence paper on the Meteorology of Curtania may seem to be doing substantially the same sort of work as any meteorologist writing a scientific paper. The requirements in each case may be called "dangerously similar." The similarities are obvious; the vital differences are hidden. Experience shows that many intelligence workers at many levels fail to grasp the intelligence point of view and that this failure is productive of much preventable misunderstanding and unhappiness.

The differences between the points of view of the different professions are mostly differences in emphasis, but this makes all the difference in the world. One example will illustrate the point; namely, the emphasis of the military profession on discipline. Discipline is a commonplace of human life encountered from earliest childhood throughout school and adult life. However, in military life it has a special importance. "Instant and willing obedience" is the ideal. No officer of the Army could hope for a successful career unless he was willing to subject himself to such discipline, and was prepared to enforce such discipline on those under him.

In exactly the same way that a military man must accept discipline, intelligence workers must understand and accept the intelligence point of view.

The military life emphasis on discipline, courage, and aggressiveness is easy to understand. The intelligence points of view are more subtle, not spectacular, easily overlooked—but just as important for the success and happiness and productivity of the worker.

The primary form of intelligence production is the intelligence paper, whether a "National Intelligence Estimate" or a "Research Aid" or whatever it may be called. A study of the procedures back of these papers will bring out in concrete form the basic principles of intelligence production and contribute to an understanding of the intelligence point of view.

CREATIVE SCHOLARSHIP vs. INTELLIGENCE PRODUCTION

The Scholarly Paper

Scholarly papers of the kind here used for comparison with intelligence papers are found in the professional journals including the journals of all the natural and social sciences. They are found in many serious books and comprise nearly all Ph.D. theses.

The scholar may be on a university faculty, or a candidate for an advanced degree, or may be in industrial or government research work.

In a typical case, the author is writing in the field in which he is profesionally expert. He therefore brings to the study much professional knowledge. He devotes much time to the preparation. It includes laboratory, field, and/or library research. It is intended to extend the boundaries of human knowledge. *Immediate usefulness is a secondary consideration, if considered at all.* The scholar expects that the work will in some degree add to his own professional reputation. He stakes his own very personal reputation on it. Accuracy and completeness within the scope intended are of the first importance.

Examples among books would be S. E. Morison's definitive life of Columbus entitled *Admiral of the Ocean Sea* (11) which took many years to produce and involved extensive field and library research. It was actually published in 1942, but it *would have been equally valuable* if published in 1932 or 1952, thereby differing from the typical intelligence paper. Another typical scholarly book is Highet's study on Juvenal (12), which took fifteen years of research and writing to complete. In the field of the natural sciences any issue of a scientific journal will supply typical examples of similar scholarly papers, where the usefulness and value of the facts set forth do not depend upon the date of publication.

The Intelligence Paper

An intelligence paper, on the present and near future capabilities of Curtania to supply its own artificial rubber requirements, has much in common with any other paper in a field of creative scholarship, whether in history, economics or natural science. In each there is a venture into the unknown. In each there is a constructive work to produce something new and to extend the boundaries of our knowledge. In each the scholar must use initiative, judgment and originality in preparing the paper. In each he must bring to this work the result of years of study in related fields. In each he must usually use some common sense in deciding at what point to discontinue the researches and complete the paper. In each there is the chance to turn in something which will barely "get by," or to turn in something of which he may be proud.

An intelligence paper may cover a small subject, such as the development of a new port for Curtania, or an exceedingly large subjcet, such as the probability of the outbreak of a general European war. It may be an item of passing current intelligence, or a long range study of probable industrial developments in the Middle East. A wider knowledge of intelligence papers can be obtained from those which are discussed in this book. See, for example, Chap. I, Intelligence Production in Action; Chap. IV, Problems A through F.

In every case we find the dominance of usefulness and timeliness, as is described more fully later.

Differences

Many of those now engaged in intelligence production have formerly been engaged in creative scholarship at educational institutions. They find much similarity. Those who have a sincere interest in their work, high standards of scholarship, and a proper pride in the finished paper find that those values are also of *great importance* in intelligence work. Many intelligence workers, therefore, quite naturally overlook the *fundamental difference* between an intelligence paper and a scholarly paper by a professor of history, let us say.

The difference lies in the *purpose* for which each paper was written. The criterion of a scholarly paper may be expressed in general terms as: Does it advance the boundaries of human knowledge or understanding? Does it present some part of its subject more completely, more understandingly more vividly, more significantly, more beautifully, or even more humorously, than has ever been done before?

USEFULNESS—THE SOLE CRITERION

> Power for engineering must always be considered in connection with *the use to which it is to be put.* The biggest waterfall in the world won't run an aeroplane.
>
> —Prof. Lucke, Columbia University, 1921.

In contrast to the scholarly paper an intelligence paper has one purpose: To be *useful* to the national interests under existing circumstances.

By usefulness we mean useful for increasing our knowledge and understanding of matters directly or indirectly connected with national security in the field of foreign intelligence. We mean especially usefulness in helping to solve the particular problem under consideration. We do *not* mean useful for the party line, nor for purely academic reasons, valuable as these may be in other settings.

Some workers, analysts and critics never accept the criterion of usefulness as fundamental in this point of view and never understand how it must change our intelligence production activities.

Many factors affect usefulness. Completeness and accuracy are of course two of them; but it is often true that some completeness and accuracy must be sacrficed to *timeliness.* Timeliness has in general a much higher priority in intelligence than in works of pure scholarship.

This, like many other concepts, stands out with great clarity in combat intelligence. The division order for the attack always contains a part devoted to intelligence of the enemy. Obviously G-2's best available intelligence reaching the combat battalions *before* the attack is more useful than a complete chart of all enemy positions published after the action. A similar example could be drawn from Strategic Intelligence.

So we can helpfully apply to intelligence an adaptation of Professor Lucke's dictum as quoted above: "An intelligence paper must always be considered in connection with the *use to which it is to be put.*"

Under "use to which it is to be put," we should consider the primary mission and the primary readers of the paper. If it is to go to a top level of a government, as to the National Security Council, as the basis for action it must be brief, convincing and non-technical. The same is true of papers for other policy-makers. If it is a training aid for reference of other analysts it may be as complete and technical as desired. The use to which it is to be put is the touchstone of judgment.

Against usefulness to the reader, two considerations must be balanced, just as one must commonly balance benefits against cost. In this case the cost is measured in a man's time.

The Reader's Time

First: Is it worth the reader's effort to read it, understand it, and keep it on hand?[1]

Under present conditions when everyone is over-busy, when the flood of documents is enormous, and time for reading is limited, any paper starts with a considerable burden of proof against it. As someone said of papers coming to one's desk, "You have to read them, in order to find out that they are not worth reading." Files are full and safes bulge.

[1] Townley (13) suggests that references to certain papers should read as follows: "Blank's paper may be ignored, for the knowledge to be gained from it is not commensurate with the appalling effort of reading it."

An analyst can do a great deal towards making a paper worth reading, if he will keep the purpose of the paper and use to which it is to be put always before him while the paper is being written. In short if he will write it with his audience always in mind. Carefully drawn conclusions have become of outstanding importance in the present competition for reader's time. The excellence of the conclusions is the factor on which many intelligence papers stand or fall—and rightly so.

The Writer's Time

The second consideration to be balanced against the usefulness of a paper is this: Is it worth the producer's effort?

Evidently a paper which is of only minor use to the reader, but which is costly in time and effort to produce, may not be justified. There are many such ill considered intelligence papers.

The economy consideration is often of great importance as it happens to be in the United States in these days of budgetary restrictions and manpower ceilings. We can seldom afford to produce an intelligence study just because some analyst or his immediate chief takes an interest in the subject. In offensive military operations the secret of success is "to be strong where it counts." A necessary corollary to this is "the ability to be safely weak where it does not count." So the strength of an intelligence production program depends in part at least on what we do *not* produce.

TIMELINESS

The concept which gives more difficulty than any other to the worker in intelligence production is the overriding importance of timeliness. Time is of the essence in intelligence, while it is usually a side issue in scholarly research. The painful necessity for the scholar to change his point of view when becoming an intelligence officer is therefore evident.[1a]

Timeliness means deadlines. Deadlines may spell hurry, lack of thoroughness, lowering of the usual high standards of scholarship and a whole flock of conditions unpalatable to the average scholarly writer.

Remedies

A partial cure for some of these difficulties may be found in the following:

First. There is a temptation when time for production is short for higher authorities to divide the total time before the paper must be published in such a way that the editorial and review staff has liberal time, while the author is very much cramped. For example, if a paper is to be written, edited and turned over for reproduction in two months, it is not uncommon to find one month allotted to the research and writing of the paper, and one month to the editing. A wiser allotment would frequently be seven weeks for research and writing with two weeks for editing and review.

Second. If the work is in the usual field of responsibility of the analyst, his surveillance of this field and the accumulation of files and understanding should have begun long before the paper was scheduled for production. With such advance preparation the analyst does not start at zero, but with a considerable part of the material already at hand. Usually, too, except for some real emergency, a little scouting will obtain advance notice of when such a paper will be required, so that some actual work can be done ahead of time. This is similar to the "Warning order" in military operations.

1a Experience shows that this point of view needs constant emphasis. Lord Strang, of the British Foreign Office, found the same difficulty in the related matter of preparing diplomatic papers, "often upon inadequate information." He says (13A): "This process (which has its dangers) is as far removed as it is possible to be from the deliberate and exhaustive methods of formal scholarship. That is why the proceedings of bureaucrats appear to the academic mind to be so superficial."

On the other hand there are many analysts who are always caught unprepared. They seem to have as their patron saint the Anglo-Saxon king, Aethelred the Unready.

Third. The author must be thoroughly indoctrinated with the necessity of deadlines, and must be taught by constant supervision to lay out the work so that it can be accomplished within the deadline, allowing some time for unexpected delays. A common fault is to lay out more than can possibly be accomplished. This results in the so-called "slide-rule effect." If there are nine parts, each of which should have approximately equal space, too much space is given to the early parts, with a constantly decreasing amount of time being available for the later ones; so that the final result is spaced like a slide-rule scale (see Fig. 1).

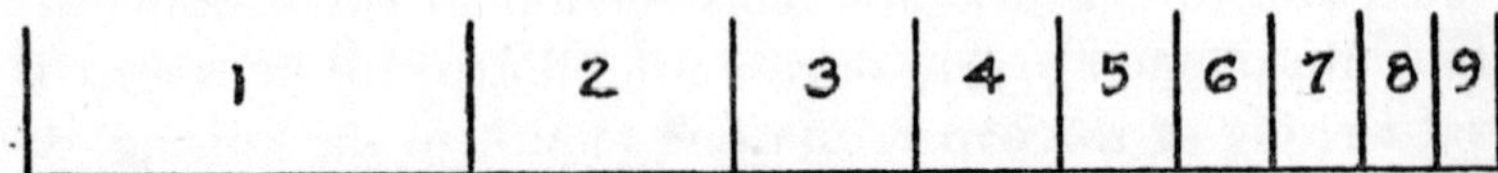

Figure 1 The "Slide Rule" Distribution of Time

Appreciation for the importance of timeliness is partly a matter of habit. Scholars have it very little. Journalists never forget it. Most intelligence papers are as much "dated" as an article in a journal like *Foreign Affairs.* For example the excellent article by Mosely on "Soviet Foreign Policy Since the Death of Stalin" has great interest and value when written; but it rapidly loses both as months slip by and new situations arise. If this point of view can be so clearly discussed with the analysts as to be fully accepted in their thinking, it helps to overcome the natural resistance to being hurried.

DEPRECIATION OF INTELLIGENCE WITH TIME

Most intelligence loses its value rapidly as it gets older. As examples, tactical combat intelligence has lost half of its value in 6 days. On the other hand, intelligence of terrain features such as roads and bridges loses half its value in about 6 years. Intelligence of basic scientific resources—manpower, education and national support of science—loses value or depreciates at the rate of 20% per year. (See Chart)

Many papers are so delayed in writing, editing, awaiting approval, and in reproduction and dissemination that they are already out-of-date when they first reach the customer.

Thus in intelligence production as in the building of battleships the correct policy is FEW and FAST[2] so that each is up-to-date when "launched." Then each paper reaches the consumer at the time of its greatest inherent value.[3] The opposite policy with the same number of analysts is to start many projects. Each one drags along over a year or more.

When these tired, old projects finally reach the consumer, the interest in the subject may be gone; many of the facts are already out-of-date. In short, the value of the intelligence paper has depreciated. The justifiable satisfaction of writer and reader has also depreciated.

The total manhours spent on a paper by the Few and Fast policy may be just the same as by the Slow and Sour policy; only in the first case the manhours for each paper are expended in a concentrated effort without interruptions.

The *inherent value* of intelligence may depreciate with time from:

Actual changes in the situation.

Possible, but unknown change—so that the paper cannot be used with the same confidence as formerly.

In addition, the *usefulness* may depreciate with time from:

[2] This was the motto of Admiral Lord Fisher prior to World War I.

[3] By "value," we mean here the "inherent value" of the paper. The usefulness of the paper to the ultimate consumer is a different matter and is governed by many extraneous circumstances beyond the knowledge or control of the intelligence production officer. As an illustration of this difference in meaning, fifty dollars always has more inherent value than five dollars. Yet, five dollars when I am broke is more useful to me than fifty dollars when I do not need money.

Loss of reader attention. Intelligence, as it grows old, quickly loses its interest and ability to attract attention, and so to influence decisions. It is of less usefulness as fewer people read or heed it.

Average Rates of Depreciation[4]

Tactical Combat Intelligence 10% per day

Artillery or other combat units may move in a matter of hours; within 10 days this intelligence has lost ⅔ of its practical value.

Strategic Intelligence in Wartime 10% per month

The economic and logistic situation changes so that within 6 months the intelligence has lost nearly one-half of its value, and in a year, nearly ¾ of its inherent value is gone.

Strategic Intelligence in Peacetime 20% per year

Changes are naturally slow. There is resistance to change. Some terrain features may change not at all. The political situation may change rapidly.

Semi-permanent Features,

such as roads, bridges, natural resources 10% per year

Note: Intelligence depreciates at the "constant percentage" rate, widely used in economics. For example: If the paper depreciates 10% a year, starting with 100, its value at the end of each year is: 90, 81, 73, 66, 59, 53, 48, 43, 39, 35. . . . At the end of each year its value is 90% of what it was at the end of the previous year. Figure 2 tells this story at a glance.

THE HISTORICAL APPROACH[5]

Intelligence is not produced in that wonderful land where "Time is a meaningless concept." The following illumin-

[4] Even though some readers would use under certain conditions slightly different percentages from those herein given, the principles and general nature of the curves remain the same.

[5] For a further discussion of the historical approach in intelligence papers, see Appendix A.

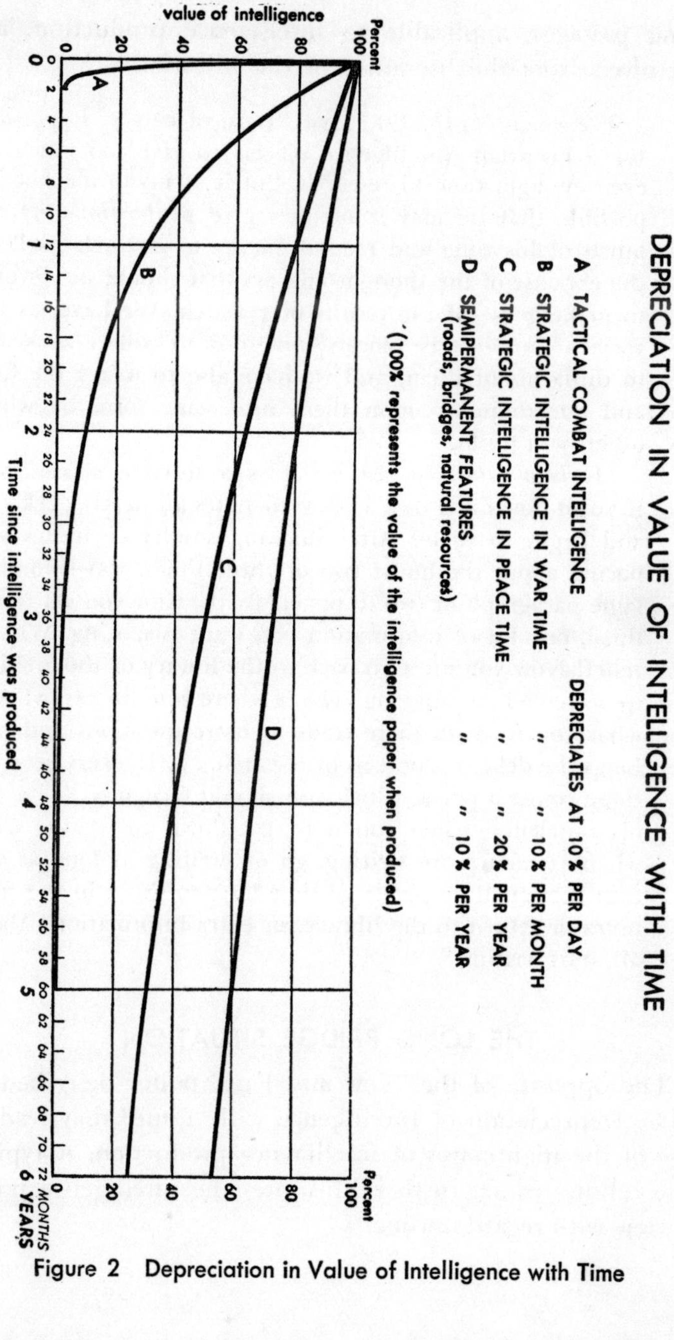

Figure 2 Depreciation in Value of Intelligence with Time

ating passages, applicable to intelligence production, are borrowed from the literature of the historian:

> *Trevelyan (4) (p. 194) says:* "It is, of course, impossible for a historian [intelligence officer] to give too much, or even enough, time to research, but it seems to me not impossible that he may sometimes give *proportionately* too much of his time and mental energy to research itself, at the expense of the thought and art that should be devoted to making use of the results of research. We have, as historians [intelligence officers] not only to collect facts, but to think about them; and we have also to weave the facts and our thoughts upon them into some form by which others will profit."
>
> *Morison (10a) (p. 293):* "It is a terrible strain, isn't it, to sit down at a desk with your notes all neatly docketed, and begin to write? After smoking sundry cigarettes and pacing about the house two or three times, you commit a lame paragraph or two to paper. By the time you get to the third, one bit of information you want is lacking. What a relief! Now you must go back to the library or the archives to do some more digging. That's where you are happy! And what you turn up there leads to more questions and prolongs the delicious process of research. . . . In every research there comes a point, which you should recognize like a call of conscience, when you must get down to writing. And when you once are writing, go on writing as long as you can; there will be plenty of time later to shove in the footnotes or return to the library for extra information. Above all, start writing."

THE LONG BRIDGE SITUATION

The opposite of the "Few and Fast" policy described in "The Depreciation of Intelligence with Time" may lead to one of the nightmares of intelligence production. A typical case follows which further illustrates the intelligence point of view with regard to time.

Suppose a comprehensive paper on the heavy metals industry in Curtania is started. A conscientious and competent analyst of the highest scholastic standards is assigned to it. The field is somewhat new. Data are few and scattered, and all in the native language. Masses of uncatalogued documents exist in libraries here and there. The analyst struggles along month after month covering the iron industry, nickel industry, etc. He takes the annual leave due him, is sick for two weeks, has the usual administrative interruptions and has to discontinue the work temporarily for a special paper due to a current emergency. He spends a quarter of his time in the office in the routine reading of documents not pertaining to this subject, but which regularly come to his desk in his general field of responsibility.

After 14 months the text and tables are finished. The all-important charts are then sent to the Graphics Department to be drawn in a style suitable for reproduction. Graphics has much work ahead and takes six more weeks to get around to finishing the job. The paper then goes to the editorial people. With their backlog of manuscripts on hand they do well to return it with editorial comments after four more weeks.

So sixteen months after the work was started it comes back for its finishing editoral touches, supposedly immediately before reproduction.

You as the supervisor say: "Thank Heaven, that paper is at last practically ready for reproduction. Let's surely get it out this week."

The analyst says: "We can't do that. Since the first data on pig iron production were collected, new and better figures are known to be available in the Library for Advanced Curtanian Studies on the Pacific Coast. As soon as I can get these new figures on an inter-library loan, I will bring my pig iron figures up to date."

When the pig iron figures are revised, all the tables on

steel production must also be changed. Then the charts must go to Graphics again to be redrawn in accordance with the new figures. By this time the copper figures are out of date. By this time nickel must be revised.

And so it goes. The paper is *always* under revision, but *never* ready. The strange thing is that the analyst is perfectly happy. He is constantly working in his chosen field. He is constantly improving his paper.[6]

He is living up to the very highest standards of scholarship. But nothing is ever finished. The paper is never reproduced. It never does anyone any good.

The situation is very much like a long wooden bridge for vehicles across a river. By the time the bridge is completed to the far shore of the river, the floor boards first laid down on the near shore are rotten and need replacement. By that time, those near the middle of the bridge must be replaced, and so on. It never is completely ready for use, and *it never will be ready* in spite of much honest and excellent work which has gone into it by competent workmen.

This is the Long Bridge Situation. This is the situation to be avoided at all costs. Once the fatal cycle gets under way, it is almost impossible to stop it. It is literally a pons assinorum.

This nightmarish situation of continual revision can only be avoided by advance planning, following the Few and Fast policy. Time necessary for completion must be estimated on a realistic approach and based on knowledge of man-hours actually needed for production of this kind, and on the proportion of an analyst's time which can really be made available for direct productive work on this particular problem after deducting for leaves, holidays, background reading, and administrative activities.

[6] Showing the truth of the saying: "The good husbandman takes as much pleasure in plowing and sowing as in the harvest."

In the case used as an example, the trouble could have been avoided by planning this as a series of three separate papers, for example, on iron, copper, and nickel production respectively, each one self-contained, and each to be *published as soon as ready.* The papers support each other by being made part of a series.

Improvement could also have been made if necessary, by having several analysts work on the paper at the same time—the group working, however, as a team under a directing head. Time can often be saved also by looking ahead and making advance arrangements to get on the docket with the Graphics Department and with the Editorial Board without delay.

An essential part of any solution would be the early indoctrination of the analysts, so that they fully understood and accepted in advance the importance of Timeliness to intelligence, and the necessity for meeting production deadlines. This result could only be accomplished by a full discussion of the general principles of intelligence at all levels, so that a common doctrine could be developed. Eventually the Principles of Intelligence might become as widely known and followed in the Intelligence Community as are Clausewitz' Principles of War in military science. Such a common doctrine would prevent many of the misunderstandings which now occur.

TIMELY TRUTH WELL TOLD

The point of view which we have here presented, including the emphasis on timeliness, is set forth in poster form on a following page.

This one-page description of intelligence as "Timely Truth well Told" could be used as a training aid for a lecture, or could be reproduced on one sheet of paper for distribution to a class.

The "Well Told" factor requires more consideration than is usually given to it. It means much more than "clearly and in correct English." The readability and the convincing quality are highly important.

An excellent example of the importance of readability was seen in World War II. In the higher levels of the U. S. Army, American officers used to grab for the British intelligence estimates in preference to those from U. S. sources. *Substantively* the American estimates were fully equal to the British. However, the American papers were formal, heavy and stodgy to the last degree, whereas the British had a light, informal, human approach in which even touches of humor could be included where appropriate.

The *convincing* quality of intelligence "Well Told" is equally important. There are many situations in which correct intelligence was produced but not heeded. Some of these were situations of crucial importance. Professor R. V. Jones, one of the most brilliant and successful of the British intelligence officers, wrote:

"But the test of good intelligence service is not merely that you were right; it is that you persuaded your operational or research staff to take correct measures." The need for a convincing quality in Strategic Intelligence is as great in peace as it is in war.

SUMMARY

The two principles of intelligence most commonly misunderstood by intelligence workers are Usefulness and Timeliness. These have just been discussed. For a given paper they both fit under the general heading "Purpose," which is one of the Nine Principles of Intelligence.

These principles are now ready for discussion and will thus round out the subject of this chapter.

Timely Truth well Told

1. "Timely Truth well Told" sums up many of the essentials of good intelligence—even more than may appear at first glance.

2. **Timely** is a consideration which many, otherwise excellent, intelligence officers never appreciate. In pure scholarship timeliness is frequently unimportant. In Intelligence, however, the value of nearly all papers lies in their usefulness—directly or indirectly—to National Security. The usefulness of a paper is closely connected with its timeliness. The value of any intelligence paper depreciates rapidly with time. (Curves are available to show this.)

3. **Truth** is, of course, fundamental in intelligence. It is harmful to overestimate, to underestimate or to hedge in the presentation of a foreign situation. Selection, proper emphasis, and real understanding are necessary aspects of truth-telling.

4. **Well Told** is the final and vital consideration. Much timely and truthful intelligence misses its mark because it is not read, is not understood, or is not believed. In presentation, great attention should be given to simplicity and clarity,—to readability, charts and illustrations. Our degree of certainty or uncertainty should be made clear to the reader. The significance of facts stated should be brought out.

5. A good check list for planning intelligence, for getting at its real meaning, and for conveying this in most helpful form to the reader is:

Timely Truth—well Told.

THE NINE PRINCIPLES OF INTELLIGENCE
corresponding to
CLAUSEWITZ' PRINCIPLES OF WAR

One of the documents which has had pronounced effects on civilized man is certainly The Ten Commandments. Published some 3500 years ago, this great Decalogue has persisted as a vital statement, and has had a tremendous influence in improving our adherence to the principles expressed.

Yet these simple commandments are subject to all the typical criticisms which critics like to raise. There was nothing original about them when written or at any time since. They omit much that is important. They are over-simplifications and do not contain the necessary qualifying statements. They are not universally applicable. But they have persisted as living words. Why?

First and foremost, because they filled a human need. They have concentrated attention and action on some outstanding points of human behavior. They led to a common understanding among human beings. They saved thought, explanation and argument. With all their faults, they were fundamentally *useful.*

Second and equally important for survival,—with great restraint and foresight Moses *restricted himself to ten* important principles. Among the hundreds of admonitions which he was tempted to include, he concentrated on ten—few enough to be remembered and to receive continuing attention. If there had been one hundred commandments they would have been forgotten within a few years.

Profiting by the above consideration, we submit *The Nine Principles of Intelligence* having all the shortcomings mentioned above, and with also some of the same claims to serious attention from the Intelligence Community.

THE MOST IMPORTANT PRINCIPLES FOR THE CONDUCT OF WAR

> These principles, though the result of long thought and continuous study of the history of war[7] have none the less been drawn up hastily, and thus will not stand severe criticism in regard to form. In addition, only the most important subjects have been picked from a great number, since a certain brevity was necessary. These principles, therefore, will not so much give complete instruction to Your Royal Highness[7], as they will stimulate and serve as a guide for your own reflections.
>
> CARL VON CLAUSEWITZ

Clausewitz' Principles of War have permeated our military literature and have had a beneficial effect on our military science.

As currently modified and accepted in United States military doctrine these principles are:

Objective	Mass
Simplicity	Economy of Force
Unity of Command	Surprise
Offensive	Security
Maneuver	

Brief explanations of these Principles of War follow.

OBJECTIVE—Every military operation is carried out for a definite objective, otherwise called a mission or purpose. The whole operation is focused on accomplishing the objective.

SIMPLICITY—contributes towards success. The "Fog of War" constantly emphasizes the importance of the necessity for simplicity in the basic plans.

[7] In place of "history of war" and "Your Royal Highness" one can substitute "intelligence" and "the present reader" for the purposes of this chapter.

Unity of Command—results in that unity of effort which is essential to the decisive application of the full combat power of available forces.

Offensive—Through offensive action a commander seizes the initiative, preserves his freedom of action, and imposes his will on the enemy.

Maneuver—brings our forces to bear on the enemy under conditions most favorable to ourselves. Maneuver often implements the principles of Mass, Economy of Force, and Surprise.

Mass—or the concentration of superior forces, . . . at the decisive place and time and their employment in a decisive direction, creates the conditions essential to victory. In short the principle is: To be strong where it counts.

Economy of Force—is a corollary to the principle of mass. In order to concentrate superior combat strength in one place, economy of force must be exercised in other places. An example of the Calculated Risk.

Surprise—when properly carried out, is one of the most fruitful of the principles in accomplishing the objective and in minimizing casualties.

Security—includes protection against surprise attacks and provision for guarding against known enemy capabilities. Some elements of security are reconnaissance, outposts, and mobile reserves.

The basic idea behind each of these principles is definite and easy to grasp. Each principle is of importance. It is of wide-spread application. In any military planning each of these principles should be given serious consideration (though not necessarily always adopted). Each is worthy of study and discussion.

These principles have been practically useful in teaching military science. They are useful as a check list to the tired and busy commander or staff officer when making plans in combat.

Most of all they have served to promote a common understanding. They make for clarity of expression. They facilitate discussion and avoid many misunderstandings. They help to build a common doctrine.

With all this they are properly flexible. There is nothing to say, for example, that a military plan *must* involve the principles of surprise. However, these principles are so drilled into the military man—from the squad leader to the army commander—that he can hardly forget them. If, as an illustration, in the presence of the enemy a unit commander neglects security (one of the principles) in a map problem, in a field maneuver or in combat, he knows that the burden of proof is on him.

So the Principles of War have proven efficient elements in our military education and in practice. They are economical of time and mental effort.

It is easy to criticize and even to ridicule the Principles of War.[8] They are not coordinate or mutually exclusive. They have differing points of view. They are not universally applicable. They are occasionally misunderstood by those students of military science who fail to think.

Overlooking these shortcomings, experience has demonstrated that the Principles of War are sound, important and practically helpful over a very wide range of instruction and of military situations. They *work.*

[8] See Lt. Col. M. L. Fallwell, "The Principles of War and the Solution of Military Problems," *Military Review,* May 1955. p. 48; Vice Adm. R. L. Connolly, "The Principles of War," *Military Review,* May 1953, p. 22; Liddell Hart, *Strategy,* N. Y., Praeger, 1954; Col. R. E. Dupuy and Col. T. N. Dupuy, *Military Heritage of America,* N. Y., McGraw-Hill, 1956.

THE MOST IMPORTANT PRINCIPLES FOR THE PRODUCTION OF INTELLIGENCE

Is it possible to develop Principles of Strategic Intelligence similar in their field to the Principles of War? Is it possible in formulating Principles of Intelligence to stick to those elements of strength, especially in simplicity of presentation, which have proven their practical usefulness in presenting the Principles of War?

If so, we could obtain with great economy, powerful aids to the development of competence in Strategic Intelligence, and towards a common understanding and doctrine within the Intelligence Community.

Benefiting by the favorable experience in using the Principles of War, we have been guided by the following in setting up our Principles of Intelligence. In all of this we are considering primarily the Principles of Strategic Intelligence Production.

1. Each principle must be of importance and widespread application.

Those who discuss the Principles of War, glory in showing that they have useful application in discussing battles from Sun Tzu (500 B.C.) to Hannibal, to Napoleon, to Patton. No claim is made that they are of universal application. Situations arise where one principle or another is not helpful.

2. They must be real general principles, guides for action in many situations.

For example the Principles of War are not framed in terms of a matter-of-fact check list such as Infantry, Artillery, Communications, etc., even though such a check list is of value for other purposes. So we do not include in our Intelligence Principles: Sociological Factors, Political Factors, Economic Factors, etc.; nor do we include a breakdown such as Persons, Organizations, Physical Factors. Factors are not principles.

3. The basic idea behind each principle must be expressible in one word or in a simple three-word phrase.

This helps the memory, facilitates use and common understanding, and is an outstanding characteristic of the Principles of War as used in United States military literature.

4. Flexibility, simple descriptions and an absence of legalistic or philosophical technicalities are essential. Remote contingencies and occasional exceptions are purposely omitted in favor of concentration on the simple outstanding ideas.

We are not afraid to incur for the Principles of Intelligence the same criticisms that have been leveled at the Principles of War, if we can obtain from the wide-spread use of the Principles of Intelligence the benefits which have accrued to military science from the older Principles, namely a concentration of attention on matters of outstanding importance and a resulting unity of doctrine.

The proposed Principles are given below. They are believed to be always worthy of consideration and frequently worthy of adoption in any case of Strategic Intelligence Production, whether in planning a project, writing a paper, or discussing the results.

The language used to describe each Principle is intended to convey the basic idea, not to be exhaustive or logically rigorous. In this it follows the general level of the current discussions of the Principles of War.

PURPOSE—The Principle of the Purpose permeates every aspect of every intelligence project. The form of attack on every intelligence project must be influenced by *the use to which it is to be put.*

This use governs the timing, the extent of coverage, the language and mode of treatment. The immediate purpose of a paper is often to solve what is commonly stated as "The Problem" as amplified in the terms of reference. A larger purpose may also exist, namely to use the solution of the problem as a guide to policy or action.

Definitions—The Principle of clear Definitions is essential for intelligence production.

Experience shows the great importance of making clear by definition or otherwise, exactly what is meant by each important word and idea, especially those used in the Title, Terms of Reference and Conclusions.

Clear definitions make for clear thinking. They concentrate effort on what is really desired, and prevent misunderstandings. Definitions are particularly needed in Strategic Intelligence. Consider for example such commonly used terms as: capabilities, vulnerabilities, intentions, near future, unconventional warfare.

Exploitation of Sources—The Principle of the Exploitation of Sources requires a thorough working of all sources which can throw light on the paper.

What are the probable capabilities and limitations of each source? To what extent do they confirm or contradict one another? The more varied the sources the better the chance for effective cross checks. With varied sources the foundations of the paper are broader, the perspective is deeper, and the chances of serious error are lessened.

Significance—The Principle of Significance requires that meaning be given to bare facts.

The Search for Significance should be vigorously pushed. The significance of facts and statements should always be shown. This is often done by comparing the fact given with a corresponding fact at the same date last year, or with a similar fact in the United States.

Pointing out the significance greatly increases the usefulness of a fact. Facts seldom speak for themselves.

CAUSE AND EFFECT—This principle leads the analyst to seek the Cause and Effect relationships in any intelligence problem.

A tracing of cause and effect is an excellent means for understanding the workings of any situation and for preventing misunderstandings. Such a study often helps in the discovery of the key factor. Pointing out causes also facilitates the use of the intelligence at the policy level.

SPIRIT OF THE PEOPLE—Any sound intelligence estimate must recognize the fundamental influence of the Spirit of the People. This Principle requires that the spirit be considered as a matter of vital importance.

The background is the culture of the group, including religion, national folklore and all those ideas which members learn from childhood on. The principle distinguishes between a vigorous, aggressive, optimistic group full of the spirit of progress on the one hand; as compared with a tired, disillusioned, pessimistic group on the other. It recognizes the place of morale and of the all-important will-to-win. It covers fanaticism, patriotism, pacifism and defeatism. "The Temper of the People" is sometimes used as an equivalent term.

An unusually aggressive spirit on the one hand or a defeatist spirit on the other hand may multiply the capability which would ordinarily be expected from a given situation by ten or by one tenth respectively.

TRENDS—The Principle of Trends is based upon the movement and patterns in human affairs. This principle requires an estimate of the probable direction of change.

Is the item under consideration increasing or decreasing and at what rate? Is the trend permanent, or cyclic, or horizontal? Trends are closely tied to Forecasting, which is such a vital part of intelligence production. A study of Trends attempts to penetrate the Fog of the Future.

DEGREE OF CERTAINTY—The Principle of Degree of Certainty requires consideration of the reliability of statements of fact; the precision of quantitative data; and the probabilities of estimates and conclusions. These three concepts are similar, but not quite the same. All three are included under Degree of Certainty.

In each case the degree of reliability, or of precision, or of probability may be very high or very low or in between. This difference makes all the difference in the world. According to this principle, one of the essential responsibilities of the intelligence production officer is to determine by critical study the reliability, precision or probability, as the case may be, of each important element of his paper and then to make this clear to the reader. This procedure greatly increases the usefulness of any paper.

CONCLUSIONS—Conclusions are essential to the full usefulness of many intelligence papers.

The Principle of Conclusions is a corollary to the Principle of Purpose. Conclusions require an answer to the question: What of it? In many papers only the conclusions are read and remembered. The greatest care is necessary so that the conclusions will convey the outstanding points briefly and clearly; but shall not be subject to misunderstanding due to this brevity. They require the best from the intelligence officer.

Implementation

These Nine Principles of Intelligence are submitted in the present crude and immature form for general discussion, criticism, revision. After such consideration it is hoped that the Intelligence Community will not wait for perfection of concept or of language; but that it will adopt and use them in their present form. Further polishing will come from use as was the case with the Principles of War.

Judging by the present state of intelligence activities, and the lack of a basic doctrine, and judging from the experience of the Principles of War—the Principles of Intelligence hold promise of real usefulness in Strategic Intelligence Production.

The Nine Principles form nine well established fundamental points around which training and practice in Strategic Intelligence can be concentrated.

This book contains pertinent elaboration of some of these principles, as follows:

Purpose: Chap. II, Usefulness

Definitions: Chap. III, The Scientific Method

Sources: Chap VI, The Letter-Figure System

Significance: Chap. III, "Facts Mean Nothing"

Causes: Chap. V, What Do We Mean by Social Science? Chap. VI, Correlation and Coincidences

Spirit of the People: Chap. V, Consistency in Character

Trends: Chap. VII, The Five Fundamental Factors in Forecasting

Degree of Certainty: Chap. VI, Expression of Degree of Certainty; Chap. VII, Adequacy and Precision of Data and Assumptions

Conclusions: Chap. III, The Scientific Method; Chap. IV, Verification

Each principle could profitably be developed into a chapter of its own.

PART II

Intelligence production as an intellectual process

We find that to study intelligence production as an intellectual process is a fruitful approach. Many of the conditions found to be favorable to creative thinking are also favorable to intelligence production. Much of logic, the theory of probability, and the methods of the social sciences can be applied profitably with modifications to intelligence production. There are many common pitfalls.

Three

FROM INFORMATION TO INTELLIGENCE

With Enough Nothings Their Sum is Something
"Facts Mean Nothing"
The Intelligence Production Process as a Whole
A Pioneer Effort : Levels of Intelligence
Some Unofficial Definitions : Judgment Still Necessary
The Scientific Method Applied to Intelligence Production

We open this chapter with a simple problem as a typical example. The problem starts with a miscellaneous lot of facts supposed to have a bearing on an everyday situation. We consider some of the questions connected with converting this raw material of information into the refined and finished product of intelligence.

This is the sort of situation which commonly faces an analyst starting out on a new project. In many intelligence production projects we find a great mass of facts, each one of small value. Should we discard them? Do facts speak for themselves, or must we explain their significance?

Progressing now to the finished intelligence we find several levels requiring discussions and definitions for clarification.

This brings us to the process of putting the facts together according to the scientific method in an effort to get the maximum benefits from the material at hand in producing finished intelligence.

WITH ENOUGH NOTHINGS THEIR SUM IS SOMETHING

In popular terms the basic principle of integral calculus has been stated: "If you take enough nothings, their sum is something."[1] This statement forms a good starting point for a study of intelligence production.

We can almost always find some facts bearing on any intelligence subject. This is a basic concept of intelligence production.

One of the experiences which never ceases to surprise and intrigue the present author is the way in which one can take a number of facts, each of which means almost nothing in itself, and get a meaningful picture by putting them together. Though this is a comonplace of the intelligence art, a few examples are worth presenting.

Examples

First in cryptography. A few words even when written in the simplest substitution cipher are impossible to decipher; but a whole page in such a simple cipher can be read very speedily. This is an excellent example of how getting more and more bits of information, each of which appears meaningless by itself, often brings out a meaningful picture. The common comparison with putting together a jig saw puzzle is also sound.

An actual example in another field (with names and places changed) is enlightening. During World War II, a military unit at Camp Claiborne, Louisiana, was undergoing active training preparatory to going overseas. There was more to be done than could possibly be accomplished in regular working hours. Much extra work was done in the evenings and week ends. Major Jones, a bachelor, was an able and

[1] To mathematicians this statement is not satisfactory.

conscientious staff officer who worked a considerable part of most week ends. Now and then he went to the nearby city of Shreveport, about a hundred miles away over a week end for shopping and recreation. His record as compiled by a lady of the post follows:

Major Jones' Calendar

Week end of May 1	Working at Camp Claiborne
Week end of May 8	Working at Camp Claiborne
Week end of May 15	Visiting in Shreveport
Week end of May 22	Working at Camp Claiborne
Week end of May 29	New Orleans, Louisiana
Week end of June 5	Working at Camp Claiborne
Week end of June 12	Working at Camp Claiborne
Week end of June 19	New Orleans, Louisiana
Week end of June 26	Visiting in Shreveport
Week end of July 3	Working at Camp Claiborne
Week end of July 10	Working at Camp Claiborne
Week end of July 17	Visiting in Shreveport
Week end of July 24	Working at Camp Claiborne
Week end of July 31	Working at Camp Claiborne
Week end of Aug 7	Working at Camp Claiborne
Week end of Aug 14	Visiting in Shreveport
Week end of Aug 21	Working at Camp Claiborne
Week end of Aug 28	Working at Camp Claiborne

An examination of this record shows nothing of significance. It is completely commonplace.

Miss Smith was a civilian employee on the post, whose family lived in Shreveport. Like most civilian employees with a limited income and no car of her own, she lived and spent most of her time near the post, where she took part in many social gatherings. Occasionally she spent the week end with her family. Her record as compiled by a lady of the post follows:

Miss Smith's Calendar

Week end of May 29	Shreveport, Louisiana
Week end of June 5	At Camp Claiborne
Week end of June 12	At Camp Claiborne
Week end of June 19	At New Orleans visiting friends
Week end of June 26	At her home in Shreveport
Week end of July 3	At Camp Claiborne
Week end of July 10	At Camp Claiborne
Week end of July 17	At her home in Shreveport
Week end of July 24	At Camp Claiborne
Week end of July 31	At Camp Claiborne
Week end of Aug 7	At Camp Claiborne
Week end of Aug 14	At her home in Shreveport
Week end of Aug 21	At Camp Claiborne

Again, nothing of significance appears.

But put these two commonplace records side by side so that dates coincide and a definite pattern immediately appears. The person who did this (let us say as a personal intelligence project), correctly deduced that the officer and girl were secretly engaged. This turned out to be reliable intelligence.

This example from real life illustrates in an undesirably simple form the present point. As the situation has been here stated, the outcome is only too obvious.

This example would correspond more closely to actual intelligence situations, and so would be more realistic (but too cumbersome to include in a book) if the calendars for *all* of the officers of the post and for *all* the girls were submitted, and if the calendar provided for each person extended over a whole year, instead of having the pertinent part *selected for us artificially* as has been done here.

If submitted in this more realistic form, this example would illustrate the fact that in *any* situation put before an intelligence officer for study there is an endless amount of information which might be studied. Most of it is irrelevant. One part of the duties of an intelligence officer is to use his best judgment to select and "nose out" from the great mass of available facts the small area of information which is pertinent and thus profitable for further study. After the more pertinent areas are discovered, it is then the duty of the intelligence officer to find their significance.

If then the records of all the persons on the post are submitted for all the days of the year, neither the mode of attack of this problem nor its final solution is over-obvious.

So, given a large number of facts related to a given situation, a keen interest in the situation, an understanding of the background, and the time to study the data from many tentative points of view, it is surprising how often the true picture emerges. (For further discussion, see Chapter IV.)

The value of large amounts of commonplace and apparently uninteresting information—provided such information is selected, studied and interpreted by a competent intelligence officer—is brought out in a review of Kulski's book, *The Soviet Regime,* 1954. The reviewer says: "It is his (Kulski's) thesis that the nature of the Soviet regime is really no secret if you read Russian and take the trouble to compare and collate enough reports, directives, theoretical expositions and apologetics. His book proves the soundness of that thesis and the indefatigable energy and good judgment of the author."

Applications to Counterintelligence

The application to counterintelligence of the piecing together of facts is evident. Security restrictions are always unpopular and often onerous. In regard to any given restriction we often say: "How can this bit of information possibly help the enemy?" The answer is, "It can't, when confined to that one bit of information." But, as we have shown, this bit of almost completely harmless information, if put together with many other bits of almost completely harmless information can often help the enemy a great deal, if he is interested in the given situation and is actively collecting and interpreting such information.

This explains the danger arising from many actions which are apparently safe from the point of view of security. It does not of course justify counterintelligence security restrictions which are not really necessary nor does it eliminate the necessity for judgment in counterintelligence regulations.

"FACTS MEAN NOTHING"

A brilliant lecturer at Oxford used to exclaim frequently in his lectures, "Of course facts mean nothing." One of his best students told me that only after twenty years did he realize what the professor meant.

I find it dangerous to quote the professor's statement orally in any conference. The audience fairly bristles with opposition in the half minute before I can explain what was intended. The professor certainly never expected anyone to take him literally.

His meaning really was: "A fact means surprisingly little, unless it is related to some other facts, or its significance is pointed out."

Related Facts

The practical importance of all this to those engaged in intelligence production can be made clear by following through one simple example which pertains to scientific and engineering manpower. (All of the facts stated may be taken as substantially correct. To simplify the problem we will here consider quantity only, excluding questions of quality.) A fact: In 1953, 40,000 engineers graduated from Soviet institutes of higher learning.

At first glance the writer of a paper containing this fact experiences a little thrill in his ability to produce this figure. He has every right to be proud, provided he does not stop at this point.

The reader is tempted to accept this and to relax contentedly. At last he knows something definite about Soviet engineering capabilities. But has the reader yet learned anything worth knowing? Unless he is one of that very few who are experts on engineering manpower, the figure as given will mean almost nothing worth-while to him if he is honest with himself. Forty thousand engineers is a lot of engineers, but the USSR is the largest nation in the world. Are there enough engineers for current Soviet needs?

As soon as the writer adds: "In 1947 the Soviets graduated 15,000 engineers and in 1950 they graduated 28,000;" then the 40,000 figure for 1953 begins to take on meaning. Then if you add that in 1947, '50 and '53 the United States graduated 21,000, 52,000 and 27,000 engineers, the situation is flooded with light. This picture can then be made easy to grasp by a simple graph.

At this point we realize how little the one figure, 40,000 engineers in 1953, really meant. We would certainly agree to the Oxford professor's statement if modified as follows: "A single isolated fact usually means almost nothing."

The constructive point here for the analyst is that he should seldom be content to state one fact. He should give related facts[2] for comparison. Then his production radiates real meaning.

One reason why related facts are not customarily added is because it entails considerably more work. Another reason is that it requires considerably more real understanding. An appreciation of this destroys the former complacency of writer and reader over the production of a bare fact; but it

[2] However, some cynic has pointed out the danger of citing more than one fact, namely that the second may contradict the first.

multiplies the real value of any intelligence paper many times.

Deeper Questions

The second point comes out when we dig a little deeper. What the reader probably wants or needs to know about the quantity of Soviet engineers includes some of the following questions: Are the numbers of engineers graduating each year decreasing, remaining substantially constant or increasing? Slowly or rapidly? How do these numbers compare with similar figures for the United States?

In considering the numbers of engineers available for each of the following kinds of duty: (a) the construction of dams, canals, roads, railroads, bridges, factories and industrial and military equipment; (b) the operation of engineering equipment; (c) research and development; (d) teaching and administration, respectively; has U.S.S.R. a severe shortage of engineers which definitely restricts their capabilities, or a nearly sufficient supply, or a liberal supply? In these respects how does U.S.S.R. compare with United States and perhaps with some other countries such as Germany?

In comparing the supply of engineers in U.S.S.R. with the supply in U.S., what allowance should be made for the fact that the economy of U.S.S.R. is in a rapidly developing stage changing from a backward to a modern condition? The U.S.S.R. needs to build more railroads, canals, dams and bridges than the United States. In making a valid comparison, what allowance should be made for the fact that United States engineers have considerably greater output per man than Soviet engineers?

The more sophisticated questions which may lead to policy and action are: How does the quantity of engineers affect the capabilities of U.S.S.R. to support their industry, and military establishment in construction, operations, research and development, and teaching respectively, now and in the near future? How does the situation compare with that in the United States, now and in the near future?

On the level of these deeper and more meaningful questions we see that facts alone *never* tell us what we must know for policy and action. Morison (11), page 294, says: "Do not fall into the fallacy of supposing that 'facts speak for themselves. . . .' Dump your entire collection of facts on paper, and the result will be unreadable if not incomprehensible."

We must have a real understanding of the relative economic and sociological conditions in the two countries. We must have some criteria for our comparison. We are getting into uncultivated fields. Only further economic or other research can give sound answers.

As a rule such basic research into unexplored fields is best carried out as an external research project by some real expert in economics, demography, sociology, natural science or other field of learning. There is a need for the very best in intelligence production obtained by combining the expert knowledge of a leader in social or natural science, with the background and judgment of the experienced professional intelligence officer. To make a successful weaving of knowledge from these two sources—the warp and the woof of Chapter I— is one of the fundamental problems of Strategic Intelligence.

The Search for Significance

A professor at Harvard in returning papers to a graduate student had the disturbing habit of writing in the margin opposite each of several paragraphs "SIGNIFICANCE?" "SIGNIFICANCE?" The student finally got the point, namely that the meaning or significance of a fact was really the important thing about it, and so should be made clear first to the writer and then to the reader.

The popularity of some excellent news commentators is due to the fact that they explain the significance of news items.

As a definite example consider the following from the author's experience in the production of combat intelligence.

During World War II, I was AC of S, G-2 with XIX Corps throughout the European Operations. I was, therefore, constantly in touch with military operations. In spite of this I had the comments of Hanson Baldwin, Military Editor of the *New York Times,* forwarded to me regularly.

About many aspects of the military situation I, being a G-2 on the spot, naturally knew much more than Baldwin. The articles coming by mail were of course many days late. I used to ask myself what made Baldwin's articles always worth reading. One reason was that Baldwin would never state an isolated fact without showing its significance by including related facts. He would never say, for example, "The new Japanese fighter plane can operate effectively at 20,000 feet," without adding: "This compares with 15,000 feet for the older model."

THE INTELLIGENCE PRODUCTION PROCESS AS A WHOLE

At this point it is worthwhile to stand back and consider the intelligence production process as a whole. We shall find that the process is, in fact, an integrated unit in which each element plays a necessary part in relation to the others. Viewed merely as a process, it is of wide-spread usefulness in human affairs entirely apart from its intelligence applications.

The dilemma faced by the intelligence production officer, by social scientists, and by those dealing with human affairs generally, arises from the fact that in many problems which these people face it is impractical or impossible to obtain the facts necessary to *prove* the conclusions which are drawn. For example: In intelligence, drawing conclusions in any problem involving future capabilities or probable courses in action; in human relations, the selection of one individual out of several for promotion.

In each case we have available for consideration a mass of data. Some are relevant, some irrelevant, some are only remotely relevant. Some are true, some false, some partly true.

In each case, data must be (1) selected, (2) evaluated, (3) interpreted, (4) integrated, i.e., a hypothesis or explanation must be formulated, which will enable us to put together a consistent picture of the whole situation, showing the relation between the parts. (5) Conclusions must be drawn and tested. (6) The final picture and conclusions must be *presented* correctly, clearly, with the proper emphasis, and with indications to the reader as to the degree of confidence which he can place in the different parts of the report.

The process described is at the core of the method by which many problems must be solved. It is in contrast to the simpler and more satisfactory method which can be used in many problems of the natural sciences and elsewhere, where facts can be obtained by industrious collection, or by experimentation, or by simple calculations sufficient to *prove* the conclusions drawn.

In the intelligence production process each of the steps—Selection, Evaluation, Interpretation, Integration, Drawing Conclusions, and Presentation—requires not only knowledge, but also judgment. Gaps exist at important places. At every step we deal with probabilities rather than certainties. In some cases an intelligent and knowledgeable man might well arrive at a solution different from ours. We deal with reasonable solutions and conclusions rather than with proofs.

Yet the result of this whole process, which involves uncertainties at every step, is far from a toss up. The odds are many fold in favor of the expert as compared with the enthusiastic amateur. Knowing how to do the best possible with the data at hand is vital for good intelligence.[3] It is *the* talent by which intelligence production officers justify their existence.

This is the process by which the crude ore of information is crushed and sifted and refined into the pure gold of finished intelligence. It is worthy of study. For the beginnings of a theoretical approach see Furfey (17).

Wanted: A Name for the Process of Fitting Facts Together

When some human activity emerges with a newly discovered unity or importance, it is helpful to give it a distinctive name. In recent cases we can see the value which a name has conferred. Consider, for example, "Automation," "Cybernetics," "Electronics," even "Serendipity."

So for the common and highly important process of taking a mass of data, partly inadequate and partly unreliable, and getting the most out of them that it is humanly possible to get: namely, for the intelligence production process, we suggest any one of the following:

The Art of Drawing Important Conclusions from Inadequate Data.
The Search for Significance.
Extracting the Meaning for Facts.
Inductive Logic (but it is more than this).
Heuristic (recently developed, pertinent in some aspects).
Orthosemantics (from Greek words indicating "True Significance").

[3] This is reminiscent of the card player's motto: "Success comes most often, not from holding a good hand, but from knowing how to play a poor hand well."

This brief examination of the intelligence production process *as a whole* is especially useful here, because elsewhere in this book much space is devoted to breaking this whole process down into its parts. Useful methods for attacking intelligence problems can be developed by studying both approaches.

A PIONEER EFFORT

Though intelligence production shares many principles with the natural and social sciences, the study of the principles of Strategic Intelligence Production as a unified systematic discipline is new. This newness governs and partially justifies the form of presentation used in this book. Best methods for the exploration of this field have not been fully developed

The present attempt to develop the principles and methods is a pioneer effort and quite evidently suffers from the usual shortcomings of pioneer explorations. However, it is true that in new territory even pioneer roads assist the bolder spirits to extend their explorations and are a first step towards better roads built by those who come after.

For several of the tables and methods of attack presented here, the maximum claims that can be made are like the familiar claims made for the performance of a dancing bear, namely, "The wonder here is, not that this is done well, but that it is done at all."

LEVELS OF INTELLIGENCE

Intelligence production includes three quite different levels which need to be discussed and treated differently. In regard to any given foreign situation these levels are as follows, aranged as a bare outline in order of increasing difficulty and importance:

1. Status—What *are* they doing?
   In simple cases this requires knowledge of facts only. Sometimes the source needs only to be able to see and to count. For example a non-technical man can report what a factory *is* making and how much, if he can see it. He can count ships or freight cars.

2. Capabilities—What *can* they do?
   This requires understanding of an art or a science. For example: A chemical engineer could tell that a factory was capable of making TNT, and how much, if it had certain equipment, materials and men. In many cases a statement as to capabilities can be based nearly altogether upon technological factors.

3. Intentions—What *will* they do?
   This question involves the Spirit of the People and an intimate knowledge of the given situation as a whole. A correct answer requires creative judgment and wisdom born of experience and mature study. Only a person well steeped in the national habits of thought and in the personalities concerned will have success in forecasting intentions—which is in part an exercise in mind reading. (See Chapters V and VII.)

Status

Questions regarding *status* are evidently answered by bare facts. Facts regarding industry, population, military equipment, biographies, etc., are naturally the foundations of intelligence production. They are supplied in all sorts of very useful documents, some of them compiled for reference or as training aids.

For reasons discussed above, facts are a good place to start, but a poor place to stop, in the study of any foreign country.

The preparation of any tables or collections of facts obviously requires judgment in selection, evaluation and presentation. Often figures stated as facts in the published paper are not found in the original literature as such. On the contrary the figures are calculated from original data by the use of factors or by other means. For example, approximate population figures for 1948 may be derived from population figures published in 1940 by means of estimated birth rates and death rates.

Except for such calculations, and the use of appropriate factors, intelligence statements regarding status require less knowledge of the social sciences and less interpretation than other levels of intelligence.

Capabilities

We now come to one of the most important, most used, and most confusing words in intelligence, namely Capabilities. "Capabilities" is used as the key word in the title of many high level intelligence papers.

Statements regarding capabilities often appear in seriously misleading forms, isolated from any limiting clauses. This is especially true in many of the Summaries or Conclusions which are often the only parts of a paper read by policy makers. Honest, but serious misunderstandings arise because two equally capable and experienced intelligence officers happen to interpret the term differently.

When applied to physical equipment the meaning is usually clear. Under given conditions a truck is *capable* of being driven at 50 m.p.h. An AA gun is *capable* of reaching an altitude of 20,000 feet, etc. No room for misunderstanding. Where there is no active opposition to be considered the meaning is also clear. The U.S.S.R. is capable of producing so many million tons of coal per annum or of building a nuclear energy submarine.

But in time of war, "capabilities" in an intelligence paper are considered to mean "*unopposed* capabilities." There are good reasons for this, but not good enough to justify the misunderstandings and absurdities which result from the adoption of the present meaning.

The reasoning is as follows: It is the responsibility of intelligence officers to know about foreign countries. For example, to say that Cuba has the capability of landing an invading force of one infantry regiment in the United States means that Cuba has one regiment properly trained and equipped for invasion. It means that she has the shipping necessary for transporting and landing the regiment and that her sailors have the training necessary for this journey, all supposing there is no opposition whatever. In short it merely means that Cuba has the physical capabilities for carrying out this operation unopposed.

Now suppose the United States has overwhelming air and naval superiority in the whole Caribbean area. Suppose the United States has an excellent network of reconnaissance planes, naval patrols, radar, etc., all in working condition. It would then be true that in spite of all Cuba's men, equipment and ships, not a regiment would actually succeed in landing on the shores of the United States. The ships would all be sunk or driven back. Yet even when the certainty of sinking is admitted, the intelligence paper will state flatly: "In case of war Cuba has *the capabilities* to land an infantry regiment in the United States."

Why do intelligence papers say that the enemy has the capabilities to land a regiment on a hostile shore, when actually the enemy could not do it? The writer of the paper knows they could not, and has no wish to deceive; but he does deceive everyone who is not fully alert to the technical limitations of the word "capabilities."

The purpose of using "capabilities" meaning, but not saying "*unopposed* capabilities" is to avoid two difficulties:

First by confining capabilities altogether to what the enemy has, and taking *no* account of United States opposition, the intelligence officer can confine himself to what is altogether his own business, namely the enemy situation. He need not pry into what is strictly speaking none of his business, namely a complete knowledge of U. S. defenses—land, sea and air. Also to take into account both the enemy and the U. S. situation the intelligence officer would have to double the volume of his information. There are likewise security reasons against spreading too widely U. S. defense secrets.

Second, by taking this one-sided approach, the intelligence officer does not require a knowledge of war-gaming. Supposing an invading force of such and such ships, with given aerial support opposed by certain other ships, shore batteries and fighter bombers, how many troops would get ashore? This problem requires tremendous technical and tactical understanding which few intelligence officers have or ordinarily need to have. Yet sound judgment on such matters is required before a simple statement can be made using the words in their commonly accepted non-technical meaning: "In time of war Cuba has the capabilities of landing an infantry regiment in the United States as an invading force."

The confusion is made worse by the fact that when considering peacetime conditions, these difficulties over meaning do not arise. When speaking of peaceful conditions our thought and language are adequate. We therefore erroneously come to feel that they are always adequate. Then when we must discuss wartime conditions, we are unprepared for the misunderstandings.

In some cases the term "gross capabilities" is used to mean "unopposed capabilities" and the term "net capabilities" is used to mean the capabilities after taking opposition into account. This is not followed consistently enough to avoid constant confusion.

There is no limit to the absurdities which result from

carrying the technical intelligence meaning of capabilities to its logical conclusion. Consider the following:

Concerning certain highly poisonous war gases public statements are sometimes made that one aeroplane can carry enough "to wipe out" so many million people. The basis for such statements usually is that a very few milligrams of this highly poisonous gas, if put up the nose and totally inhaled by a man would kill him. One plane could carry enough gas to have the capabilities to kill millions of people *under these conditions.*

As a case in point the *New York Times* for September 19, 1946, carried a story having the heading (I quote the whole headline exactly. There is no qualifying sub-heading.): "Ounce of New Super-Poison Held Able to Wipe Out U. S., Canada." Please note that killing every person in the United States is not enough. Canada is thrown in for good measure. Such are the absurdities to which the concept of capabilities and what a munition is "able" to do if unopposed, can lead us.

Or as an extreme (and this time hypothetical) example consider: The United States has two million men under arms. Curtania has two million rounds of small arms ammunition. One round of small arms ammunition can kill one man in less than one minute. *Therefore,* Curtania has the capability of killing all of the defense forces of the United States in less than one minute!

Practical Considerations

As a reader, whenever you see the word "capabilities" view it with suspicion. Take a critical attitude. What does the writer really mean by capabilities? Under what conditions will his statement be true? Under what conditions will it be doubtful or false?

As a writer, always make clear the conditions under which your statement will be true. If your statement has a wartime context, and if you mean to talk only about *unopposed* capabilities, always so state. Never leave it to the reader to misinterpret your statement. Avoid this term altogether and use an alternative whenever possible.

As for editors and supervisors, study critically all statements involving "capabilities." And insist on clarification when necessary.[3a]

Enemy Intentions and Probable Courses of Action

When we take the next step and say not "What *can* the enemy do?" but "What *will* the enemy do?" "What are the enemy's probable courses of action?" then we are in quite a different realm.

"Status" and "Capabilities" both rested upon objective facts that could, in theory at least, be measured and counted. With intentions or "probable courses of acion" we bring in the crystal ball and set it right in the middle of the table.[4]

As we get further from combat intelligence and more into Strategic Intelligence the terms "intentions" and "probable

[3a] The difficulties above mentioned arising from the use of "capabilities" are neither imaginary nor out of date. That these difficulties occur at the highest levels is shown by the serious misunderstanding which occurred regarding the remarks of Admiral Carney then CNO. A *New York Times* despatch of 13 April 1955 states: "Admiral Carney later told Congress that he did not predict—as was alleged—that the Communists would attack Matsu in mid April. He was speaking, he said, of enemy capabilities, not their intentions."

[4] No one has written so clearly or so devastatingly about enemy intentions as Schwien. (7) His excellent book, which is devoted altogether to combat intelligence, had a very salutory effect in pointing out the dangers of common glib references to enemy intentions. See his Chapter II, "Capabilities vs. Probable Intentions." Our Army FM 30-5 Combat Intelligence Feb. 1951, par. 47, says: "Commanders must be certain that they base their actions, dispositions, and plans upon *estimates of enemy capabilities rather than upon estimates of enemy intentions.*"

courses of action" become more reputable. Kent (5) for example says: "Probable Courses of Action: Estimates." "I have urged that if you have knowledge of Great Frusina's strategic stature, knowledge of her specific vulnerabilities, and how she may view these, and knowledge of the stature and vulnerabilities of other states party to the situation, you are in a fair way able to predict her probable course of action.

"To strengthen the reliability of your prediction you should possess two additional packages of knowledge. First, you should know about the courses of action which Great Frusina *has followed in the past.* Does the history of her *foreign policy reveal a pattern* which she will adhere to? Has she followed certain lines of international behavior for so long that they have hardened into *traditions with proven survival value.* Or are they myths founded in irrationality? Will these traditions or myths exert an influence—even though an illogical influence—upon her probable present course of action? Has Great Frusina an old friend with whom she will never break; has she had over the years a real need for an 'eastern ally': has she a traditional 'life-line of empire' to maintain, or the urge for 'ice-free ports?' Knowledge of this order is important, but must be used with caution For while the force of tradition is strong, the present moment may be the very one in which Great Frusina is girding herself to break with the past.

"Second: You should know, as closely as such things may be known, how Great Frusinans are estimating their own stature in the situation. . . .

"One may say in summary that if intelligence is armed with the various kinds of knowledge which I have discussed in this chapter, and if it commands the welter of fact which lies behind them, intelligence ought to be able to make shrewd guesses—estimates, they are generally called—as to what Great Frusina, or any other country is likely to do in any circumstances whatsoever. Note that intelligence does not claim infallibility for its prophecies. Intelligence merely holds that the answer which it gives is its most deeply and objectively based and carefully considered estimate.

"In such fashion intelligence should have a reasoned opinion on what policies a country is likely to initiate within the next year of its own free will."

Usually in Strategic Intelligence there is more time to study the situation than in combat intelligence. The preliminaries to strategic action carrying out a country's intentions often involve thousands of citizens, massive action of industry, etc., and so are harder for that country to hide. So a statement of "intentions" is much more often justified in Strategic Intelligence than it is in combat intelligence.

A Parody

Early in 1945 the London *Daily Express* published the following as a take-off on our efforts to explain away the deficiencies in the use of intelligence at the time of the Battle of the Bulge in Europe. It touches on the concept of capabilities and intention without using these terms. The *Daily Express* military commentator wrote:

"While it cannot be said that Rundstedt's offensive achieved its object of changing the Allied time-table, it has undoubtedly made some alteration necessary in that time-table.

"It has rather postponed than delayed an offensive, and in that sense alone, may be said to have lengthened, but not prolonged, the war. The Allies were not surprised, because they knew the possibility of a surprise attack. What surprised them was that the Germans thought it worthwhile to make a surprise attack in spite of the fact that such an attack, though deemed possible, was not deemed probable, in view of the fact that we knew they would try to surprise us."

SOME UNOFFICIAL DEFINITIONS

As a continuation of the line of thought of the past few pages, and with the specific purpose of helping to eliminate some existing misunderstandings the following additional definitions are proposed:

Vulnerability

The vulnerabilities of a nation are the weaknesses which make it susceptible to any action through which its war potential may be reduced or its will to fight diminished. This includes also those activities indirectly related to war potential such as industrial, scientific and political potential.

Vulnerability implies that one nation *could really carry out* successfully the hostile action against the vulnerable nation.

As examples, from the situation discussed in the preceding paragraphs, Cuba is vulnerable to a military invasion from the U. S.; but the U. S. is not vulnerable to a military invasion from Cuba.

Estimate

An intelligence estimate is a paper which either assesses a present situation or makes a prediction about future developments.

Every forecast is an estimate. Estimates frequently deal with the future, but not necessarily so. A study of the Arkadian Army extending over the past five years and noting progress in some departments, and loss in others, might end with an estimate in the form of a conclusion that "all things considered the combat effectiveness of the Arkadian Army is significantly greater than it was five years ago." This would be a correct use of the term "estimate," though dealing only with the past and present.

If a statement of present status is based on rather direct counting or measuring, or simple calculations, it is not considered an estimate. For example: Tables of soundings, biographical information, facts about crops, exports, bridges are not estimates. However, if we are studying some subject on which facts are difficult to obtain, such as many subjects behind the Curtain, and on which understanding of many related circumstances and judgment of the over-all result play a vital part in final conclusions, then we may have an estimate even though based altogether upon present status.

This definition of an intelligence estimate differs from a meaning of the word used in non-intelligence activities in connection with measurements. In reporting figures (for example distances or weights), it is customary to indicate that some were ascertained by actual measurement or weighing and others were "estimates"; that is, approximations based upon experience, but without actual measurement. In fact in the Army an important part of training is "range estimation" in which distances on the terrain are guessed at, if you will, and the guesses then checked against measurements, so that the guesses or estimates may improve with experience.

Potentialities

Capabilities which do not now exist, but which are possible of development in the foreseeable future.

Potential carries no implication as to whether such development is probable. Thus a nation with undeveloped copper deposits has the potential for a copper mining industry.

JUDGMENT STILL NECESSARY

One essential for sound judgment of a paper as a whole is mature thought from a broad point of view.

Many people spend their lives in some field of endeavor without ever attempting to get at any of its fundamental philosophy, or exploring the boundaries, or thinking the problems through to clarify their own point of view. People who fail *to think about* their field of primary responsibility and to *think all around it* certainly miss many of the deeper satisfactions and probably accomplish less than they would otherwise do. Trevelyan (4) emphasizes the same point.

This is certainly true of intelligence production on foreign countries. We have here the problem expressed in the title of Mead's book, *The Study of Culture at a Distance,* (19) namely to study a foreign situation when we cannot get very close to it.

For example, consider the case of the historian trying to understand and to depict the life of the Middle Ages. This cannot be done on the fifteen-minutes-before-lunch basis, which is the bane of sound intelligence production. One must soak oneself in the atmosphere of the age and country whether as a historian or as an intelligence officer. Furthermore, one must *constantly think about it.* During such rumination, patterns form and trends emerge. (See Chap. IV). There is no substitute for mature thought. Following thought should come discussion.

Sherlock Holmes and the Forcing of Conclusions

In learning what to do in any process, the consideration of pitfalls to avoid, i.e. what not to do, is always helpful. Awful examples have their place. The foregoing discussion has described the process of putting scattered scraps of information together; so that a meaningful picture will emerge and sound conclusions can be drawn. Examples of these same principles carried to extremes are given in the publications of the Sherlock Holmes Society of London and of the Baker Street Irregulars in the United States. These two affiliated societies are devoted to a study of Conan Doyle's writings regarding Sherlock Holmes. "Learned papers" are published by these two societies on various questions pertaining to the lives of Holmes, Dr. Watson and other characters mentioned in the Sherlock Holmes stories.

The papers are based upon an extraordinarily thorough study of the stories; research into the cultural, geographical, meteorological and political background, and are probably the most completely documented papers in existence. They exemplify the processes commonly used for the production of intelligence. Sherlock Holmes studies are in fact caricatures of learned papers, and are written entirely for fun with a remarkable display of wit and originality.

As a warning to intelligence production officers, consider the paper which focuses on the question: From what university did Dr. Watson graduate? This is a question that never entered the head of Conan Doyle, the author of the Sherlock Holmes stories. The writer of the paper above mentioned is studying a situation which never existed, even in Doyle's imagination. The writer of this paper, therefore, cannot possibly have any sound basis for drawing conclusions. Nevertheless, he writes a convincing paper, thoroughly documented, to show that Dr. Watson graduated from Yale! (As an example of his reasoning he quotes with proper references to the text, several cases where Dr. Watson had committed errors in grammar. This proved he could not be a Harvard graduate. And so on for other deductions.)[4a]

Seriously speaking, this paper is well worthy of study by intelligence officers as a warning as to how easy it is to build up a glib, convincing case out of next to nothing, and so to reach conclusions which are entirely unwarranted.

For a discussion of the "Logic of Sherlock Holmes" see Ruby (23). So much for Holmes.

[4a] Winthrop Wetherbee, "The Third Continent: Further Light on Dr. Watson," *Baker Street Journal* (New Series) *2* (1952), 129.

Turning back now to the intelligence officer, the problem regarding the drawing of conclusions is aggravated by the fact that most writers are happier when they can draw definite conclusions from their researches. Most supervisors of intelligence workers are happier when a conclusion is drawn. Nearly all readers experience a feeling of satisfaction when the author offers them a strong conclusion which they can tie to and relax. They feel a mild resentment when an author presents them with no conclusion. So there is a psychological pressure in favor of conclusions, which in some cases is dangerous.

THE SCIENTIFIC METHOD Applied to INTELLIGENCE PRODUCTION

The Scientific Method—Straightline or Feedback?

The so-called "scientific method" means different things to different people, but the basic features are much the same. These features are: collection of data, formation of hypotheses, testing the hypotheses, and so arriving at conclusions based on the foregoing which can be used as reliable sources of prediction.

In the collection of data and the testing of hypotheses, observation or preferably experiment plays an important part. References to discussions of the scientific method are given in the Bibliography, including an illuminating statement of the two extreme positions.

The scientific method has had a large share in the progress in the natural sciences. Much of it is also applicable to the social sciences and hence to research for intelligence production. A study of the method (or more correctly, methods) will assist the intelligence officer by giving him a better understanding of the research process, and in providing him with some specific applications. Furthermore, some applications of the method to a typical intelligence problem will bring out two points which have been overlooked in this field and will show their outstanding usefulness.

As a background problem for all of our present discussion, we will suppose that you, as an intelligence officer, are required to produce a paper on "The effect of the supply of scientific manpower on the present and near future scientific capabilities of Curtania." Methods will be described here in simplified form, so as to eliminate all details which do not bear on the points under discussion.

Sir J. A. Thomson (20) as quoted by Gee (21) gives as the steps in the scientific method:

Collecting the data
Measurement
Arrangement of the data in workable form
Analyses and reduction
Hypothesis
Formulation.

This list of steps may be criticized on two points, both having practical importance to the intelligence officer.

First, it does not *start* with a step which includes the idea of a General Survey and Plan of the Whole Problem. Without such a general survey at the very beginning there is little to guide the collection of information and other research activities.

Second, and here is the vital point of this whole discussion —nearly all lists of steps prepared by those who have discussed the scientific method lead one to believe that scientific research is essentially a streamlined succession of one logical step after another until the final result is reached. We get the idea that eddies in the stream, or backtracking, or feedbacks as they would now be called, are the exception and are to be avoided so far as possible.

Conant (22) and some few others have mentioned the fact that the actual course of scientific research, like the course of true love, ne'er runs smooth, but the important *advantages* of the eddy currents have certainly not yet been pointed out in such a way that they are constantly utilized by intelligence officers.

The contention of the author is that for intelligence production research, the straight line flow fails to utilize the highly valuable *guidance* which comes from eddies or feedbacks at nearly every stage of the process.

The feedback in scientific research was brought out by

Gibson (10) in an article which has many applications to intelligence. A detailed description of the process is justified, because each detail has a useful application to intelligence production.

For intelligence research the most useful selection of steps is that given in the following list. In this list the short title of each step, as given in the chart (Figure 3) has been underlined. Details refer to the Curtania Scientific Manpower Problem already described.

The Major Steps

Step 1. *General Survey*. A Survey of the whole problem and of adjacent fields from which help might be obtained. A general plan for the conduct of the work, including time, men and principal sources of information believed to be available.

For example, as a start in the consideration of scientific manpower in Curtania, it might become evident that we would need to consider as a guide what is known about scientific manpower in the United States and how our knowledge of U.S. manpower is organized and expressed.

The understanding, judgment, common sense and realism devoted at the beginning to this general survey and plan will have a powerful influence on the success of the whole project.

Step 2. *Definition of Terms*. A definition and explanation of what we do and do not mean by each term and concept, which will be clear to ourselves, our reviewers, and our readers is *essential*. Defiinitions are, in fact, one of the Nine Principles of Intelligence.

In the present instance some questions of definition are: Does "scientific" include "engineering"? Does it include secondary school students of chemistry and physics? Does "scientific capabilities" include capabilities for scientific research only? Or does it include also capability to support all the other principal scientific activities such as: industrial scientific research, scientific control of manufacturing processes, and teaching science? How many years are included "in the near future"? Should a careful numerical comparison be made with the U.S. scientific situation, so that results can be expressed comparatively?

We see at once, that a clear definition of each term and concept which can be misunderstood is essential at the very beginning.[5]

Step 3. *Collection of Data.* Some data are readily available in the U.S.; other data must be requested from overseas.

In this step we include getting the data together, but not field collection.

Step 4. *Interpretation of Data.* This is a short title for studying and working over the data so as to get out of it all that there is in it, and to see the progress and limitations of our work as we go along. This step includes evaluation, classification, analysis, and interpretation of the data. Data may sometimes be helpfully plotted, subjected to statistical analysis, etc., at this step. In many discussions of intelligence per se, evaluation is treated as a separate step; but for this discussion of the scientific method, evaluation can conveniently be considered as part of interpretation.

Step 5. *Formation of Hypotheses.* From our interpretation of the data we can formulate tentative hypotheses. For example, it may seem that Curtania has an unexpectedly large number of railroad engineers. We ask ourselves why. Does this mean that Curtania is far ahead of us in railroad transportation capabilities; or does it mean that it is so far behind us that it has an urgent need for more railroads in order to catch up with other civilized countries? The tenta-

[5] A military maxim states: What *can* be misunderstood, *will* be misunderstood.

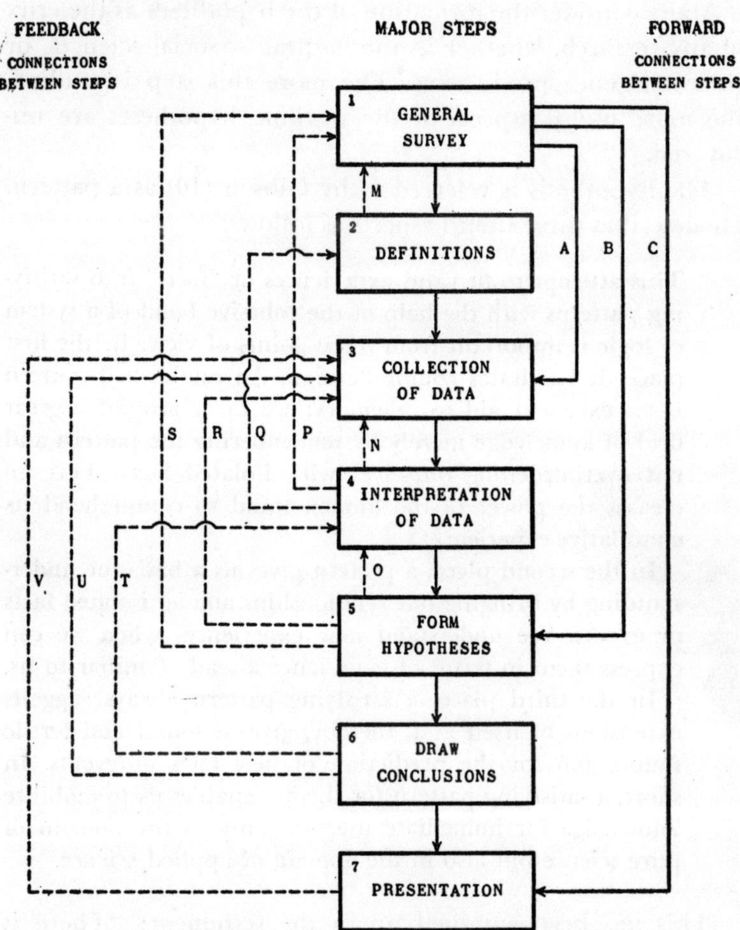

Figure 3 Flow Chart for Intelligence Production

tive hypotheses which we set up at this time generally point to specific questions by which they can be tested.

Many consider the formation of the hypotheses as the crux of any research, whether in the natural or social sciences, or in intelligence production. The more this step is studied, the more useful aspects of the working hypotheses are uncovered.

The hypothesis is referred to by Gibson (10) as a pattern. He describes three useful aspects as follows:

> This attempt to fit valid experiences or "facts" into satisfying patterns with the help of the cohesive bond of a system of logic is important from three points of view. In the first place, it facilitates comprehension. An established pattern is an excellent aid to memory; we carry around a great deal of knowledge merely by remembering the pattern and not overburdening ourselves with isolated facts. This increases the power of the human mind to comprehend its cumulative experience; . . . .
>
> In the second place, a pattern gives us a basis for understanding by bringing our relationships among isolated facts or events. We understand new experiences when we can express them in terms of experience already familiar to us.
>
> In the third place, a satisfying pattern always suggests extensions of itself and, thereby, gives a sound and fertile foundation for the prediction of new facts or events. In short, a satisfying pattern (or theory) enables us to mobilize knowledge for immediate use, not only in the domain of pure science but also in the domain of applied science.

This has been summed up in the statement: "There is nothing so practical as a good theory."

Viewed in its broadest sense, forming hypotheses is an ever-present part of any research. At the very beginning, when we lay out our general plan, we start with certain assumptions (or hypotheses) as to which factors are probably important and which are almost certainly extraneous. Similar hypotheses guide our collection of data, interpretation, conclusions and presentation.

Hypothesis is a term well established in scientific research literature. Intelligence officers more commonly use "integration" for this step, even though the meaning is not exactly the same.

Step 6. *Drawing Conclusions.* This step includes the investigations necessary to prove or disprove the tentative hypotheses set up in Step 5 and to draw the final conclusions which are the heart of most intelligence papers. (Conclusions form the last of the Nine Principles of Intelligence.)

Step 7. *Presentation.* Drawing up the final report. The writer must not only have clear ideas, he must express them clearly. The degree of certainty to which each important statement is entitled must be indicated. Tables and charts will probably be a part of a manpower paper. Valid comparisons between nations are difficult to make, but in this case a comparison of the scientific manpower situation in Curtania with that in the United States may be the most illuminating part of the paper.

The above steps in the scientific method as applied to intelligence production are parallel and closely similar to the steps ordinarily considered by the intelligence officer. A comparison is given in the table on page 82.

The principle differences are:

(1) Evaluation is a definite and necessary step in intelligence production where so many of the raw data are unreliable.

(2) "The Formation of Hypotheses" is one of the favorite phrases in discussions of the scientific method.

It seemed best, therefore, to recognize and retain these differences in this chapter rather than to try to force these two quite similar lists of steps into exactly the same form.

A Comparison

Steps in Intelligence Production As Ordinarily Considered By The Intelligence Officer[6]	Steps in Intelligence Production Following The Scientific Method[7]
	General Survey of the Problem
	Definition of Terms
Selection of Data	Selection of Data (sometimes Collection)
Evaluation of Data Interpretation of Data	Interpretation of Data including evaluation
Integration	Formation of Hypotheses (and their verification)
Conclusions	Conclusions
Presentation	Presentation

The essence of the scientific method is that each step when taken is considered as *tentative*. Each may be modified by what is learned in later steps as the work proceeds. For example, the collection of data is not carried out once and for all and completed at one time. After some of the data are collected in Step 3, the data are interpreted in Step 4. The interpretation will doubtless point to more collection in certain directions and less in others, thus giving guidance as the research proceeds.

Each of the other steps is similarly treated. For example, the plan for the whole project is tentative when adopted. We should be willing to set up a tentative plan, and *equally ready to reopen the case* and to modify our tentative plan whenever new evidence points to the need for modification.

6 Discussed in this chapter under "The Intelligence Production Process as a Whole."

7 See Fig. 3.

This will all become clear in following the method step by step as given below.

The Function of the Feedback

The attached flow chart (Fig. 3) shows how the work actually proceeds. The flow chart must be closely followed in connection with this discussion.

We first consider one specific example and show, for the purposes of illustration, some of the channels of thought that would probably be used. It should be evident that in other cases other channels of thought would be followed, making useful connections (not shown in this figure) between almost any one of the Major Steps with almost any other one.

The work goes forward in sequence from Step 1 to Step 2 to Step 3, etc. It *also* goes forward by leap-frogging over some of the steps as shown. For example, General Survey to Presentation.[8] At the very beginning of any project it is helpful to form some tentative ideas as to what the nature of the final report will probably be. This plan for the final report like everything else is subject to change as the work progresses. In the present instance a general survey will show that a comparison of Curtanian scientific manpower with that of U.S. will be desirable. This knowledge *at the very beginning* is a guide to collection. The initial survey indicates that charts will probably be needed for the final report. So in our thinking we deliberately skip from the very beginning all the way to the very end. (Step 1 to Step 7. Channel C.)

The General Survey nearly always brings tentative hypotheses to mind. (Channel B.) In the case given as an example we might form a hypothesis that scientific research is *the* crucial item in scientific capabilities. We might take

[8] See alsc Chap. IV., Useful Procedures, "Beginning at the End."

as a hypothesis that if we can find enough high grade original research workers, the other categories of scientists will take care of themselves. We investigate this hypothesis from the beginning. Following out such hypotheses will influence all of our work on the project.

We will now examine how some of the ideas when fed backward to earlier steps in the method help to modify some of those earlier steps and the tentative conclusions that we may have reached for any given step.

As examples it is evident that ideas derived from Interpretation of Data, or from the Formation of Hypotheses, or from final Conclusions or from an attempt at the final Presentation of our project may all disclose the need for more data in certain fields. The new data may, of course, in turn modify any of the thinking dependent upon them. All of this is shown by the feedback lines on the flow chart. (Channels N, R, U, V respectively.)

As another example shown by the chart (Step 5 back to Step 3, Channel R) a hypothesis might indicate that the number of scientists with advanced degrees was the real key to scientific research capabilities. So we then go back to the selection step and focus our attention on these advanced-degree scientists which are few in number, but important in assessing future scientific capabilities.

Again our interpretation of the data collected may show us that some definitions we had made at the beginning of the work were not in accord with Curtania categories. So we change these definitions as a result of the feedback shown. (Step 4 back to Step 2, Channel Q.)

Useful results from the feedbacks between other steps constantly occur. Some of the more common are shown on the chart. For example, Step 5 back to Step 1, and Step 6 back to Step 4, Channels S and T respectively. Different connections not here shown will occur in different problems.

Each of the forward and backward connections between

the steps as shown by the lines on the chart has a meaning. they are worth following through and understanding. Then we can be on the lookout for them when they occur in our work, and can get the maximum benefit from the irregular, but highly useful, mental connections between the Major Steps of the scientific method as applied to intelligence production research.

A More Generalized View of Research

We have just presented a simplified picture of the Major Steps in the scientific method, and have followed through briefly the intellectual operations required by one example. The picture given is logical and sufficiently simple to bring out the main points. The list of Major Steps is easy to remember. It is certainly logical, for example, to start with the General Survey and Plan of the Project and to end with the Presentation or Final Report. We are now ready to extend our study of the scientific method beyond this simple outline in three useful directions indicated below as Sections A, B, and C.

A. *The Order of the Steps.* In a research project each of the seven Major Steps listed is generally present by the name given or by an approximately synonomous name. Groupings and Subdivisions of these steps do not change the essence of this list. But surprisingly enough the highly logical order just given is frequently changed.

Often the whole train of events starts with the hypothesis as the first step. In your own field an original hypothesis may occur to you as a first step. The more you think of it the more you become convinced that the hypothesis opens a new and promising line of attack. You then collect some data (Old Step 3) in this direction which seems to support the hypothesis. Thus encouraged, you plan a systematic research project Old Step 1).

Many researchers have started with the selection of facts in one field, but with no dominating hypothesis and no plan, thus starting with Old Step 3. Darwin started in this way to collect data which eventually led to the theory of Evolution through Natural Selection, ending with his publication (Old Step 7) in 1859.

Gibson (10), less simply, but perhaps more correctly than myself, presents the scientific method with its feedbacks as a cycle, in which you can start at one step just as logically as at any other. My own chart presents the method as proceeding predominantly in one direction with Step 1 as the *most usual and mentally satisfactory starting point.*

B. *Secondary Effects from Feedbacks.* We can now profitably consider more fully and more seriously the secondary and tertiary effects of the feedback. Let us follow further one of the effects already mentioned, taking one specific case as illustrative of many.

As an example suppose:

Step 3. We collect scattered biographical data on some leading Curtanian scientists.

Step 4. We interpret the data and thus find that nearly all of the limited number of biographies at hand show that the subjects hold advanced degrees.

Step 5. We form the tentative hypothesis that advanced degrees are the controlling factor in Curtanian capabilities for scientific research and development.

Feedback. Step 5 to Step 3, Channel R, we greatly increase our collection of biographical information on Curtanian scientists.

Step 3 to Step 4. Interpretation of these data leads to a question regarding how closely the Curtanian Ph.D. degree corresponds to the U.S. Ph.D.

Secondary Feedback. Step 4 to Step 3, Channel N, we collect data on the meaning of the Curtanian Ph.D. degree.

This is a new direction for our studies not previously contemplated.

Step 3 to Step 4. Interpretation of the new data shows that the Curtanian Kandidat degree corresponds the most closely to the U.S. Ph.D. and that the Curtanian Ph.D. is relatively rare

Tertiary Feedback. Step 4 to Step 2, Channel Q, we correct our definitions of Curtanian higher degrees This correction applies throughout the whole paper.

In this simple example the feedback has served to guide and improve our research activities *as they went along*. Far from being a nuisance to have to return to the library for more information, it is the most economical way in which our collection and selection could be guided.

The only rivals in efficiency would be first the assumption of omniscience on our part whereby we knew all the answers at the beginning. In this case the project would not be a *research* project at all, in the sense of exploring the unknown, but would be merely a *compilation* of well-known information. The second alternative would assume uniform good luck in our collection. In the infinite amount of material which might conceivably be collected, we would have to assume that we would habitually stumble into the most pertinent facts.

It is a commonplace that new facts may lead to new hypotheses, which may point to new areas of inquiry with new avenues of attack all beyond the original project. In the present discussion, however, we are showing how these eddy currents in our work feed back into additional methods for *attacking the same problem*. Our increase in knowledge of the original problem is definitely on the compound interest principle, where we *get interest on the interest*. The benefits build up—if we make full use of them—in a manner which mathematicians describe as exponential.

C. Finally is the outstanding place of the *Formulation of the Hypothesis* in the whole process (or cycle) of an intelligence research project.

We have seen that all our preliminary planning for the project was unconsciously based upon assumptions as to what was pertinent. In fact, without hypotheses, we cannot even *think* about a research project. Sometimes a listing of these hypotheses and a critical examination of the validity of each will uncover some long-standing errors and set us on the road to a more successful approach. The large number of assumptions with which we start is seldom realized by research workers. Among these assumptions some are probably seriously in error.

The formulation of hypotheses is the most purely intellectual operation in intelligence research. The intellectual aspect is covered in Chapter IV. The Formulation of Hypotheses can, in fact, be shown as the dominant step in the research cycle, with all of the other major steps as subsidiary. This point of view can be fruitfully pursued.

Four

INTELLIGENCE PRODUCTION

An Act of Creative Thinking

Examples of Intelligence Production Problems
Requiring Creative Thinking
General Principles of Mental Activity
Stages in Creative Thinking : Useful Procedures
Six Types of Research Minds : General Summary

There are three things no man can stand to be told, namely that he has bad taste, that he can't handle people, and that he can't think.

Richard Weil, Jr.,
past president of Macy's, New York

Much of intelligence production is essentially a compilation. With great industry we get together a large number of facts bearing on a given problem and present them in some logical arrangement. We fill in blanks and add up columns. This is highly useful work, but is not of the kind which is to be considered in this chapter.

Problems of the kind mentioned above can be completely solved—in theory at least—merely by hard work and a knowledge of appropriate techniques. Little or no inspiration or judgment is needed. For example a map can be made of a piece of land with any amount of detail desired, purely by spending enough time on it, provided one is a map maker. The same thing is not true of some other kinds of problems where the possible solutions are multitudinous, and where a correct answer can only be expected as the result of experience, judgment, and wisdom. Examples: To prepare a piece of creative writing; or like Kekule in organic chemistry, to explain the configuration of atoms based on the benzene ring; or to develop polio vaccine; or to estimate the probable courses of action of a nation as a reaction to our new airfields in Africa.

Problems of this latter group cannot be solved by set techniques plus hard work. It is here that the art of creative thinking which mobilizes our mental resources, and applies them most effectively, is essential.

Most of what has previously been written on the subject of creative thinking has had primarily in mind the solution of problems in mathematics, of other natural sciences, or of making inventions. Among such publications in chronological order are Poincaré (26), Bancroft (27), Platt and Baker (28), Rossman (29), Polya (30), Conant (31), and Beveridge (32).

A considerable part of what these authors have written, including nearly all that they have written about mental operations, can also be applied to the problems of intelligence production. Such applications will be pointed out in this chapter.

Material will also be drawn from those fewer writers who considered other kinds of objectives when discussing creative thinking. Such as: A. A discussion of the psychological background of creative thinking—James (33), Dewey (34), Humphrey (35), Wallas (36). Only the necessary high-spots of the psychological background will be covered here. B. Creative writing—Lowes (37). C. Originality in business or advertising—Osborn (38).

We know that the readers of this book can think. If intelligence production is really an intellectual process then it will be profitable to make one of our attacks on its problems from this point of view. What are the steps in an intellectual process? What procedures have been found to be generally helpful?

So the purpose of this chapter is to present some interesting principles applicable to scientific discovery, intelligence production, and other forms of mental effort.

We first consider certain types of intelligence production where creative thinking is necessary. These types form a background of specific instances to which our general principles of mental activity discussed later in the chapter can be applied.

We then consider the general process of mental activity as an introduction to the four well-recognized stages in creative thinking. An understanding of these stages may help us to carry out each of them more effectively. Based on this foundation we then consider several procedures which have been found especially beneficial in intelligence, borrowing ideas freely from others wherever we find anything which can be adapted to improve intelligence production.

Finally we quote from a distinguished scientist who has made a study of types of research minds. Since we find the same types of minds among intelligence researchers, this study helps us to utilize each type to best advantage (including assistance to each reader to help him to recognize and best utilize his own type).

EXAMPLES OF INTELLIGENCE PRODUCTION PROBLEMS REQUIRING CREATIVE THINKING

Some typical examples of intelligence production problems are listed below.

When reading later in this chapter about any one of the

stages of creative thinking, say illumination, the reader can ask himself: How would this apply to the formation of a hypothesis, or a prediction, etc. in the intelligence examples given? This serves to tie this whole discussion right down to the desk of the analyst. Pointing out the applications of this chapter directly to intelligence problems is the more necessary because most of the examples of stages in creative thinking here quoted arose originally from scientific research rather than from intelligence research.

In giving examples of intelligence problems we are only following the excellent advice of Dale Carnegie, namely: Never state a general principle without including several specific examples to which the principle applies.

Problem A. Devising a Method of Approach

Let us suppose that the question put to the analyst is: What is the quality of the engineers currently graduating from institutions of higher learning in Curtania? To solve this he must evidently obtain a method for the determination of quality.

Some aspects of this problem which soon come to mind are:

What do we mean by quality in engineers? Is it ability for research and development; or ability to teach? Must these each be considered separately? Must we also consider separately the different branches of engineering such as mechanical, civil, electrical, etc.?

Can we helpfully study quality of engineers in one country except in comparison with engineers in other countries?

Even if we knew the quality from intimate professional contacts with the engineers under study (impossible in the case of Curtania) how would we measure and express it?

Supposing a reasonable number of facts can be dug up, is the quality of Curtanian engineers a promising subject for study? Would the answer be useful if we could get it? Can we obtain a reliable and meaningful answer with the time and the intelligence workers available? or are the difficulties so great that this is essentially an unprofitable and probably a hopeless problem for intelligence attack?

If a critical difficulty exists it lies in our shortage of understanding of the fundamental principles and of the critical points for attacking the problem, somewhat as stated above. The original "simple" question is seen to bristle with sub-problems of creative thinking.

Problem B. Formation of a Hypothesis

The question: In case of an early war, what are the capabilities of Curtania in long range artillery?

If the Curtanians have good models for their guns, what is the situation as to fire control, artillery shell manufacture, training? Is there some critical limiting factor which controls the whole problem? For the efficient collection of data you *must* form at an early stage of the research some tentative hypothesis as to the critical factors. This tentative hypothesis will guide the selection of data unless and until a better hypothesis is formed.

Problem C. To Give a Correct Picture of a Foreign Situation

For example, Control of Science from the Top Down in Curtania.

This is not a static situation which can be properly depicted merely by organization charts. The picture is that of a huge organization of human beings, each with his ambitions, capabilities and limitations. How does it really work? Where do the decisions really come from? To what extent can a scientific worker far down in the hierarchy make his scientific ideas heard? Is the political control really fatal to bold, creative, scientific progress?

How can this be described clearly, correctly and with the proper emphasis, so that the reader gets a true picture of what the situation really is and how it really works?

These last questions require the best creative thinking and creative writing.

Problem D. A Prediction

Will the Communists return to power at the coming elections in Arkadia?

Our mind would range over many possible key factors: the size of the wheat crop; the attitude of a local leader; the amount of Soviet support, etc. In the selection out of many possibilities of a few key factors for further study, all of the stages of creative thinking play their parts.

Problem E. Another Prediction

Probable Developments in Curtanian Internal Transportation Facilities by 1965.

Here the key factors and possible modes of attack are fairly evident. Positive factors would certainly be need and motivation. Limiting factors possible shortages of steel, manpower or money. The creative intelligence problem for the analyst is how to balance the positive against the limitations so as to arrive at the probable net result.

Problem F. Creative Writing

Having been given our problem, having solved it somewhat to our satisfaction, having by long thought and study formed *in our own mind* a clear picture of the situation, then how should this be presented in the final report? How extensively or briefly should we report our findings? How definitely, or with what limitations should we state our conclusions? What charts, pictures, quotations should we use? A finished presentation is a work of art. Here is a problem for the creative artist, and hence in creative thinking.

GENERAL PRINCIPLES OF MENTAL ACTIVITY

The General Picture

Much has been written about various aspects of the thinking process. This forms a part of the general subjects of logic and of psychology and is included in studies on education and related subjects.

All of this is described in any of the books on logic as by Whitehead (1) or Ruby (23) for example, or on psychology, James (33) and others. One that is readable, modern, but very elementary, and which has the same general approach as the present chapter is Humphrey's *Directed Thinking.* (35)

Only a few of the high spots directly connected with Creative Thinking are given below. *This is done in general terms and without any attempt at rigorous definitions or highly technical psychological modes of expression.*

When left to itself the mind flits more or less aimlessly from one subject to another. When nothing is required of any stage of the thinking process, this undirected flitting about, or day dreaming, is carried on without appreciable effort. It is no effort for me to think that it is a long way to Tipperary, if I have no responsibility for finding out how to get there. The mind can and normally does touch on a great number of subjects one after the other in a fraction of a second each and without noticeable effort.

When the mind is motivated in one direction, we make an effort to concentrate our thoughts on one general subject.

Even then there is a tendency for our mind to wander, so that it must be constantly brought back to the question before us.

Motivation may be very mild like a passing interest in a lecture; increasing to an earnest desire to master a lesson; or at the extreme to a burning desire which completely dominates the mind and sweeps all before it. Such a burning motivation may be negative—fear, a desire to escape, intense discomfort, etc. It may be a positive passion, anger, greed, an overwhelming desire to attain some goal. Motivation is often a complex of several factors, some of which may be subconcious. The degree of motivation in any instance has influence on the final outcome of the thinking.

Some of our various bodily activities are conscious, like the movement of our limbs; some semiconscious, like breathing; some completely unconscious, like the movement of the heart. So with our thoughts and ideas. Some are completely conscious. We recognize them and know that they are there. Some are unconscious. We are not aware of them. We are not aware of the contacts which are constantly being made between these unconscious thoughts, though we may later become conscious of the integrated result.

As a result of our whole living experience, including our reading and our thinking, our minds contain a huge number of ideas which we accept as facts. Most of these are correct as far as they go, some are based upon prejudices which may be unfounded. Some of our ideas are definitely erroneous.

To live ordinary daily lives, men (as well as animals) have constantly to take this enormous body of ideas at their face value. Ordinarily we cannot take the time to re-examine the thousands of common assumptions in our daily life.

Most of us have acquired into our personal culture many acts that we find natural and pleasant to do; others that we would find most unpleasant to do—this entirely apart from bodily needs or tangible benefits. For example, a Christian finds it natural to kneel in prayer. An old soldier would be very reluctant to perform any act disrespectful to the flag. Our acquired culture, habits, and prejudices are a part of us and of our mental content.

When a problem is presented to the mind, the mind considers one possible solution after another in rapid succession, in fact almost instantaneously. Most of these solutions are rejected as promptly as they are thought of. One or two are reserved for more serious consideration. Finally one is adopted.

Two Examples of Consideration and Rejection in Problem-Solving

You have three weeks for your summer vacation. Being broke you were planning to spend it quietly. Opening your mail you are surprised to find a check for $1,000 from your uncle, sent to you for use on your vacation. Where shall you go?

At once your mind considers a number of places and instantly discards them one after the other. Florida? Too hot. Friend John? He is rather a bore for three weeks. Egypt? Too far away, too expensive. England? Too expensive. The round trip fare by air or a good liner is $800. It would be a foolish way to spend your money. So you temporarily and sensibly decide on Cape Cod where you have friends. This is Decision No. 1.

But you give the matter another thought. There is a friend in England whom you would greatly like to see. You make a serious investigation and find that there are some ways of getting to England and back by ship in which you perform some services on shipboard and pay only $300 in cash. This makes the trip to England possible in time and money. You decide to go there as Decision No. 2.

Please note the overriding importance of a critical re-examination of the assumptions of Decision No. 1. *Should*

I go to England and back, having $1,000 and 3 weeks? Correct answer, No.

Decision No. 2 (Same situation, different approach). *Can* I get to England to see that friend and come back, having $1,000 and 3 weeks? Correct answer, Yes.

The new decisions is made possible by a serious *reconsideration of my former assumption* that a round trip to England would cost $800. Challenging assumptions which are commonly accepted will often lead to new conclusions or to a better solution of the problem.

One more equally simple example of mental activity in problem-solving. Suppose on going over my accounts I come to the inescapable conclusion that I am spending considerably beyond my income. I cannot increase my income. I must make a marked reduction in my expenses. The universal experience in such cases is as follows.

I go over carefully each major item in my budget.

Rent? No. It would cost more to move all my belongings than I would save.

Clothes? No. One of man's business assets is a good prosperous appearance.

Sell the car? Certainly not. How could I get about for work and for play? My way of living is built around the use of a car.

So I go through the entire list. There is a good reason in each case against any substantial reduction of expenditures; but still I must cut down. The money is just not there.

I must go over the same list again. The facts are the same; but this time I challenge the original assumptions. Earlier I approached the problem on the basis that I would not cut down any given item of expense when inconvenient. I naïvely hoped to find some convenient budget cuts. *Now* I go down the list persuaded that I *must* cut whether convenient or not. I get a totally different answer from the same facts. I find that I can substantially reduce many of my expenses. Again a reconsideration of my first assumption leads to quite different results.

Conclusions Applicable to Intelligence

The conclusions from this cursory discussion which are useable in intelligence production are these:

The mind is full of ideas which we accept as facts and treat as such in our instantaneous mental reactions. In seeking a solution to an intelligence or other problem the mind glances at these stored facts, combines, recombines, and discards them in rapid succession.

The answer that we get, or whether we get any answer at all, depends in large measure upon the degree to which we accept or challenge the data usually accepted as facts.

The great majority of the ideas stored in our heads which we regard as facts are reliable. Some however, are prejudices which may distort our thinking. Some supposed facts are partly or wholly wrong.

In any inquiry it is helpful to *write down* the assumptions from which our conclusions are drawn and examine each assumption critically. What is the possibility that this assumption may be incorrect? What is the possibility that we could get a different answer by stating the assumption differently? Supposing I desired a different answer very much, what changes in wording would I make?

One reason for *writing down* the assumptions rather than just thinking them over is that the act of writing holds the attention to each assumption for an appreciable time. If not written, the consideration of some opposite interpretation may be tossed out unceremoniously.

Challenging Axioms

One great scientific discoverer said that he achieved his original advances in human knowledge by "challenging axioms." This is a very helpful approach when attacking a difficult intelligence problem. You suppose the existence of conditions widely different from those commonly accepted for the situation. If these different conditions existed, what results would follow? What indications which could be detected by our intelligence system would follow? Can we get positive evidence that these indications do or do not occur?

Challenging axioms is merely carrying one step further the matter of challenging lesser facts as just decribed. In intelligence it is sometimes helpful to consider the possibility of the existence of conditions *radically* different from those commonly accepted as true.

For example, at one time it was customary to consider the Soviet leaders as motivated in their foreign policy by arrogance and an aggressive spirit. It was helpful to consider the opposite (whether finally accepted or not). In other words suppose they are motivated by fear due to the fact that they find themselves with a low standard of living, barely enough food, and surrounded by hostile airfields.

STAGES IN CREATIVE THINKING

In this section, we get to the very core of our central problem; namely, the intellectual part of intelligence production.

In preparing an intelligence paper the mass of data which the analyst is to consider may come to him without any logical order. It is usually incomplete—often lacking in some of the most important parts. It contains both truth and falsehood. The analyst has the responsibility of creating from this miscellaneous mass a logical and meaningful report.

Creative thinking in the solution of problems or in other constructive activities as described earlier in this chapter, is the mental part of the process by which a mass of data is treated constructively, so that it results in the solution of a problem or the development of a meaningful picture of a situation. More often, of course, a whole problem is broken into parts, so that a single given unified act of creative thinking results in the solution of only one *part* of the problem at a time. The parts are solved one after the other to form the whole.

Creative thinking, whether in the fields of the natural sciences, of creative writing, or of the social sciences (including intelligence production), is conveniently considered as taking place in four stages, in chronological order as follows:

Accumulation
Incubation
Illumination
Verification

The list of stages will recall and is parallel to the seven steps in intelligence production described in the last chapter.

The purpose of this section is to break down thinking as related to intelligence into these four stages which are *the most useful for studying the mental process.* Each stage will be discussed in turn for its practical applications. This is illustrated by Figure 4.

The Creative Thinking Process as a Whole

(A quick survey of the whole process of creative thinking is given at this time. Then, when each stage in the process is later discussed more fully, its relation to the whole will be understood.)

We start by assuming as an example that we are confronted with a problem pertaining to Curtania. This may be to estimate the quantity of Curtanian engineers; or to picture the over-all control of scientific research there; or to report on the top personalities in their new government.

In the *Accumulation* Stage, as part of our general knowledge we have been accumulating basic ideas and prejudices touching on these subjects since high school days. For example, we have seen engineering achievements, have read about shortages of scientific manpower, and have seen the effects of top level control in school and elsewhere. We now collect information on our *specific problem* and read widely in this field.

This is followed by Stage 2, *Incubation.* We think over what we have read. Consciously and unconsciously we put the facts together in various ways so that some logical picture begins to emerge.

Then after long study if we are full of the problem and the facts bearing upon it, and if we are keenly interested in the results, the real meaning of the facts and a solution to the problem may present itself to our mind, often in a flash of *Illumination* as Stage 3. This is closely related to the Interpretation of the Data and the Formation of Hypotheses described as steps in intelligence production.

The fourth Stage is *Verification* in which we seek to prove or disprove the solution presented to us in the act of Illumination. Verification corresponds to the checking of hypotheses and the drawing of final conclusions step in intelligence production.

The outcome of all this effort at intelligence production may be definitely misleading, or mediocre. On the other hand, it may contribute a brilliant new insight into an important problem. The quality of the production will depend upon (1) the data available, (2) how we treat these data. The latter step constitutes the creative thinking.

Experience shows that there are certain conditions which are definitely favorable to success in creative thinking and certain conditions which are unfavorable. These conditions are described below. By fostering the favorable conditions we improve the level of our production and increase the chances for success many fold.

For convenience in presentation and for the assistance of

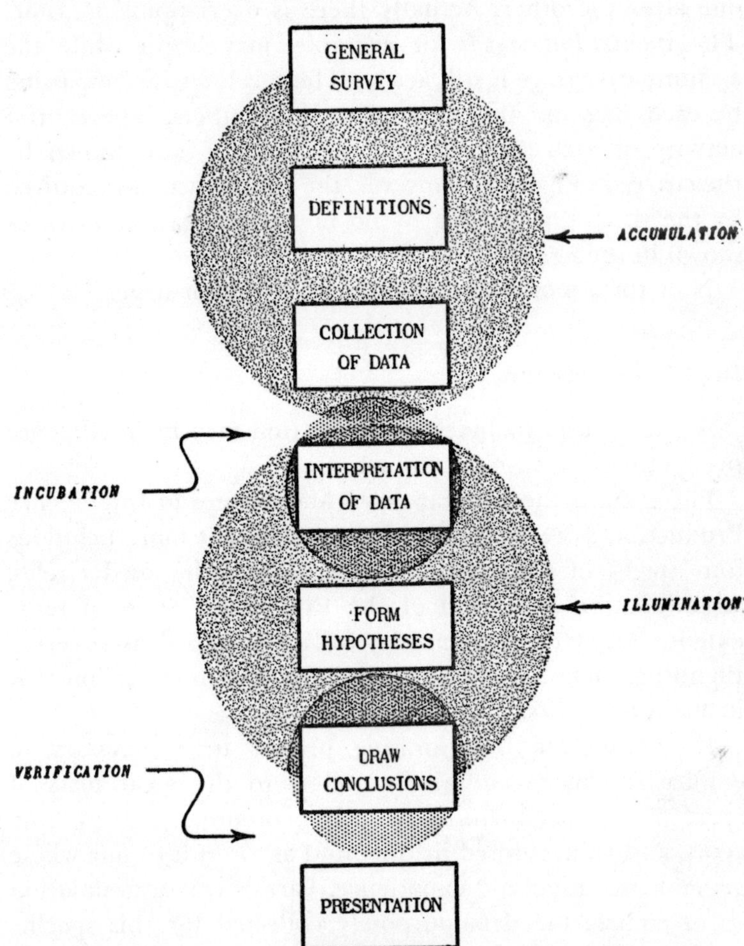

Figure 4 The Four Stages in Creative Thinking
in relation to
The Seven Steps in Intelligence Production

the reader the four stages in creative thinking are here considered separately and are treated as though they occurred one after the other. Actually there is overlapping in time. The incubation stage, for example, may begin while the accumulative stage is still active. There is likewise trespassing by each stage on the areas covered by others. The central activity of each stage in creative thinking is as shown by the circles in Figure 4. However, the borders vary as required by the situation, and are by no means so clear-cut as those shown in the figure.

Now for a more detailed discussion of each stage.

Stage 1. Accumulation

Accumulation includes the Collection Step in intelligence production, but also very much more.

Fig. 4 shows the familiar seven Major Steps in Intelligence Production as rectangles, with the somewhat more nebulous four stages in Creative Thinking as superimposed circles. Accumulation affects all of the Production Steps to some extent, but it can be most usefully considered as covering Planning, Definitions and Collection. It is in collection that its main focus lies.

In considering the thinking process it is necessary to emphasize that Accumulation refers to the great mass of more or less pertinent facts, errors, prejudices, ideas, concepts, and values stored in the mind as a result of our whole general education and experience. Part of this accumulation is, of course, the data purposely collected for this specific intelligence project. Another large and influential part started to accumulate in our childhood.

Some ideas definitely relevant to the given problem may have permeated the conversation and literature in our own country for several generations. Phrases like the "unspeakable Turk," "a dog of a Jew," "damned Yankee," etc., were at certain times and places universally heard, and all but universally accepted in certain places. It is hard to escape their influence.

In research in the natural sciences we are not troubled by prejudices formed in childhood regarding such unemotional subjects as barium sulphate or the square root of minus one. However, in the subject matter of intelligence, the very heart of the problem may depend upon race, religion, politics, economics, or other subjects where life-long prejudices hold sway. These enter into our basic assumptions and in all of our conscious and unconscious thinking. This emotional background makes essential positive and vigorous efforts to guard against prejudices and preconceived notions.

Accumulation therefore includes substantial contributions from our whole personal and national culture and experience. It includes many and specific contributions from our educational specialty whether chemistry, economics or history. The difficulties of applying high professional critical standards to this mass of facts, opinions and prejudices which have been accumulating in the mind for many years is obvious.

By contrast suppose that in the Collection Step of Intelligence Production we industriously collect data on the numbers of Curtanian engineers from wide-spread sources. Each item collected is systematically listed on a separate card with proper references to sources. It is easy to see that a critical examination of this mass of raw information could be made with a rather definite degree of thoroughness. For example we could individually restudy *each card,* and by this means *know* that all cards had been critically assessed. We could place some estimate of precision after each figure. We could submit each card to some outside expert to accept or reject. In other words we have some *finite* material before us in written form. We can process it in quite definite ways, and we can make clear to other professionals just what we have done.

Now consider a related problem bringing in the Accumulation Stage in accordance with the broad meaning used in this section. Suppose for this problem I am given the task to estimate the quality of the engineers of Curtania and their capabilities for research and development.

I collect data from various sources. However, the whole background for my judgment of quality in engineers is strongly conditioned by my own experience in studying and teaching engineering and by my own dealings with engineers of high and low quality. My judgment of capabilities for research is also strongly influenced by my own experience of over twenty years in industrial research. Many of the crucial ideas pertinent to this project have been "accumulating" in my mind for years before I ever heard of intelligence or took any interest in Curtania.

It would be impossible to get together for checking any written collection of the data *already in my mind* upon which my judgment would be based. In fact I am probably unconscious of many of my own experiences which actually influence my judgments.

These simple examples illustrate the distinction which we have made between Collection and Accumulation. The examples emphasize the huge, indefinite and partly disorganized body of material which accumulates in the mind and which may well strongly influence our decisions.

If this accumulation contains great quantities of misinformation and prejudices it may be a fatal handicap to sound intelligence judgment. Even if most of the facts in my mind are essentially correct, the resulting effect on my thinking may still be incorrect if the proportion or emphasis is not representative. For example if I know five Frenchmen, and by pure chance four of them are crooks, it takes an effort of the mind to avoid the conclusion that most Frenchmen are crooks.

On the other hand a mind in which the intelligence officer has accumulated a large body of essentially correct information in a given field of knowledge and where mature thought and discussion have arranged this in sound and meaningful patterns, constitutes a valuable asset for intelligence production. In fact such accumulations—including mature mental digestion are *essential* to good intelligence production. As Pasteur said: "In the fields of observation, chance only favors the mind prepared."

"Preparation" is another word for this stage which we have called accumulation. As used by Graham Wallas (36) the word preparation emphasizes all the preparation through education and experience which should precede the collection proper in attacking an intelligence production problem.

One of the great factors favoring such an accumulation in any field is a lively interest in the subject, even though it be amateur. In this case every chance reference to the subject in reading or conversation is noted and mentally filed in its proper connection. Opportunities are seized to discuss the subject with informed persons. One's knowledge is constantly increasing, developing and correcting itself.

An interesting question arises here about the possible danger of knowing too much about a subject. The danger arises from the fact that a person bearing so much knowledge becomes so weighted down by the conventional point of view that he may be prevented from developing originality. In the history of natural science research, there are many examples of outsiders or amateurs, like Bessemer in the steel industry, who saw the possibilities of new developments which ran counter to the judgment of the old timers. Certain it is that in science and in industry most of the successful developments have been made against the opposition of many well informed experts. This point of view is summarized by Beveridge (32):

> Wide reading is no substitute for thinking. Shaw's quip "reading rots the mind," is characteristically not quite so ridiculous as it appears at first. . . .
>
> Thus in subjects in which knowledge is still growing, or where the particular problem is a new one, or a new version of one already solved, all the advantage is with the expert: but where knowledge is no longer growing and the field has apparently been worked out, a revolutionary new approach is required, and this is more likely to come from the outsider. The scepticism with which the experts nearly always greet these revolutionary ideas confirms the idea that the available knowledge has been a handicap.
>
> The best way of meeting this dilemma is to read critically and maintain a healthy scepticism.

For the intelligence worker there are obviously great advantages in a thorough grounding in the general principles of the natural and social sciences. Wide reading in fields only distantly connected with the immediate problem will often stimulate the imagination and bring out interesting analogies when further study of a narrow problem would only deaden the mind.

Continuing now specifically in intelligence, many well considered and firmly held opinions of experts on vital matters pertaining to foreign countries have turned out to be wrong. As examples, the Germans believed that England would not come to the support of France at the beginning of World War I. France believed that the Germans could not make a tank attack through the Ardennes in World War II. The Allies continued to believe in the existence of a Japanese army of a million men in Manchuria towards the end of World War II. The Soviets evidently believed that Tito could not maintain his power in the face of their own unfriendly attitude. So again a fresh look, and a critical re-examination of the situation is often essential in intelligence.

Stage 2. Incubation

After Accumulation comes Incubation as the second formal stage in creative thinking. In this period the mind goes over the information acquired for the specific problem as modified by the general background formed by the lifetime of accumulation. Much of this mental action is unconscious and is, in fact, a sort of mental digestion and assimilation of facts available in the mind.

Quiet thoughtfulness in which one's ideas are sorted out, arranged in logical fashion and their connections discovered need not wait till the collection of the facts is completed. It may take place at the very beginning of an intelligence or other project. In the usual hurly-burly of intelligence production some of the following quotations regarding quiet thought, which may be considered examples of incubation, have a special appeal.

Hans Zinsser wrote of the great French bacteriologist, Charles Nicolle:

> Nicolle was one of those men who achieve their success by long preliminary thought before an experiment is formulated rather than by the frantic and often ill-conceived experimental activities that keep lesser men in ant-like agitation. Indeed I have often thought of ants in observing the quantity output of "what-of-it" literature from many laboratories. . . . Nicolle did relatively few and simple experiments. But every time he did one, it was the result of long hours of intellectual incubation. . . . Then he went straight to the point without wasted motion.[1]

[1] Quoted by Beveridge (32)

The action of our unconscious mind during Incubation may also be even more helpfully compared to the action of our eyes. In the case of human vision, only a small part of what is within the range of our sight is seen in clear detail. This part is technically said to be in the "fovea," that is, the direct focus, while a much larger part is in the margin of vision where it is perceived, but only indistinctly.

Similarly, at a given instant, we are fully conscious of only a small part of our mental processes. A larger part is on the margin of our consciousness.

There are many mental processes which are as completely unconscious as the functions of the liver. For example, you meet a man on the street of whom you have not thought in any way for years. Instantly your mind sorts out his name from the thousands of names stored in your memory, and presents this name to you in time to speak it. Your mind associates the face with the name. As Jastrow says: "The associative mechanism finds its sphere of activity largely in the subconscious realm."

Oliver Wendell Holmes (39) has presented this proposition clearly and convincingly.

> I will give some instances of work done in the underground workshop of thought. We wish to remember something in the course of conversation. No effort of the will can reach it: but we say, "Wait a minute, and it will come to me," and go on talking. Presently, some minutes later, the idea we are in search of comes all at once into the mind, delivered like a prepared bundle, laid at the door of consciousness like a foundling in a basket. How it came there, we know not. The mind must have been at work groping and feeling for it in the dark: it cannot have come by itself. Yet, all the while, our consciousness, so far as we are conscious of our consciousness, was busy with other thoughts. . . .

> The more we examine the mechanism of thought, the more we shall see that the automatic, unconscious action of the mind enters largely into all its processes. Our definite ideas are stepping-stones; how we get from one to another we do not know....
>
> Persons who talk most do not always think most. I question whether persons who think most—that is, have most conscious thought pass through their minds—necessarily do the most mental work.

As was pointed out in the first part of this chapter, the effort to solve a problem mentally is a constant series of trials and errors. Finally we more or less accidentally stumble upon an answer to which the objection is not so obvious. The smooth course of trial and rejection is brought to a halt. Our attention is arrested. Further consideration only confirms the plausibility of the solution which we have momentarily under consideration. Instead of rejecting the possible answer which we have now stumbled on, we stop, consider further and finally accept it. The closely allied mental condition when working a puzzle is described by Ruger (39A).

Bentley (39B) says:

> It appears that the transcendent accomplishments of genius are due in large measure to condensations and ellipses on a large-scale which reduce the elaborative procedures to their lowest terms. Intuition frequently means only defective observation of the rapid process of thinking.

Types of mind differ in the proportion of their thinking which is carried on consciously, on the margin of consciousness, or unconsciously.

A comparatively large part of our time is spent in such a way that the fovea of our conscious mind is just sufficiently occupied to keep it from interfering with our real thinking. These periods include shaving, dressing walking to work, routine mechanical operations which no longer require close attention, etc. Many forms of recreation likewise occupy the fully conscious mind just sufficiently "to keep it out of mischief," as for example easy exercise, riding on a train, attending a concert, etc.

It is under these conditions that our marginal consciousness, being free from conscious direction, usually turns either to those things that trouble us or interest us the most. At such times much progress may be made in digesting and assimilating the details of our research problem.

The amount of time spent in this marginal thinking and its importance have been largely overlooked. Possibly much thinking that has been considered unconscious is really in the margin of our consciousness.

What are some of the conditions for helpful action of our minds when on the margin of consciousness and beyond?

First, we must have a great interest in the problem and a desire for its solution. This gives our minds the impulse to pursue this particular problem and assists in excluding other conflicting ideas. Furthermore, the problem should be clearly defined. "A question clearly stated is half answered."

Second, and closely allied, there should be an absence of other problems which would tend to crowd out the first. To paraphrase, "Where your treasure or your trouble is, there will your subconscious mind be also." No matter how diligently you apply your conscious thought to your work during office hours, if you are not really wrapped up in your work sufficiently to have your mind unconsciously revert to it frequently, or if you have personal problems of so much more urgency that they crowd out the intelligence problems, then you can expect little in the way of illumination or hunch.

Third, the mind must have available a large store of

pertinent information. Just as when looking up a question in a library, the larger the library, the more chance there is to find what is wanted. Poffenberger (39C) says:

> How shall we explain the great differences among people in their capacity to think and in the value of their thinking?
>
> One difference is in the *number* of suggestions that come to mind and in the varied relationships that are noted between the problem and previous experiences. A problem that would suggest to the mind of the genius many recollections and ideas would seem to the ordinary mind to have no connection whatever with the problem in hand. Such differences rest in part upon differences in natural curiosity which drives the individual to find out about things and look for relationships.
>
> Another difference has to do with the speed and facility with which the suggestions come—some too rapidly and some too slowly.

Fourth, the material should be stored in the mind in a systematic fashion and it should be well digested so as to be useful. A mass of isolated facts is as inefficient as a great pile of books without order or catalog. It is much better to have fewer facts well digested.

Fifth, the investigator should have a sense of well-being and a sense of freedom from interruptions. Woodward (39D) says:

> We see in this experimentally studied case some of the conditions that favor invention. Good physical condition, freshness, mastery of the subject, striving for some result and hopefulness. Now what is this last? Confidence, enterprise, willingness to take a chance, eagerness for action and readiness to break away from routine?

Benger (39E) in an excellent article on "The Organization of Industrial Research" states:

> Research work is more sensitive to the atmosphere surrounding it than most types of work. . . . I know of nothing that will inspire a man to do his best as much as expression of confidence in his ability to do his job.

Stage 3. Illumination

At several important points in working on an intelligence problem, just as in a scientific problem, there comes a time when a tentative solution must be selected from a very large number of possible solutions. Here we must formulate one or more hypotheses for further study, and abandon, permanently or temporarily, many other possible modes of attack which seem less promising. At this time the mind in a moment of illumination focuses attention on the one or two crucial points and forms hypotheses to explain their part in the whole picture.

Some of the typical occasions in our work at which such selections must often be made are as follows, using as examples the types of intelligence production problems described earlier in this chapter.

The selection of a method as described early in this chapter, is a typical example. We cannot possibly try all conceivable methods. We must select one or two for further study. The specific problem cited in the example is to devise a method for evaluating the quality of engineers graduating from Curtanian institutions of higher learning. Evidently real insight into the important aspects of quality in engineers requires judgment and even a flash of illumination to single out the crucial part of the problem.

The next example is an estimate of artillery capabilities. In any estimate of foreign capabilities success is achieved by the ability to select the one or two critical limiting factors.

Similarly in the example where the requirement was to present the picture of a situation, a good intelligence officer must fix on the one or two critical factors. Sometimes those selected are different from the factors commonly accepted as most important.

In any part of an intelligence problem where the mind must make a selection of the critical points described above, the selection is sometimes made by considering in turn all promising possibilities and so arriving methodically at a decision. For example, Charteris (40) in describing Haig, the Commander in Chief of the BEF, says: "To Haig the essential method of arriving at a decision was complete knowledge and study of all the factors, and then a considered and most firmly held judgment."

The study of all possible factors has the advantage of apparent thoroughness. It has the disadvantage that it is very time-consuming. Often the number of hypotheses which might reasonably be considered is impossibly large. Then judgment must select a few for further study. Often too, by attempting to be "thorough" and to study everything, we devote so much time to the relatively unimportant points that we can go deeply into none of the aspects of the problem, including those most critical.

In contrast to the plodding, cover-everything, approach is the guidance sometimes given by judgment, intuition, illumination (as used here), the New England guess (as used by Bancroft), or the scientific hunch (as used by Platt). The meaning is the same.

The important conditions are: (1) a specific problem for which one greatly desires a solution (e.g. a method for evaluating engineers in Curtania); (2) A long study of the problem, Accumulation; (3) A period of Incubation in which the problem may be turned over in the mind; (4) Favorable conditions for the Illumination or flash of an idea which brings to the conscious mind the results of the accumulation and incubation often free from some rather sticky misconceptions.

Once a promising point is singled out by such illumination, it is framed into a hypothesis and tested by further study.

A questionnaire on the appearance of Illumination or the Scientific Hunch was sent out by Platt and Baker (28) to a number of leading research scientists in the United States. Although research in the natural sciences was primarily considered, those parts pertaining to mental processes are probably equally applicable to intelligence research.

In the report of the study many specific examples are given. For instance in regard to general conditions favorable to mental illumination as an aid to the solution of a problem, several research workers say their best ideas come to them while walking between their home and the laboratory morning or evening. Several mentioned walking in the country. A considerable number state that hunches have come when listening to music and a few refer to the related condition of listening to a sermon.

Abel relates:

> It is an old saying ever since Archimedes solved the problem of specific gravity in his bath tub . . . that discoveries are not made in laboratories but in the bath tub, or during an afternoon or evening walk as in the case of Helmholtz, or in the watches of the night when the puzzled brain will not quiet down, as has been the experience of so many investigators.

In these cases, the essential features, common to all, are evidently pleasant relaxation and freedom from mental interruptions.

One of the research workers who replied to the questionnaire expressed his idea when he wrote:

> I think most of my hunches have come to me in the early morning while in bed thinking about some problem on which I had done considerable work and studying. I am physically relaxed and rested; mentally, I am enjoying

myself, thinking and planning the day's work. I have often said that I do more work before getting up in the morning than after.

Another wrote:

> I must say that my hunches come as the result of deliberate purposeful thinking about the problem, drawing consciously or unconsciously upon a broad knowledge of other closely allied fields. Any condition favorable to such thinking yields results but owing to the nature of my work which involves a great deal of administration, such periods can only come at night after the day's work is done. *Any employer of my services who wanted creative thinking oftener THAN ONCE A DAY, SHOULD RELIEVE ME OF MY ADMINISTRATIVE WORK, otherwise I might describe myself as a hard worker during the day on the mechanics of the job and a creative thinker at night on my own time.*

Dr. M. H. Ittner replied in similar vein:

> In my experience, the most helpful thing is to talk with other chemists who have been successful *in other lines,* and to visit large factories engaged in *different lines* from my own. It is always an inspiration to see how others have solved their difficulties and it causes me to consider my problems less difficult than I had thought before. I can never go through a factory no matter how different from my own line without starting new lines of thought that are only vaguely related in their final conclusion to the suggestions that started them, though worthwhile things of some kind are apt to result.

We find a remarkable unanimity of opinion. Many of those who replied spoke very feelingly of the unnecessarily unfavorable conditions under which their mental activities must be carried on.

There are, of course, some general conditions, partly unavoidable, which are well understood to hamper mental activity. Many mention, for example, mental and physical fatigue, petty irritations, noise, worry over domestic or financial matters, depression, anger. There is nothing new in all this. As James said, "Worry means always and invariably inhibition of associations and loss of effective power."

We can all sympathize, though perhaps not agree, with George H. Gibson, an inventor, who lists among particularly unfavorable factors, "having to get to work on time."

The one thing that is more detrimental than anything else to creative thought of the best kind is interruptions of all kinds. This is stressed in the replies again and again. Equally bad is the *feeling that one may be interrupted at any time.* With such a feeling it is impossible to relax and let the constructive portion of the mind have full sway.

This is expressed by another respondent to the questionnaire of Platt and Baker who said:

> Yes, the distractions of executive work, the straightening out of snarls arising from human perversity, being compelled to listen to contentious or gossipy talk, are "conditions definitely unfavorable." Folin has well said that the research man "does not need a director, and should not be expected to become one."

Another research worker wrote:

> Someone has said that the function of a bishop is to "suffer fools gladly and answer letters by return mail." Such functions have their reward; but they are not conducive to scientific concentration and revelation.

The examples given above all pertain to research in the natural sciences. In each case an important part of the research consisted in selecting tentatively for further study one or two approaches out of many. This is an intellectual process greatly facilitated by the stage of illumination. In many parts of intelligence research a similar selection must be made. A wise selection is facilitated by the same intellectual processes. All of the above examples can apply helpfully to intelligence research.

Stage 4. Verification

This stage in creative thinking corresponds to the checking of hypotheses and Drawing Conclusions which is Step 6 in intelligence production. As the result of our study of an intelligence project and perhaps in a moment of illumination, a bright and promising insight into our problem appears to us. It fits many of the facts and appears to provide the solution to that part of the problem.

Basing the present discussion on the types of intelligence production problems given in the earlier part of this chapter, having arrived at the verification stage of our problem, we now ask ourselves: Is the method which suggests itself to us a good one? Or, is the hypothesis which comes to our mind and which seems at this moment so brilliant, really sound and fit to be formulated as a final conclusion? Or, is the picture of the whole situation which we now see so clearly in our mind's eye the true one endowed with correct perspective? Or, is the prediction which presents itself the most probable; are there any serious objections?

Evidently only when a *particular* solution presents itself, can we then devote special and critical study to this one solution. Then and only then can we verify it or modify it, or discard it. In physical science we often carry out this verification stage by one or two key laboratory experiments. In intelligence we verify (or discard) by seeking additional and crucial facts, and by *mental experiments.* In these we ask ourselves, supposing our solution is correct, then what indications should there be? What other conditions must exist? Are these other conditions possible or probable? What results would follow? Is the overall picture which would exist, in accordance with known conditions, and with good judgment and with past experience?

Note that just because a new solution leads to apparently bizarre results is no reason for summarily discarding it. Such an outcome is merely cause for greater caution.

Summary

From the foregoing discussion of creative thinking we find that there are some conditions generally favorable to such creative effort which can be directly applied to intelligence production.

The intelligence officer should start with a good background of knowledge in the field to be covered. He should have had a chance to read widely (accumulation), but not to satiety. Then on receiving any specific intelligence production problem he should have a chance to think the subject over, to try putting the facts together in various ways, to make several outlines, and best of all to talk the problem over informally with a few interested and well informed colleagues (incubation).

As a result, the solution of parts of his problem may come to him in a flash of illumination which furnishes a promising hypothesis or solution. This hypothesis is subject to verification by further study.

USEFUL PROCEDURES

Procedure I. Stimulating the Imagination

A group of students of Professor Doriot[2] has published an interesting book (42) *Imagination—Undeveloped Re-*

[2] Brigadier General USAR-Ret. and Professor of Industrial Management, Harvard Graduate School of Business Administration.

source which discusses various methods which have been used to develop original thoughts. Here, as in many other cases, we are borrowing for use in intelligence some ideas intended primarily for another field (in this case for business and advertising). A few quotations applicable to intelligence production are:

"Most of us will go to any length to keep from thinking persistently about our problems. We turn on the radio, we read, we talk, we do anything rather than think."

A new idea is "a new combination of old entities. . . . Facility at combination is at the heart of the creative process. Here the imagination really comes into play."

The central suggestion for bringing out new ideas is that already practiced and advocated by Alex Osborn (38). He calls this procedure "Brain-storming."

A Brainstorming session is a discussion of a problem for the sole purpose of bringing out new ideas. It consists of 4 to 12 persons preferably with varied backgrounds. The sessions proceed at a rapid pace lasting only from 15 to 45 minutes. There is a leader who briefly explains the problem, and a recorder (preferably a non-participant).

The essence of the method is that no difficulties or objections to any idea put forward may be brought up at that session. The motto is "all contributions gratefully received." An original idea put forth by one participant stimulates a better idea from another participant. And so the discussion goes in a wide-awake, optimistic, stimulating atmosphere, favoring competition in spontaneous originality. No one need fear that objections or ridicule will be directed towards his new, but half-baked idea, because no such objections may be brought up at the meeting. In some respects the wilder (that is the more original) the idea the better.

As a method for stimulating the imagination and bringing out original ideas when applied to a specific problem, this method has a record of success.

Later, at another session, probably by other persons, the ideas proposed at the Brainstorming session are studied and sifted. All are given a sympathetic hearing. Most of them have such obvious objections that they are discarded almost immediately. Out of the whole session one solution often emerges, which is much better than would probably have been obtained by routine methods. The Brainstorming procedure has the added advantage that it is a means for combing out those unexplored pockets of the terrain where the truth may lie hidden unless we occasionally go off the road and beat the bushes in a cross-country reconnaissance of this kind.

One memorable statement in this study of "Imagination" has applications in intelligence production beyond the Brainstorming procedure. Speaking of the wide open stimulation of new ideas and the exclusion of any cautious criticism *at the same session* one group leader said: "If you try to get hot and cold water out of the same faucet at the same time, you will get only tepid water. And if you try to criticize and create at the same time, you can't turn on either cold enough criticism or hot enough ideas."

This point of view could be applied to many intelligence conferences at which criticisms are often over-emphasized. Such an over-critical atmosphere results in what has been called "the apprehensive" type of discussion.

The method of starting with a wide open, optimistic, aggressive point of view is widely applicable to planning and especially to writing. For most of us, it is better to write the first draft with vigor and enthusiasm, retaining momentum and putting blanks for facts not available. Then at a second sitting, dig up the additional facts needed, consider critically everything that has been said. Revise much of it. As someone said long ago: "It is better to write with vigor and correct with care, than to write with care and correct with vigor."

Procedure 2. Discussions

After an analyst has done some of his own thinking, it is surprising how stimulating to thought, corrective of shortcomings, and illuminating is a discussion with others.

This provides that all-important outside viewpoint. The one person who cannot possibly know whether a paper is clear is the author. He knows what he is trying to say. Only a second person can tell whether he has made himself clear. The author thinks his own ideas are important, of course. Does anyone else think so?

At the start, one of the best discussions is with a friend having some competence in the field in which the paper is written. This provides the necessary outside point of view, without that unfriendly critical atmosphere which is so destructive to enthusiasm, and which indeed may be fatal to originality in the early stages of a paper. There is furthermore something very stimulating in presenting ones ideas orally to another, and in arguing them out in a friendly fashion. Solitary writing lacks this kind of stimulus. Every graduate student, for example, finds this out in going over the progress of his research with his graduate advisor. Occasionally the professor will ask a question which will bring out an entirely new point or will call attention to a fallacy.

Speaking of research at the General Electric Co. Saul Dushman then Associate Director of Research said:

> We have no regular staff meetings. Usually the most successful staff meetings occur when somebody gets a hunch and talks to somebody else and gets a third man interested. By the time they get through talking to him, there may be quite a change in the original idea. We find it good to discuss things together at various times. There is no doubt of the value of laboratory discussions of problems.

A helpful literature exists regarding discussion groups. See Bibliography.

Procedure 3. Beginning at the End

Another type of useful procedure is provided by Polya (30). In intelligence a lively exercise of the imagination will often enable us to visualize the probable outcome of an investigation before it is begun. In particular it enables us to visualize whether any of the modes of attack which we have in mind have any chance to solve the problem. It is thus usually essential to study the end at the very beginning, just as the conquerors of Mt. Everest studied the peak with telescopes from afar as a guide to all their planning.

Polya uses several mottoes to point out the value of thinking a problem through to its final outcome before work is started. He quotes: "A fool looks to the beginning, a wise man regards the end." More caustically he quotes, "A wise man begins in the end, a fool ends in the beginning."

Polya's stimulating book is entitled *How to Solve It*. Though written primarily in regard to mathematical problems, some parts are most useful for intelligence production. He is a great advocate of analogies. He also emphasized the value of analyzing a problem and making a special effort to determine which are the one or two critical parts.

Polya's book is typical of the many books containing ideas useful to the intelligence officer which do not suggest this fact in the title or stated purpose of the book.

Procedure 4. Balancing of Pros and Cons

In the social sciences in general and in intelligence particularly, the truth of a hypothesis or the wisdom of a course of action can seldom be decided by a simple experiment. The conclusions of an intelligence problem are usually drawn by the author as a result of his best judgment. In contrast to the conclusions of the natural sciences, the conclusions in intelligence are seldom susceptible of actual proof. If the preliminary conclusions are attacked in a subsequent discussion, the final decision is usually reached on the basis of the general impression resulting from the discussion. There is seldom any *systematic* balancing of pros and cons.

For most purposes a general impression is sufficient. There is some danger however that the decision between the adoption of two opposing points of view may go to the person who cares the most about one side or the other. He may be very enthusiastic for one view; or he may regard the opposing view as highly objectionable.

In either event there is a good chance that the Truth (though mighty according to Harvard) will *not* prevail against the good talkers who may have sincerity, but faulty information.

This difficulty is wide-spread. Intelligence discussions are no worse than discussions in business, politics or the social sciences where reliance must usually rest upon discussion, rather than upon experimental proof.

Conant (31) has carried to its logical conclusion his desire to have both sides fully and fairly presented when decisions are to be formed, and his feeling that unless this is done enthusiasm may prevail over good judgment.

Conant's ideas are best presented in brief extracts from his own words:

> First of all, a healthy skepticism is in order in listening to an expert, particularly an enthusiastic one. The next step is to try to find a person of equal technical competence but with an opposite emotional bias. If such a one is not at hand, some competent individual hitherto unconcerned with whatever project is in question should be asked to undertake the job of being "devil's advocate," as it were. He should be asked to devote himself to preparing the case for the reasoned opposition to what has been proposed. Such procedures for balancing the bias of technical men . . . have been worked out almost without plan in the

> successful industries of this nation. But similar methods of operating have not yet been evolved in other areas; they are absent in the United States Government.
>
> It is inevitable that in any technological undertaking, conservatism must continually face enthusiasm. In so doing, emotions are aroused and personal fortunes become entangled with technological considerations.
>
> This is not the time nor place for me to outline in detail my remedy for what many feel to be a bad situation. I will content myself by saying I believe that if the Department of Defense would gradually introduce a quasijudicial system of review which provided forced opposition to new projects, the taxpayers' money would be more wisely spent. When a question came up to be settled, even if three or four echelons from the top, one or two referees or judges might hear the arguments pro and con. The important point is that there should be arguments against the proposal; they should be vigorous but candid; . . . Then adequate briefs for the two sides could be prepared (not compromise committee reports). With opposing briefs, arguments, and cross-questioning, many facets of the problem, many prejudices of the witnesses would be brought out into the open. The forced opposition is the important point.

His proposal in conformity with legal theory, is that the whole truth is more likely to be brought out if each side has an advocate. It is in accordance with the military experience with a *two*-sided map problem or two-sided maneuver as far superior to a one-sided exercise controlled by umpires. The two-sided exercise is also much more trouble in both military or intelligence problems, but the extra trouble is more than justified by the higher quality of the results.

It is interesting that the two-sided problem is now being carried out as a regular part of Operations Research by CONARC. Operations Research has some similarities to intelligence research. Further use of the two-sided problem in cases of special importance is probably one of the most promising opportunities for making substantial improvements in the results of Strategic Intelligence Production.

Procedure 5. Writing the Report

Writing a good intelligence report is certainly an example of Creative Thinking. Writing the report should be done in the first draft with more consideration for the ideas to be expressed than for smooth wording.

As previously stated, for the first draft of a paper the author's imagination should range widely and the writing should flow freely. Then the author should review his own work from a critical point of view. He should have his paper carefully studied and criticized by others. Finally an author should always stand off and review his own work as a whole. In view of the background situation, and of the specific information available, and in the light of common sense he should ask himself does the paper together with its conclusions have the proper perspective and convey an overall impression which is justified?

SIX TYPES OF RESEARCH MINDS

In the natural sciences and to some extent in the social sciences, observers have noted several distinct types of research minds. The existence of these wide differences is much more than a matter of passing interest; it is a matter of vital, practical importance in getting the best results out of a group of research workers.

Each type of research worker has his capabilities and limitations. Each needs a different kind of guidance. Certain scientists are successful and happy in working at certain kinds of problems, but would be quite unhappy with other types even in their own field of science. All of this is now widely recognized by some directors of research, especially in the larger scientific laboratories. See for example Platt (43) and Wilson (44).

The types of research minds, and the capabilities and limitations of each type, are just as evident in intelligence research as for other fields of research. This difference has not yet been recognized so explicitly in the field of intelligence.

Dr Ralph E. Gibson, Director of the Johns Hopkins Applied Physics Laboratory, in an article on "Some Implications of Scientific Research" (10) has a description of types of "productive research workers" which applies just as well to intelligence research workers as it does to others. He says:

"Among productive research workers there are to be found at least six types of mind, which we can recognize by studying the authors of articles in the better journals or more penetrating works in the history of science. (The following classification is backed by no professional authority, but is merely the conclusion of an unsophisticated observer.) These kinds of minds are: (a) the Promethean; (b) the critical or analytical; (c) the cumulative and inductive; (d) the cumulative and descriptive; (e) the meticulous; (f) the routine-industrious. It is evident that more than one of these attributes will be found in any given individual, although one will generally predominate.

"The Promethean mind tries to inject something radically new into anything it does. It may provide the flash of genius that shows up a continent of knowledge or gives rise to a new all-embracing theory. It may just invent an easier and better way way of performing an experiment or making a commodity. It is a mind that transmutes ideas from one field of experience to another and sketches in the broader patterns.

"The critical or analytical mind takes nothing for granted, but examines keenly all statements presented to it, probing deeply into their consequences for consistency and rigor. It is the questioning mind so needed for clarification of complex situations, for establishing the validity of experience, and for determining the consistency of patterns.

"The cumulative-inductive mind ranges in the literature and in experiment, collecting facts and attempting to put them roughly in order. It is a type of mind that has contributed, for example, largely to physical chemistry. It is a type of mind that invents local elements of pattern.

"The cumulative and descriptive mind is that of the trained and keen observer who remembers what he sees and describes it clearly for others to read. It is the mind that has laid the foundations of the complex sciences of astronomy, geology, and natural history. It is always evident on the frontiers of knowledge and is the stock-in-trade of the effective teacher.

"The meticulous mind is concerned about the correctness of all details in observation, procedure, and processes. It is concerned with the search for accuracy and precision. Finally, we have the routine-industrious mind that follows through relentlessly, especially where many experiments are needed to establish one fact and where repetitive processes are of the essence.

"History has shown that all these mental attributes have important roles to play in the sound and steady growth of all branches of science and engineering, and we should be guilty of crass intellectual snobbery if we discounted any one of them. The meticulous worker who spends years in establishing the real facts in a complex phenomenon or in perfecting a technique, or the routine-industrious man who explores an area thoroughly by a long series of measurements, provides means and materials for the creative artist and inductive thinker, materials they might not be able to get for themselves. The critical mind keeps thought and observations on the track, saving costly detours along false trails.

"Each has his place, and the secret of the efficient use of man-power either on a laboratory scale or on a nation-wide basis lies in assigning to each mind a job suited to its attributes and carrying with it the recognition of contributions to a worthwhile objective."

One indication of the usefulness of a consideration of these types of minds is shown in Gibson's last sentence, as given above. It offers a challenge to all intelligence supervisors.

GENERAL SUMMARY

The central theme of Part II of this book is that intelligence production is an intellectual process. A study of the intellectual processes involved makes a profitable approach to the study of the principles of intelligence. The present chapter focuses the attention on that particular part of the intellectual process known as "creative thinking."

Creative thinking requires more than plodding industry—essential as such industry is. Creative thinking requires that flash of insight which can be obtained from the right kind of people working under conditions favorable for the cultivation of such insight.

By an understanding of the principles involved each research worker may make more favorable the conditions under which his own thinking is carried out. Supervisors of intelligence production officers can do even more to provide for the analysts under them the conditions found favorable for creative thinking.

We have accordingly in this chapter broken down our studies of creative thinking for practical purposes into four stages, Accumulation, Incubation, Illumination and Verification. We then present five procedures which are often found helpful at different places in an intelligence problem.

Finally we recognize the widely different capabilities and limitations of the various types of research minds, so that each one may be used to best advantage.

Throughout this chapter we benefit from what has been profitably worked out for other related disciplines. This is in accord with one of our central themes, namely: Because intelligence production has only scanty literature of its own, let us poach aggressively on the fields of the more mature disciplines.

Five

HELP FROM THE SOCIAL SCIENCES

Natural vs. Social Sciences : Does History Repeat Itself?
Methods as Tools for Intelligence Research
Consistency in Character of Groups or Nations
How Foreign Are Foreigners?

When 'Omer smote 'is bloomin' lyre
He'd 'eard men sing by land an' sea,
An' what he thought 'e might require
'E went an' took—the same as me.

KIPLING

This chapter has the definite purpose of giving to the intelligence officer a working knowledge of the general nature of the subject matter and methods of the social sciences; so that he can make more use of the great treasury of knowledge and understanding pertaining to human activities which the social sciences have brought together.

This chapter cannot make an intelligence officer into an economist or political scientist, for example, if he is not one already. It can, however, indicate the kind of wares each social science has for sale. It can describe the general methods of the social sciences, so that proper applications can be chosen by the intelligence officer for his work.

It is not the function of this chapter to give more than working definitions of each of the social sciences. More adequate discussions of many aspects of the social sciences are easily available in the professional literature of these subjects. The coverage of each social science as such in this book is purposely held to a minimum.

The social science approach to any given intelligence project will usually help in one or more of the following ways:

1st By providing *an understanding* of the general principles of the project, the extent of our knowledge of it, and the problems involved.

2nd By providing *specific suggestions* as to methods which can be applied with necessary modifications.

3rd By pointing out *common pitfalls* to avoid.

4th By providing *references* as a start for further study.

In nearly all problems confronting the intelligence officer some help, even if not necessarily a complete answer, is available from those who have already wrestled with similar questions.

The intelligence officer will profit by considering what use others are making of analogies, case histories, and condensations—all as tools for his own trade. Each officer must find his own well-considered answers to the questions: Does history repeat itself? Is there a National Character? How foreign are foreigners? Unless he does so he may adopt some common fallacies, or he may discard useful intelligence tools.

The literature dealing specifically with the principles of strategic intelligence is scanty, and does not reflect even the best of what is now known. This is in part due to the newness of the systematic pursuit of strategic intelligence, and in part to the lack of graduate courses and graduate students.

A negligible number of Marco Polos, like Sherman Kent and George Pettee have, of course, ventured out of the lush, civilized areas of history, or of military sciences into the unknown land of Strategic Intelligence, but the number of these hardy explorers has been insufficient to conquer the wilderness.

So, as Strategic Intelligence officers, having little of our own, like Homer and Kipling in the verse quoted above, what we think we require, we go and take—and present to the reader.

NATURAL vs. SOCIAL SCIENCES

We have found that Strategic Intelligence includes some components like scientific intelligence, the subject matter of which is 100% in the field of the natural sciences; political intelligence, the subject matter of which is altogether in the field of the social sciences, and some like geography or transportation which are a mixture of both. To get the most of what the methods of the natural and the social sciences respectively have to contribute to Intelligence, it is important to distinguish between the two, and to understand the strong points and the limitations of each.

While history and geography, for example, are some of the oldest studies of mankind, the idea of forming a new group comprising these two disciplines together with economics and some others under the general heading "Social Sciences" is quite recent. Calling these subjects "sciences" and the related attempt to make them into quantitative sciences has resulted not only in certain beneficial results, but also in considerable confusion.

As the intelligence officer will continually encounter in his reading and discussions ideas, terms, and methods derived from the social sciences, he will find it worthwhile to avoid this confusion by taking a look at the area covered by them. That is the purpose of this section.

Broad Classifications

In this section we have drawn heavily on the excellent summary of the social sciences presented by Gee (21).

Terms such as natural sciences, physical sciences, social sciences, etc., are commonly encountered and must frequently be used by intelligence workers. Because there is no universal agreement about what each term includes, it will be useful to present a simple classification as they will be used in this book. The present section is a very broad brush treatment of the picture, showing where most of these terms fit. No attempt is made to discuss many controversial border lines, such as that between mathematics and logic, or that between anthropology and sociology.

The classification here given claims to be first of all convenient. Next, clear and in accordance with the usual (but not universal) practice. It is not completely rigorous or mutually exclusive; but it is believed to be more useful than a more elaborate classification with all of the refinements. The overlapping, where it occurs, is so obvious that there is little danger of confusion.

To start with a very broad background, we notice that some universities divide their studies into natural sciences, social sciences and humanities. This division is useful, though the boundaries are by no means clear-cut.

Passing over the humanities, the classification may be continued as follows:

I. Natural Sciences
   A. Mathematics (sometimes listed under the physical sciences)
   B. Physical Sciences—the study of energy and matter in their relationships
      1. Astronomy—the science of the universe outside of our own planet

2. Geophysics—including Physical Geography, Geology, Meteorology, Oceanography, the large-scale physics of our planet
3. Physics—to include nuclear physics
4. Chemistry

C. Biological Sciences

1. Botany
2. Zoology
3. Paleontology
4. Medical Sciences—including Microbiology
5. Agricultural Sciences separately or to be included under Botany and Zoology

II. Social Sciences—the life of man in the group

A. History
B. Cultural Anthropology
C. Sociology
D. Social Psychology
E. Political Science
F. Jurisprudence
G. Economics
H. Cultural Geography

These are arranged very generally in an order from the most discursive and descriptive, such as history and sociology, to the most definite and measurable, such as economics and geography. Some of the other disciplines which are occasionally found among the social sciences include, for example, ethics, philosophy, and the education. Evidently any of the subjects named, whether natural sciences, social sciences, or others, can be further divided and subdivided ad infinitum. This is no way affects the broader divisions given above, even though it may introduce a multitude of additional names for the various sciences in the subdivisions.

What Do We Mean by Social Science?

Stuart Chase (50) in a very general way defines social science on a high level, as "the application of the scientific method to the study of human relations."

We are now ready for definitions and a more detailed discussion of the Social Science area. The problem is a tough one. Usually the definition breaks down into two parts: one concerning the appropriate subject matter (i.e., the *social* part) and the other, the appropriate analytic method (i.e., the *science* part).

The social scientist is not so much interested in persuading or even predicting as he is in laying out the elements of a situation; identifying the critical factors which will bear on the working out of the situation under given circumstances; and, when he can, drawing dependable cause-consequence relationships. He does not so much solve problems as he does assist in sharpening the solver's understanding of the nature of his problem.

What kinds of problems are we talking about here? Anything having to do with the physical world, with matter, with life-forms, with universal natural laws; such are *not* the data of the social sciences. Anything having to do with human individual or group action, with decision-making, with markets, with the organization of formal and informal associations—such clearly are the data of the social sciences.

What, then, is the appropriate analytic method for a particular problem? The most open-ended answer might be: *the appropriate method is that closest approximation to the "scientific method" permitted by the nature of the data that the social scientist deals with.* This surely includes such characteristics of the scientific method as: definition of key terms; verbalization of major assumptions; systematic progression from hypothesis through collection and evaluation of data to conclusions; careful attention, at every step, to internal logical consistency.

Perhaps most important of all, the social scientist can only *hope* to maintain strict neutrality toward his data which will almost always be something that he, as a social human being, cares a great deal about, directly and personally and emotionally. Always, the social scientist must be as rigorous as his data allows.

We can, then, come to the conclusion that social science is the study of human beings in groups; it is a method of analysis; it is a means of throwing light on complicated situations and contributing thus to understanding of them; it is a useful tool for the manipulator of individual and group action; perhaps one day it will also be a means of precise predicting—even as, already, a few of the social sciences (e.g., economics) are able to predict general trends (e.g., market behavior) with considerable accuracy. In fine, social science is the systematic application of analytic techniques as rigorous as the data and the situation permit toward the end of increasing our understanding of individual and group behavior.

Cohen (15) states, however:

". . . We must not conceive the social and the natural sciences as mutually exclusive. Rather should we view them as dealing with parts of the same subject-matter from different standpoints. The social life of human beings is within the realm of natural events; but certain distinctive characteristics of the social life make it the object of a group of special studies which may be called the natural sciences of human society. In any case the empirical or historical fact before us is that many questions are clearly in both the physical and the social realm. . . ."

Why Should an Intelligence Officer Read Widely in the Social Sciences?

First, because the social sciences deal with human activities in groups—just such activities as these which are the most important to intelligence.

Second, because many of the problems, concepts and methods of the social sciences can be borrowed and adapted for intelligence production. Readings in the social sciences give breadth and perspective to our understanding of intelligence problems by providing examples, analogies, and contrasts.

Finally, such reading is valuable because it contains so many statements in which we cannot concur. It is challenging to come upon statements so much at variance with our ordinary ways of thinking, that we summon our mental resources to refute the statements. The social sciences are still in a sufficiently fluid condition, with many claims sufficiently vague and hence difficult to disprove, that the "lunatic fringe" can still publish in reputable journals. Encounters with questionable statements keep our critical faculties alert.

Capabilities and Limitations of the Social Sciences

The study of the social sciences is in general helpful because it contributes to our understanding of how mankind behaves. Also in particular it may be said that as a result of much good work by many good men, *each* social science has developed improved methods for the study of problems in its own field. Each social science can, therefore, contribute valuable expert knowledge and techniques to Strategic Intelligence. We contend that this expert knowledge can be valuable even in those cases where it cannot be completely objective, or reliably quantitative.

Experimentation and Quantification

The study of many of the phenomena of history, economics, political science and other fields of learning pertaining to man's life in a group is thousands of years old; but the application of the scientific method, as Stuart Chase says, to the study of these subjects in a systematic way plus the attempt at measurement and at the discovery of general laws is quite recent. So we are not surprised to find in the social sciences many evidences of immaturity. Within reputable professional literature extremely pessimistic statements co-exist alongside of extremely optimistic statements regarding the progress and value of the social sciences.

In the past 50 years there has been a great drive towards objectivity and quantification in the social sciences; and towards the separation of opinion and moral judgments from objective facts. The hope has been expressed that some day our knowledge of the laws of the social sciences would be comparable to our knowledge of the laws of the natural sciences, so that given certain known starting conditions, we could predict the outcome with confidence.

Spengler says: "The early sociologists . . . viewed the study of society as a sort of social physics." Some substantial progress has been made along the direction of applying to the social sciences those methods worked out so successfully for the natural sciences; though the inherent limitations of the social sciences for predictions are evident.

Spengler introduces a healthy note of caustic criticism when he says ironically: "Today methodology has been elevated to the level of a fetish. He who would be a real scientist must obey rigorously the three authentic canons:

1. Only those studies are scientific which are quantitative (statistical) in nature.
2. The sole aim of any science is to predict.
3. No scientist dares, as a *scientist,* to express a judgment as to what is good or bad. . . ."

He then shows the fundamental difficulties and ends with the conclusion: "It follows from what has been said that *social science differs categorically from physical science.* The three canons laid down fit no one of the social sciences. No amount of pretended exactitude or assumed impersonalism can transform social science into physical science. The social scientist, therefore, is condemned to be an artist who must rely on common sense instead of upon an esoteric methodology, who must be governed not only by the standards of the laboratory but even more by those of common sense and common decency. He cannot even act *as if* he were a physical scientist."

So for the present and the foreseeable future the social sciences have the following *fundamental handicaps* as to progress and predictions as compared with the natural sciences.

Natural science conditions are reproducible (e.g., the vapor pressure of water at 70° C.). We do not have to start always at the beginning, but can build with confidence on what has been done by our predecessors. The water that we use will act exactly like the water by the previous experimenters. By contrast the conditions of a social science situation are inherently *not* reproducible. Each situation that we study is in part new. We do start with a knowledge of what has happened in previous somewhat similar situations and with a knowledge of available methods. Such knowledge represents the solid contribution of the social sciences towards further progress.

In the natural sciences most of the factors important in the study are measurable with some precision (e.g., temperature, quantity, pressure, voltage, etc.). In the social sciences many of the important factors are measured with a degree of uncertainty that limits the utility of all quantitative conclusions (such as any quantitative statement of degree of motivation, of ability as a military commander, of leadership, etc.).

The whole question of measurement or quantification in the social sciences is one of fundamental importance. This is particularly true of applications to intelligence production.

I am not here saying that many factors vital to intelligence production cannot be measured; but that their measurement is time-consuming, difficult, and often of debatable validity; so that results are not so easily useable as the measurements of the natural sciences. This point, which is so vital to intelligence production, is considered more fully elsewhere in this chapter.

Quantification is useful. It is of great assistance in making predictions, but it is certainly not everything. In life, most considerations, including some which are of the highest importance, have never been measured nor balanced in quantitative terms against opposing considerations. We have never measured our confidence in our friends, our love for our country, nor our interest in our profession. So with the social sciences; their greatest contribution consists in their enabling us to understand the inner workings and controlling factors in many situations of great importance to intelligence. Their next greatest contribution is in the methods which they have already developed for future study.

A very helpful discussion is that of Sorokin (85A).

Contributions to Intelligence

Let us consider the inherent value of the social sciences to the intelligence officer. From their very nature, why should he turn to the social sciences for help, and what general kind of help can he rightfully expect which he cannot hope to obtain from any other source?

Pettee (6) has said: "Effective strategic intelligence in the future will depend on the application and development of social science . . . there exists in the modern social sciences a body of knowledge, much of which measures up to the most severe standards of truth and has been demonstrated to be practically useful."

Gee (21) sums up his conclusions about the future of the

social sciences by saying: "While there are inherent in them difficulties innumerable, yet the social sciences do seem to present the greatest intellectual challenge of the present age, as well as the promise of greatest immediate achievement for *mankind.*"

History. The story of mankind is in a class by itself. Intelligence evidently is one aspect of history—past, present, or future, if one may speak of future history. With some exaggeration it could be said that if an intelligence officer could master the riddles of history he would need to know little else except current facts in order to understand foreign situations. Many historians do not think of history as one of the social sciences, or feel that history owes much to social science methods. However, most formal lists of the social sciences properly include history as one of them (25).

Cultural Anthropology. Anthropology, literally the study of man, has been divided into physical anthropology which considers the physical measurements of man, and cultural anthropology. From its name, cultural anthropology might be considered to cover all forms of culture—economics, political, etc., of all mankind. Actually cultural anthropology has covered mostly the culture of ancient and primitive peoples. This has thrown light on many modern problems.

Kimball Young (52) writes: "In time cultural anthropology and sociology will be united in one common discipline." An intelligence officer can obtain from cultural anthropology light on such problems as: Customs of primitive peoples with which the United States or other nations must deal: or the problems which Curtania will probably experience in exploiting certain primitive tribes within its borders.

Sociology. The study of men in groups. It includes especially folkways, customs, accepted ways of thinking, and culture in general. Sociology shares parts of these fields with psychology, political science, jurisprudence and economics, ethics and education in which cases sociology plays the minor role. It is in group relations which are not primarily political, economic, or legal that sociology has made its major contributions.

It happens that sociology has concentrated less on *primitive* cultures than has cultural anthropology. Nevertheless help on many of the problems mentioned under cultural anthropology might well be found also under sociology. The intelligence officer could look to sociology for help in problems involving a deeper understanding of the general place of custom, folkways and "culture" in human behavior and of the workings of groups and institutions which are not primarily political or economic in purpose. Such other institutions include for example the church, educational institutions, social organizations. Among the components of Strategic Intelligence all of those listed under sociological intelligence are covered, including the important subject of population. Evidently some of these fields are at times vital in intelligence problems.

Social Psychology covers the psychology of man in his relation to others. It covers also a study of collective responses or the behavior of groups. L. G. Brown (52A) writes: "Social psychology is a study of the interaction between organic and social processes which results in human nature." This field of study can contribute to our understanding of National Character which is discussed later in this chapter.

Political Science relates to the evolution, the organization, and the activities of the governing authorities. Munro (54).

Much progress has been made by political scientists in a study of the factors for example, which have an important influence on election results or on governmental processes, including those groups which resist the efforts of their own government. Careful field studies have produced reliable information which can often be applied to specific intelligence problems. Intelligence officers can look to political science to help them to identify the key factors in a coming political campaign and to estimate the effect of each. Political science can throw light on the strong and weak points in different systems of government and the results to be expected in given cases.

Jurisprudence. Law in four syllables. Intelligence can profitably make use of some of the methods of jurisprudence, especially the procedure by which both sides of the case are presented. Lawyers often make good intelligence officers.

Economics deals with social phenomena centering about the provision for the material needs of the individual and of organized groups. It touches on supply and demand, prices, wealth, etc. Industry is one of the foundations of national strength in peace or war. The fundamental importance of economics to foreign intelligence is obvious.

Cultural Geography (sometimes called Human Geography). Geography may be divided into physical geography—rivers, mountains, air and ocean currents for example; and cultural geography—the aspects due primarily to man. For example, cities, roads, dams, canals, etc. Cultural geography includes most of economic geography. Its close relation to economics is evident. Among the components of Strategic Intelligence cultural geography contributes heavily towards foreign intelligence regarding geography, transportation, telecommunications, military capabilities.

Comparison with Biology

In defense of the optimistic view of future developments in the social sciences it has been pointed out that the ability of the social scientist to establish general laws and to predict is more like that of the biologist than that of the chemist. The biologist like the sociologist deals with living things which are far from uniform, yet he has made great progress in his ability to establish laws and to make predictions based on large numbers. This comparison with the social scientist is not entirely accurate.

The fundamental discrepancy is as follows: In many of the generalizations and predictions of a biologist he is dealing with an average. For example we may consider the yield of successive acres of wheat as affected by experimental factors such as water or fertilizer. Then each individual stalk of wheat contributes to the average on an equal basis. Outstanding individuals have no effect—there are no *leaders* in the wheat field which persuade all other stalks to act in one way or another.

In other cases a biologist deals with a distribution as when he predicts a certain mortality from an epidemic. He is quite successful in predicting 10% mortality, partly because he is not required to specify which individuals will make up the 10%. He has the benefit of dealing with large numbers and is not concerned for the success of his laws or predictions applied to individuals.

By contrast in the social sciences, even though the social scientist is at first glance dealing with thousands, the outcome of any given situation often depends upon the *decisions of a very few individuals* who influence the thousands around them. Thus the soldiers in Lee's army were individually roughly equal in fighting ability to those under McClellan. The difference in results was due to the great difference between General Lee plus a small group of his officers as compared with Gen. McClellan plus a few of his officers. Similarly the decision of one man, Hitler, led millions of Germans into World War II.

So the social scientist in some cases (but not all) misses the factor of safety conferred by large numbers. Even when superficially he is dealing with large numbers, the *effective decisions* are so often made by a few. The factors of imitation, persuasion and compulsion, of individuality and leadership, which exist among human beings are usually absent in the studies of the biologist. Thus for many of his problems the social scientist cannot draw much encouragement from the progress in prediction which has been made by the biologist working with large numbers of variable individuals, but treating them en masse and without consideration of leadership within the group. In other cases the social scientist like the biologist can ignore individuals and deal only in totals. We must be careful to distinguish between the two.

A Summary of Differences

To sum up, much has been gained in the social sciences by the efforts at clarity (in defining terms, for example), by the efforts at objectivity, by the application of statistical analysis to the planning of studies and to an interpretation of the results. Some success at deriving laws and making predictions has been achieved where large numbers were involved and where leadership did not influence the results; where we were concerned with the overall distribution of the qualities under study within the group, and did not have to make predictions regarding the action of previously selected individuals. Yet in so many situations considered by the social sciences it is the action of *certain individuals* which affect the outcome.

DOES HISTORY REPEAT ITSELF?

This question continues to be asked and is of course of great importance to intelligence. Many say that definitely history does repeat itself. See for example Farago (54B).

The broader question is: Does any situation studied in the social sciences repeat itself?

In history we find many situations which have striking points of similarity with each other. As two fairly recent examples Napoleon was astonishingly successful in his wars with nearly all of Europe. His invasion of Russia proved fatal to his eventual success. The experience of Hitler can be made to seem quite similar. Other examples will occur to the reader.

When we ask the question: Does history repeat itself? we may have any one of the following questions in mind, these being arranged in order of decreasingly definite answers to be expected.

A. Does history repeat itself, somewhat as a natural science situation repeats itself? In natural science we can say sulfuric acid plus a solution of barium chloride always gives a white precipitate of barium sulfate. Can we say for example, in history that if a peasant population is subjected to a stated degree of undernourishment for a given number of years it will always revolt? No.

Can we get a positive answer if we substitute "in 80% of the cases" for "always"? No.

Evidently if we give our specifications in such detail that it *covers exactly* one case where the population did revolt, no other case will probably occur sufficiently similar to fill the specifications, so we would not have a generalization broad enough to be of any practical value.

So for all practical intelligence purposes we can say that history does *not* repeat itself.

For an interesting modern discussion of this question which has such fundamental importance in intelligence production see Frankel (54A).

B. Does any given aspect of history (economic, political, cultural) have an overall pattern which establishes a common succession of events as implied by Toynbee? Even on a much smaller scale than Toynbee's "Civilizations," can a historian, expert in the given field and in the most nearly related history, predict the outcome of a given situation on the basis of his knowledge of patterns and "laws" of history, or economic development, etc.? In the opinion of the present author: Seldom.

There are few cases, economic, political or otherwise, where the pattern is so clear that the prediction can be made essentially on the basis of what has happened in similar cases in the past. Some use can be made of a knowledge of the outcome of other similar cases, but the part which an understanding of the special conditions of the particular situation under study plays is large.

C. Do historical situations have many elements in common? If so, then in any given situation the elements which are common to historical situations can be sorted out, these can be considered as modified by certain factors peculiar to the given situation; so that a final prediction can be made by using judgment to weigh both the old and the new factors. In other words even if history definitely does not repeat itself *is there any practical value in the study of history?* Emphatically yes.

Let us consider some analogies. Do military campaigns repeat themselves? Of course not. Are there many elements of past military campaigns which are helpful in planning future campaigns? Of course there are. Other things being equal, does a commander who is well acquainted with military history have a distinct advantage over one who is not? Certainly he does. Do the outstanding features of many military campaigns from the Battle of Cannae to the first Battle of the Marne play a live role in the thinking and decisions of our military commanders? Yes.

Even if military campaigns never repeat themselves, is there an unquestioned advantage in being an experienced campaigner? Yes.

Even if no two law cases are exactly alike or should be handled exactly alike, is that an advantage at the bar in legal experience? Yes.

Even though two sales interviews do not repeat themselves, is there an advantage in being an experienced salesman? Yes.

In each of the above examples there are *single factors which repeat in part and which can be usefully remembered and applied to the new situation.*

The great service of the social sciences is to contribute that *understanding* of each situation considered; so that the research worker, equipped with the expert methods and understanding peculiar to his own field of social science, and provided by memory with a wide knowledge of more or less similar past situations, can pick out the common factors, recognize the divergent factors, and so *get the full benefit from his study of the history of his own field.* In this way the solid knowledge of the professional will score far ahead of the occasional lucky guess of the amateur, even though *history does not exactly repeat itself.*

The notion that history repeats itself in any meaningful way is so intriguing that the author cannot resist the following wild flight of fancy. Suppose for practical purposes history did repeat itself. Then historical situations could be coded and punched on IBM cards.

When confronted with a live situation in the form of a current intelligence problem, we would only have to set the machine, run through the cards, and that past historical situation most similar to the current situation would be sorted out. We would merely have to read off the outcome of the previous history, make appropriate changes in dates and nations, in order to have the inevitable outcome of the current situation delivered to us on a silver (IBM cardboard) platter.

This flight of fancy has some grains of sanity in other fields. The method described has been seriously used in attempting to predict weather changes by starting with the previously recorded weather situation most like the current situation being studied, and learning from the records what sort of weather followed this sort of a situation in the past. We could expect that the same sort of weather would follow when the same meteorological situation came around again as a current problem requiring a weather prediction. This method has been similarly applied also in a few other directions.

So even though history does not repeat itself, the intelligence officer can profit by a wide knowledge of history in his own field.

But to the intelligence officer the facts of history are not enough; he must know the significance of these facts, not only what happened, but why it happened. He needs not only knowledge, but also understanding or wisdom. Then he can make full use of those elements of historical situations which do repeat themselves in part, using judgment to integrate them with special new factors to arrive at the best prediction possible.

METHODS AS TOOLS FOR INTELLIGENCE RESEARCH

Critical and constructive studies are constantly being made of methods for carrying out various human activities. In the natural sciences, engineering and in the industrial arts, the advantage of improved methods is universally admitted. We find, for example, studies of methods in education, in military science, and in the writing of history. In the social sciences a vigorous study of methods has recently developed. Recent books include *Methods in Social Research* (18), *Social Science Research Methods* (21), *The Language of Social Research, a Reader in the Methodology of Social Research* (58), etc.

In intelligence production as yet we find little study of methods as such. Yet a systematic study of methods in any given field by an open-minded expert in that field nearly always leads to worthwhile improvement. We shall now consider several metnods as useful tools in intelligence production.

Analogy as a Tool—From the Known to the Unknown

Analogy is one of the most useful tools in intelligence production. In fact it is one of the most common forms of our everyday thinking. "Last August was unpleasantly hot in the city, so next August will probably be the same. We should make plans to go away." "The last Yale engineer that we employed was well-grounded in his profession, (so the next one will, probably, also be above the average). Let's hire another Yale engineer." In each case we go from the known to the unknown.

Reasoning by analogy is so usual, easy, and superficially convincing that we use it all the time. We sometimes do not make the best use of this method. Many times we fall into some of the numerous pitfalls. Like nearly every other intelligence production procedure named in this book, in order to get the most out of the procedure, it will pay to consider its capabilities and limitations.

In reasoning by analogy we start with a situation about which we wish to know more. (For example, the temperature in the city next August.) As one means for learning more we look around for a somewhat similar situation about which we already know something (in this case, the temperature last August). We think that, in the absence of evidence to the contrary, the unknown situation will probably be somewhat like the known. Except in the physical sciences, two situations for practical purposes are never exactly the same. We can never know all the governing factors, hence the use of the terms "probably" and "somewhat like."

We see at once that we can do better than this. As in nearly every intelligence operation there is no substitute for a real understanding of a situation—the background and governing factors. The more thoroughly we understand the situation, the more exactly we can speak and the greater the degree of certainty of our estimate. The more confidence we can have that we have avoided common pitfalls.

The first of the common pitfalls is that two situations which have great superficial similarity and which are, therefore, considered analogous for the problem before us, are actually not similar in the factors which govern this problem and, hence, are not analogous for the purpose.

Taking the Yale engineering graduate for example, the standing of a young engineer in his class is probably a much better criterion of his ability than whether he graduated from Yale or from some other first-class educational institution. There is probably much more similarity in engineering competence between a Yale mechanical engineer in the upper tenth of his class and a MIT mechanical engineer in the upper tenth of his class, than there is between a Yale mechanical engineer in the upper tenth of his class and one in the lowest tenth of his class. So for the purposes of engineering competence, young Yale engineers, though superficially similar, are not soundly analogous.

The second pitfall is that many analogies are pushed too far. The similarity for the primary purpose of the study may be so good, that we erroneously extend the analogy and the inferences therefrom far beyond any real justification. The primary successes in the use of our analogy overcome our caution and lead us on to all the greater disaster.

Taking now the positive approach, what can we do in an intelligence problem to derive as much benefit as possible from analogies?

Based on a statement of the Social Science Research Council as quoted by Gee (21), with modifications of our own, we may say that the usual requirements are:

1. Sufficient preliminary study of the problem at hand so that one can state clearly the elements in which a parallel is sought.

2. Singling out an analogous known situation in which the important factors for the purposes of this problem are sufficiently similar to make this sound analogy. There must be no important factors for the purposes of this problem which are so radically different that they would destroy the usefulness of the analogy.

3. Study of the unknown problem situation compared with the known analogy and arranging the likenesses and differences in parallel columns. Then they can be checked and weighed against one another. It is always useful to bring the differences out into the open.

It has been well said that in working by analogy, time spent on the differences is more fruitful than that spent on the similarities.

Frye and Levi (59) have pointed out that analogy plays a principal role in the formation of hypotheses. They say: "The capacity to discern fundamental similarities between things superficially very different is one of the outstanding attributes of the theorizing mind. . . ."

Evidently, too, if several analogous situations can be found they provide a more solid foundation than just one.

Analogy—The Percentage Method

A familiar rough and ready method for utilizing analogies is the percentage method. Starting with the known—for example, this year's sales or costs, or production—we arrive at a figure for next year's sales, costs or production by estimating that they will be 90%, or 150%, or what you will, of this year's. Or that Curtania output per man-hour in a machine shop will be 60% of that in a United States machine shop of similar size. This is not a lazy man's method.

It is not a method by which "we can find out something without knowing anything."

Obviously, we have to understand the whole situation, so as to be sure that the two activities being compared are sufficiently similar that a valid comparison can be made. We have to understand the differences, so that allowances can be made for them. We need a critical independence of thought and maturity of judgment in fixing the percentage factors which are evidently the crux of the whole method.

When foreign information is scanty the analogy method is often the best method—sometimes the only method for obtaining a partial picture of the foreign situation with some degree of reliability.

Analogy—A Specific Example

One of the very few studies, directed primarily at the development of improved intelligence production *methods,* was one carried out on a foreign manufactured product.

The intelligence officers concerned faced a situation common in intelligence, namely there was very little positive information. What information there was seemed so scattered, that little or no meaning could be derived from it. The situation looked so discouraging that no definite steps had been taken to make it better.

The workers realized that there were two distinct parts to the problem. First, to get more information. Second, to get more meaning out of the information at hand. Their study was confined to the second part. It was all in the field of intelligence production.

Their experience and conclusions justify the systematic study of methods in this field, and are of wide application to other intelligence production problems. What they point out as helpful procedures and what they point out as pitfalls are both worth-while parts of their study.

In view of the tremendous shortage of information which they encountered, and in order to give the scattered bits some order and possible meaning, they used "the analogy" method. This starts with the tentative assumption that, *in the absence of any information to the contrary,* in many cases the Curtanian problems and eventual solutions will probably be much like those of the United States. In the field of certain manufactured products part of this assumption *must* be true. The principles of physics, metallurgy and engineering are the same the world over.

This analogy method leads directly to a systematic study of the United States research and development program on these products. We learn the U. S. successes and unsolved problems and the direction of their efforts. All of this gives us the best possible intimate understanding of the whole problem pertaining to the type of product covered by this intelligence study. Intelligence officers are able better to visualize the Curtanian problems by having seen the actual tests of U. S. products.

Then the scanty facts known about the whole Curtanian industrial research and development program are studied in the light of our comprehensive knowledge of the corresponding U. S. program.

Right away we see clearly how the foreign information can form part of a consistent picture. Knowledge of our program enables us not only to specify more clearly what foreign information we especially want, but also to state how and where it can most probably be obtained.

So, though this study of methods did not directly cover field collection methods, yet it sharpened, and made much more effective, our directions to the field collector. In fact, an important part of the mission of a worker in intelligence production is to provide helpful guidance to field collectors in the form of clear and definite requirements, pointing out critical items and suggesting where the information may be found.

In the project which we are discussing here, more information appeared when better requirements were sent to the field: and on the basis of our better understanding of the whole manufacturing activity through close contact with the U. S. program, the information which appeared had added meaning.

This method, at least, starts us on our search provided with very large assets, namely information derived from a study of the underlying principles, the achievements, the difficulties, and the plans of the United States. Some of these are practically certain to have a close parallel in Curtania.

As an extreme example, let us take manned earth satellites. Even if we knew very little about Curtanian research and development in this direction, we could still be fairly certain that Curtania would not have such a manned "space ship" in 1957. We come to this conclusion merely from our knowledge of the tremendous difficulties connected with this problem based on United States' experience.

A Check on Analogies—The Home Comparison Method

Analogies can also be used as a healthy check on the methods we have adopted for drawing conclusions about Curtania. For example, we may have developed a method for estimating the quality of Curtanian engineering education; or we may have adopted certain critical factors in judging the effectiveness of Curtanian anti-aircraft fire; or in evaluating the quality of the medical care available in foreign rural districts. In all of these cases a useful check on the soundness of our proposed method would be: How successful would such a method, or such criteria, be to distinguish high quality from low quality in similar activities in the United States? As a vivid but humorous example see Jerome (60A).

In some cases where the foreign situation is radically different from that in the U. S., this method will not be decisive or even pertinent; but in most cases this method will shed much light on the effectiveness of the criteria that we are using.

Case Histories—An Intelligence Tool

In many studies in the social sciences there are two contrasting approaches—the statistical approach and the case history approach. These are so different that each one supplements the other and makes contributions towards the truth which the other lacks. Almost any study is stronger if it can include some elements of both approaches.

Let us take as an example an economic, sociological or other study of families in an American community (a county, town, state, rural area, etc.).

One part of the strength of the statistical study lies in the fact that it includes large numbers. It may include all the families in the area, or it may include large samples. The results are principally expressed in the summarizing parameters, especially averages and distributions. For example in statements such as: The average family income is $5,000. These are distributed so that 10% receive over $15,000, etc., 40% have automobiles, and 5% have two or more automobiles in the family, etc. Figures of this kind are familiar and can be continued ad infinitum.

By contrast the Case History Method selects cases typical of the whole groups or typical of subgroups and presents a *fairly complete picture of each case*. For example the report may say: "Let us now consider the Jones family, a typical family in the median income range. Mr. Jones has a wife, two sons and a daughter. They own a farm worth about

$20,000 on which there is a $15,000 mortgage. They have one Chevrolet on which $500 is still to be paid. Mr. Jones, 35 years old, is a graduate of the Texas A&M. His sons are active in the 4-H Club and expect to become farmers, etc., etc."

The number of facts pertinent to any situation is so large that summarizing devices have become essential somewhere in the whole study. Totals, averages, and standard deviations serve a useful purpose as far as they go, but they are subject to two serious objections. First, as they stand they may be misleading and may even seem absurd without some interpretation. For example the average Harvard graduate has, let us say, 2.2 children and .9 of a wife. The average cafeteria patron at lunch eats .1 of a slice of apple pie, .2 of a dish of ice cream, .25 of a salad, and so on. The average stockholder in the given corporation owns 300 shares of stock, whereas actually no stockholder is in this range at all. Several directors hold 100,000 shares or more each. Thousands of employees hold 5 to 10 shares each. (See Chapter VI for a discussion of averages.)

The second objection to lumping individual cases into totals and averages is that these parameters lack the flesh and blood, the emotions that are the essence of real life. We can form a mental picture approaching the truth of 9 Harvard men, each with his own wife, and of one unmarried Harvard man; but none of us can visualize the *average* Harvard man with .9 of a wife (or perhaps in the interests of truth and high standards of scholarship we should be more exact and say with .937 wives).

So statistics and summaries are valuable; but it is highly desirable to *supplement them with case histories* giving specific examples of persons, groups, farms or what not—each with its past, present and future, its successes and failures, its warm living existence. We bring back into our intelligence picture the one most important single factor in any living organism or dynamic situation, namely *the life.*

When making a social science study of an American community the social science worker can select his own method to a considerable extent. He can decide in advance the relative emphasis which he wishes to place on statistics, on case histories, or other methods.

In intelligence, on the other hand, we often have to take what we can get. For example, in some comparable study of collective farms in Curtania we may have to rely nearly altogether on statistics published in the Curtanian daily papers. Then part way through the study we come upon one or two defectors who can throw a kind of light on the situation *quite different* from that of the official statistics; namely, case histories of themselves and a few of their neighbors.

Thus it is highly desirable to use *both* methods in most studies in the social sciences, including intelligence. Case histories are particularly important in intelligence on account of the wide reliance on interviews with prisoners of war, defectors, and occasional contacts of various kinds.

In considering the case history method as an intelligence tool we can profitably discuss the advantages and the limitations.

We will begin our discussion of the advantages of case studies by quoting Goode and Hatt (18). "The case study then . . . is a way of organizing social data so as to preserve the *unitary character of the social object being studied.* Expressed somewhat differently, it is an approach which views any social unit as a whole. Almost always, this means of approach includes the *development* of that unit, which may be a person, a family, or other social group, a set of relationships or processes . . . or even an entire culture." Thc case study preserves the development or changes, in other words the dynamic as contrasted with the static approach.

It is interesting to remember that the case study is the original method used from the most ancient times in story-telling, history, and parables. At its best it conveys a vivid human picture, and one side of the truth *not obtainable to this degree of perfection by any other method.*

As Bernard (60) points out, "A case description is, if accurate, always a true record of what occurs, while a statistical generalization, except in those instances when all included cases are identified, is only an abstract approximation."

Case histories are usually more useful in the early or exploratory stages of a study than in the later stages.

The weaknesses and consequent dangers of the case study method stem principally from two causes. The first is the small number of cases which can be *effectively* included. Even if the writer should include hundreds of case studies in his report, the reader cannot possibly carry more than a few of these in his mind.

When we depend upon a few cases there is a particular danger of bias or unreliability in the sources. Thus if each of ten defectors separately describes highly unfavorable conditions in the country from which they came, their unanimity may seem convincing. Actually each one may be separately influenced by the same factor; namely, dislike of the new regime in the country from which he has just escaped, and by a desire to justify his leaving his native land. The 90 who remained at home, and whom we do not hear from, may be quite contented.

The cases selected may not be a fair sample of the "population" or situations under study, as in the above instance. This may well happen even when each case is correctly evaluated and accurately described. Only when a population or a *part* of a population is fairly homogeneous can a few cases properly depict the whole, or any substantial part.

There is, however, a tendency for the reader to remember

and so to exaggerate the importance of the few cases selected for inclusion in the written report, and to think of them as necessarily representative of the whole. There is the related danger of over-emphasizing unusual events.

The second danger from the use of case studies arises from the fact that the vivid and intimate nature of a case study increases the difficulty of the author when trying to view these cases objectively. Goode and Hatt (18) express this: "The basic danger in its use is the *response of the researcher*. The researcher comes to feel a false sense of certainty about his own conclusions . . . each *case* which is developed as a unit takes on complete dimensions in the mind of the researcher. It is quite comparable to our feeling of . . . certainty about our close friends. There is, in short, an emotional feeling of certainty which is much stronger than in the case of other types of research."

Means to avoid these pitfalls may be summed up as: (1) A vivid consciousness of the dangers and an active determination to combat these dangers; (2) Great care in selecting cases which will fairly present all of the important aspects of the situation, taking special care that views opposed to those of the author should be fairly represented; (3) An active search for probable bias in the source; (4) An advance criticism of the author's ideas and of the draft of his paper by colleagues who have not been influenced by the close and sympathetic contact which the author has had with the cases cited.

The intelligence production officer has special difficulties due to the fact that the "cases" available to him may be very few and by no means representative. However, with all their faults, these few intimate, perhaps biased cases, present a side of the subject of his intelligence report probably not covered in any other way. Such cases should not be discarded on account of the limitations just mentioned. The author should first get clear in his own mind the usefulness of these cases and their limitations. He should then make these elements of usefulness and limitation clear to the reader of his intelligence report.

All of the above may be taken as a typical example of the utilization of the social sciences for intelligence purposes as described on the first page of this chapter. We see that in considering Case Histories the work already done in the social sciences assists the intelligence officer: "First, by providing an understanding of the general principles; Second, by providing specific suggestions as to methods; Third, by pointing out common pitfalls; and Fourth, by providing references for further study." as stated in the introduction to this chapter.

This implementation in fact pervades the entire present book, though it is not always so clearly spelled out as in this chapter. The intention to provide an understanding of general principles, to contribute specific suggestions as to methods applicable to intelligence, to point out pitfalls, and to give study references is always present. In some places it did not seem necessary to label each step.

CONSISTENCY IN CHARACTER OF GROUPS OR NATIONS

> Of all the books that no one can write, those about nations and national character are the most impossible.
>
> JACQUES BARZUN
> quoted by KLINEBERG (61)

The reader may find the above quotation rather discouraging as a beginning for this section. He will find some rays of hope near the end.

The purpose of this section is simple. We find frequent reference at the highest levels to national character. We read, for example, of German thoroughness, Oriental cruelty, Gallic wit, etc. How reliable are such concepts? How can we best use them in intelligence?

Evidently, if reliable differences exist in the character of different nations, an understanding of such differences would be a great help in estimating probable courses of action or in forecasting long-term capabilities. On the other hand, if such national differences have no consistency or reliability, then we must be on our guard against being misled by such statements which are commonly assumed to be true without critical examination.

We can start our present discussion with the analogous case of *personal character*. A knowledge of the character of the Commanding Officer of the opposing military unit has been used in combat intelligence for many years. Intelligence on this subject was systematically distributed and used in World War II, especially in Europe. For example, one German commander was known to be very aggressive and to make bold and skillful use of tanks; another was known to put up a stubborn defense; a third could be induced to withdraw by a vigorous demonstration of force. Such knowledge of personal character was specifically useful.

If we had failed to make full use of the personal characteristics of enemy commanders, we should have thrown away a valuable intelligence asset. Widest use of such knowledge was perhaps made in our own Civil War, where opposing commanders were often well known to each other personally. Civil War memoirs are filled with such references. Napoleon, also, made extensive use of his knowledge of the character of opposing commanders. See Farago (54B).

Is There a Group or National Character?

We turn now to groups or nations. We will use the word "group" as a general term to include a nation, or a group within a nation, such as the British upper classes, the German General Staff, or the French 18th Century Intellectuals.

We are surprised to find the wide-spread use and general acceptance of phrases, such as the group "character" or group "mind." An intelligence officer must decide to what extent he is willing to accept the idea of the group character as useful intelligence on the same basis that he holds quite definite opinions as to the character of his acquaintances and of individual public figures. To show the prevalence of the idea of group character or mind on a high professional level, we will cite a few examples out of many. A recent visit to the Columbia University Book Store showed no less than five more or less recent books on display having the group or national "mind" in the title.

In an excellent and thoughtful discussion of National Character by Klineberg (61),[1] he says, "In a symposium on 'Psychological Considerations for Making Peace' in the April

[1] Klineberg unwisely entitles his article, "A Science of National Character." There is certainly no *science* of national character, any more than there is a real science of personal character. However, his conclusions are of interest. "I am reasonably pessimistic about the present status of our 'science,' but I have considerable hope for its future. Difficult, yes; complicated, certainly; but impossible, no. . . . We can have a science of national character."

1943 number of the *Journal of Abnormal and Social Psychology,* more than half of the writers find it necessary to make direct references to the problem of national character in one or another form."

In that truly excellent history, *The German People,* Veit Valentin (62) says, "Thus a sort of petty self-seeking was developed in the National character—envy, touchiness, jealousy, ambition without generosity. . . . All of which contributed to a second very typical component of the German national character; to wit, respect for power, for the authority of the uniform, the title, the office, the inside information."

The last chapter of Commager's (63) *The American Mind, Thought and Character Since the 1880's* contains some general statements on the American character which appeal to the present author as true, and significantly different from statements which would be made about any other nation, and hence as having definite intelligence value to a foreign nation wishing to understand the U. S. and its probable "course of action."

As another example, Santayana (64) has a chapter on "The Best in English Character," which is true of the English, but not of any other nation known to the present author.

As an example from another field, a serious professional study of British infantry tactics (65) starts with the postulate that infantry tactics "must be based on national characteristics." The British author then lists five fundamentals of English character pertinent to this study. One is "lack of imagination involving absolute faith in ultimate victory." (The English soldier cannot imagine that he may be beaten, so he holds on and eventually wins. In a more brilliant nation the soldiers can see more clearly all the dangers and so they surrender promptly.) Again we feel that the author is saying something worth saying. An intelligence officer is the better for reading it.

Finally the well-known British diplomat Nicolson (66) makes some definite statements about the Greek character in classical times. He implies that Greek national character consistently affected national actions.

In order to make more plain what we mean by character in nations or groups, we list below some of the traits of character which seem to be consistent over a sufficiently wide range of conditions and over a sufficiently long period of time to be of importance in intelligence:

Industry	Will-to-Win
Thoroughness	Reliability
Progressiveness	Truthfulness
Enthusiasm	Generosity
Patriotism	Brilliance
Warlike Qualities	Visionary Qualities
Courage	Spirituality
Tenacity	Spirit of Cooperation
Spirit of Fair Play	

and their OPPOSITES

It must be admitted that the idea of a national character is convenient. Many glib statements can be made about it. Any reader will think of many examples to support almost any such statements. They are sufficiently vague to be easy to accept. A list of references, giving various interpretations of the American character, is given in Appendix B to show how varied and, hence, how uncertain our estimates of national character may be.

An analogous case may serve as a warning. For years literature was full of statements about human facial charcteristics. The "lofty brow" indicted "the keen intellect." Admirals had "a strong chin" and certain ladies "a voluptuous mouth." All of these phrases were convenient to writers and reader. They helped to paint a vivid word picture of a person.

They were used by the best authors and were almost universally accepted as reliable.

Unfortunately a critical study shows that they have no reliability at all. Otherwise by a study of the face we would have a useful method for reading individual character. They are worse than useless, because misleading, in judging individuals. Will the convenient and attractive ideas of national or group character suffer the same fate when critically examined?

Many take a dim view of using the concept of "group character" as a serious factor in intelligence. Others voice more active criticism. We repeat that the purpose of this section is to get out of the group character concept whatever real value there may be in it, and to avoid any pitfalls which it may present. We repeat also that as this phrase occurs with ever-increasing frequency in the best professional literature, an intelligence officer *must* make up his own mind about it. Otherwise he may unconsciously accept it as a reliable concept.

Some Definitions and Explanations

First let us further define what we mean and set forth some of the practical limitations of this concept.

We are talking about character, not skills or even customs as such. Under character we would include such qualities as aggressiveness, stubbornness, daring, caution, the will-to-win, the willingness to quit and so on as listed above.

In intelligence we often deal with nations, so it is convenient to consider national character. Modern social scientists like to point out, however, that nations often have little unity except the geographical area and their central government. Within a given nation there may be a wide diversity of ethnic groups, cultures, and even languages. The classes may differ widely as between peasants, industrial laborers, upper classes, etc.

So we admit that it greatly simplifies the question as to whether there is or is not a group or national character, and even in some cases makes it meaningful when it would otherwise not be meaningful, if we consider the character of groups within a nation, rather than the character of a nation as a whole. We may often consider the character of selected groups *first,* and *later* try to describe the character of the nation as a whole if desired.

As we all know, in any nation the great majority of people will and must follow along with any policy set by the government. They go to war, make friends with certain neighboring states, pay high taxes for welfare, etc., as the government decides. By breaking a nation down into groups, it is often possible to select the *controlling groups* and so to get at the *effective national character* and to predict the national course of action. Such prediction was much easier 50 years and more ago than it is today.

For example, in the nineteenth century the British upper classes were a well-defined group which effectively dominated the government. By understanding the character of the upper classes one could certainly understand much of the English national character as regards war, diplomacy and many other matters.

As another example a group of families on our western frontier would be called adventurous if a small percent were constantly venturing into unknown territory and so creating an aggressive, adventurous atmosphere on that part of the frontier. Again a whole group might be called "warlike" if the leaders were warlike in the strict sense of the word; and if a large proportion of males of the proper ages were willing to follow the leaders and could be made into good soldiers, even if they showed little eagerness for battle; and if there was no organized active pacifist minority.

So the effective action of the group may be taken to reflect the character of the group for the purposes of this discussion.

Usually the standards are set and the decisions are made by a minority of any group, which minority is aggressive and vocal. (See Chapter VI, The Three Part Rule.)

A comparison will now be made between our knowledge of an individual's character together with the applications that can be made of that knowledge on the one hand; with the knowledge which we can gain of the character of a group and the applications that we can make of that knowledge for intelligence purposes on the other hand.

The present author believes that each individual has elements of character which are knowable and quite reliable in indicating what to expect from him under given conditions, and that most readers will agree in this. Similarly in other days the character of the German General Staff, and to some extent of the German Officer Corps, set the standards for the character of the German Army.

The comparative simplicity of those days is gone, but the effective[2] national character and probable courses of action of many civilized nations can probably still be foreseen by considering the character of the few groups which are *decisive in a given situation.* The problem can be simplified, too, by eliminating from our consideration some of the groups—sometimes quite large groups—which are not effective in a given situation. Thus in studying Canada, one could eliminate the Eskimos, but not the French Canadians. Sometimes one group such as the farmers, or the labor unions, will have an effective veto on certain kinds of national action.

Furthermore in describing the group character we never mean that all members of the group think or act or have

[2] Effective character in an individual or a group is an aspect of character so definite and so strong as to make itself effective in action to a notable extent. Thus a man is not effectively quarrelsome because he feels quarrelsome, but only when he indulges in quarrels to a notable extent. A group is not effectively progressive because it yearns for progress, but only when it manifests evident progress.

the character stated. We only mean that *a sufficient number* have the given character to affect the character or even the reputation of the group as a whole.

We start by admitting that it is easier for any of us to learn something about the character of another individual than to learn something of the character of a group. We began in infancy by learning about individual members of our family, and we continue the process of learning about the character of individuals every day of our lives.

By contrast, it is not a natural daily experience for us to learn the character of a large group which may be widely dispersed geographically. Furthermore, though there is no doubt that every individual has a character, yet the skeptic may fairly question at this stage of our discussion whether a group has a group character, any more than those who happen to be in Grand Central Station, New York, at a given moment have a group bank account.

We will leave two questions for consideration later in this section. The questions are: (1) Is there a group character useful for intelligence purposes? (2) If it exists, can we gain reliable information about it?

Some Objections—Partially Met

For the moment we will tentatively assume that the answer to both of these questions is affirmative. Based upon this assumption, let us examine some of the objections which have been raised against attempts to use group or national character for intelligence purposes.

1. *Objection.* Group character is not sufficiently definite and consistent so that we can be sure that the group will react in accordance with its accepted character: that is, for example, industriously, conservatively, stubbornly, courageously, as the case may be.

Answer: Neither does an individual always act "in character," yet an individual's character pattern is sufficiently reliable that we can bet on the individual under certain circumstances with great confidence. It is valuable to know the character of an individual with whom we must deal, and we throw away a valuable advantage in our dealings with him if we disregard knowledge of his character and consider him only as an average human being.

2. *Objection.* The character of a nation or group changes with time. (Modern Italians are far different from the ancient Romans, for example.)

Answer: The same thing is true of the individual. The reckless youth becomes the cautious old man. Changes in group character occur more slowly than changes in individual character. If group character remains substantially constant over the period of an intelligence estimate—say ten years—we can disregard how it may change in one hundred years. The warning here is that one must question the value of remote history as evidence of present group character. The British aggressiveness in Elizabethan times may not be pertinent today.

3. *Objection.* Nobody has clearly defined what we mean by group character. No one has a clear understanding of the elements of character nor of their genetic, psychological, cultural or other origins.

Answer: The same thing is true of individual character, which has never been adequately defined. We can use empirical knowledge of a phenomenon long before we understand it. We could warm ourselves in the sun, long before we understood the composition of the sun or the nature of radiant heat.

4. *Objection.* Similar miscellaneous objections claim: "There are no rules for using national character studies for prediction. There is no rule of thumb to tell a good character description from a poor one."

Answer: We are equally deficient in systematic studies of personal character, yet we can utilize our knowledge of personal character effectively.

5. *Objection.* More fundamentally: "To be a meaningful tool 'national character' must . . . give an understanding of [the people's] basic premises and the reasoning behind their actions and attitudes of approval or disapproval."

Answer: Agreed that it is highly desirable to understand the underlying reasoning behind group character. Such an understanding multiplies the useableness of our knowledge of group character several times.

However, an understanding of such reasoning is not *necessary* to usefulness in intelligence. Suppose we see that for the past 150 years the British have stuck it out in all their important wars and have carried on to final victory in spite of disastrous earlier defeats. We can call this *tenacity* an element of national character. Suppose we see no reason to suspect a change in their character. It will be a safe bet for an intelligence forecast to say that if Britain were attacked tomorrow she would not fold up in a matter of months; but would very likely "muddle through" to victory. We can take this from the behaviorist point of view. This point of view considers only *what happens.* Why it happens is regarded as mere speculation.

The predominant motive for sticking it out may be fear of the enemy, or pride. We should like to know what it is; but lacking this knowledge of motives, a knowledge of national character as evidenced solely by recent past behavior is still a reliable intelligence asset.

The Crucial Questions

We return to the two crucial questions mentioned above. Namely: (1) Is there a group character useful for intelligence purposes? (2) If it exists, how can we gain information about it?

We admit that the present development of the social sciences and of the art of intelligence production does not give us any sound scholarly foundation on which to base answers to these questions. Methods for attacking these problems and for presenting the results have not been worked out. No systematic and critical consideration of the usefulness of national character for intelligence purposes has been developed by intelligence officers.

However development of methods, carrying out of projects, and critical application of results to intelligence forecasts are just the *sort of achievements* that the social scientists have demonstrated that they can do. It is just the sort of thing that they have already done soundly and beneficially in other closely related fields.

In fact a critical study of national or group character is a field just ripe for cultivation. The fruit would find a ready market among intelligence officers, diplomats, and others. So we may feel sure that ten, twenty, or thirty years from now much progress will have been made and helpful answers to questions based on competent studies will be available. But would it be wise to wait thirty years before making up our minds whether to make any use of national or group character as an intelligence tool?

The present author believes that in this case, as in so very many others, we must make the best use that we can of what we now have. However, we make wisest use of doubtful concepts when we frankly face the sketchiness of their foundations. Furthermore, we do not propose to stake our all on our understanding of national character in a given case, but use the national character as we see it as *one bit of evidence* which we put together with other bits before we draw conclusions.

So to answer the question on the basis of the sketchy evidence at hand: Is there usually a group character useful for intelligence purposes? Yes.

Although this question has never been made the subject of a thorough on-the-spot research, we believe that there is such a thing with meaning and limitations *closely analogous* to individual character. With groups as with individuals, there are certainly adverse conditions which will nullify the usual traits of character. There are some dangers before which even the boldest will quail. There are some discouragements which will cause the most industrious to step out of character and to lose interest.

Occasionally a great cause may move an individual or a group to vigorous action in marked contrast to their previous disillusioned character. We admit that characters may also change gradually with time. But within the periods of time considered for intelligence purposes, group character is a valuable lead, and one which we can in general count on for consistency.

To make the possible contrast between the character of groups more clear, let us consider pairs of groups as specific examples; each group mentioned having sufficient unity to make it worthy of *study as a group*. These groups are selected so that there are significant differences between the characters of the two groups in each pair. Examples mght be:

The farmers or peasants in two areas of roughly comparable size. These areas might be two widely separated counties in the U. S., or areas in U. S. compared with those in Russia, or in France compared with Germany.

Coal miners of U. S. compared with coal miners of England.

Total inhabitants of two towns of roughly comparable size but in contrasting locations.

French Army compared with German Army at outbreak of World War II.

U. S. research chemists compared with German research chemists in 1930.

Members of U. S. labor unions compared with members of English labor unions.

Graduates of colleges and universities in U. S. compared with those in U.S.S.R.

Inhabitants of Italy compared with those of France.

Origin of Differences in Group Character

The differences in effective character between groups in the same pairs must be due to one or more of the following factors:

1. Genetics. The tendency of science is to minimize dependence on the *inborn* differences other than physical between different races, ethnic or other groups as a whole.

2. Culture. In the broadest sense. All that background of ideas which members of a group learn from each other. This includes customs, folklore, religion, education, values.

3. Selection. Out of the larger population of which the group is a part what selection has been made by any means—conscious or unconscious—so that one group contains a markedly larger proportion of those who are physically strong, intellectual, brave, etc.

4. Physical Environment. Weather, soil, isolation. They may make life too easy; or on the other hand may be stimulating and rewarding to effort; or at the other extreme may be so difficult as to exhaust all of the group merely in the struggle to keep alive.

5. Constructive Intragroup Cooperation. Rewards within the group may be based upon favoritism, or upon merit. There may be a dead level of reward or free competition. There may or may not be recognition and reward for merit and punishment for antisocial acts. Leadership may bring out certain qualities of character and discourage others.

Next, how can we gain reliable information about group characters in general, or about a specific group character in a given situation?

Part of the answer is that government and other agencies should sponsor research projects into methods and as pilot projects, to get information about the character of specific groups. But again, what should an analyst do while he waits for such research to be undertaken and completed?

Methods for Using Group Character as an Intelligence Asset

Supposing the intelligence problem for some given foreign country was concerned with: (1) economic recovery in which the industry of the people as a national character would play a part, or (2) to likelihood of war in which the warlike quality would play a part, or (3) to the prospects for a treaty to settle international differences on a fair basis in which a national spirit of friendliness and fair play would play a part. In such cases what would be the general procedure for answering the question: What influence (if any) will the so-called national character (if any) have on the outcome of this intelligence question?

First break down the question from the character of the nation to the character of certain pertinent groups. What group or groups within the nation will have an important influence on a given situation? What groups have substantial power to instigate action? What groups have the power to prevent action?

Second, considering now pertinent groups only, what is the mechanism by which the action of each such group is decided and implemented? Are there one or two leaders, or a relatively small "executive committee" which makes the decisions? Will the rest of the group nearly always follow? Does a small percentage set the fashion and set the pace which others more or less willingly follow? Is the decision substantially by majority rule? Or is the character evidenced by the total net action of all individuals rather than by the leadership of a few? For example, a thrifty group gives evidence of this character by its total net savings, lumping together those who save much and those who save nothing.

Third, what has been the history of each group as to any given character in the past?

Fourth, have there been any important recent changes in the make-up, or control, or the conditions under which the group acts, which would lead us to expect that the character of the group would be different in the near future from what it has been in the not too distant past? If so, what has been the direction of the change? Will the change probably continue?

So even in the imperfect state of our knowledge about national character and methods for attacking problems depending upon national character, we can attack a given problem of probable courses of action of a group by a process of analysis and narrowing the problem down to the critical situation of the sub-group that has the power to act. In some cases we must also consider sub-groups whose opposition could *prevent* the nation from taking action successfully.

So we reiterate: we may consider group character as a real usable factor in intelligence forecasting, even if it is still in the development stage.

Here again we are following our announced pattern of attempting to get dividends out of a concept regarded as a possible intelligence asset. Again our implementation is to understand the fundamental principles, to discover sound methods, to point out pitfalls and to furnish references.

HOW FOREIGN ARE FOREIGNERS?

Closely related to the question of national character is the question: How foreign are foreigners? In other words, to what extent do they differ from Americans in their reactions?

This question is fundamental in much of our intelligence thinking. Every intelligence officer has to adopt some sort of a point of view on this question. Most do so unconsciously. However, the matter is so important, and it is so apt to be influenced by personal prejudices, that it is worthwhile to bring it into the open and to shed upon it all the light which psychology and the natural and social sciences and perhaps the humanities can provide.

As America is somewhat isolated from other countries, it is not surprising to find that many Americans are provincial in outlook. Millions of Americans live most of their lives without ever encountering a person who cannot speak English, and without ever living in a foreign country. When these Americans finally do travel they are somewhat outraged to find that foreign parts are infested with foreigners. Like Mark Twain, they are surprised to find that in Paris *even the children* speak French.

As General Doriot says: "Many Americans think that all other nations look at problems from the Anglo-Saxon point of view; or at least, if other nations don't, *they ought to.*"

The question has been put: Are foreigners just Americans with beards? Are the differences merely superficial like language, clothes and mannerisms, or do they react *fundamentally* differently?

In estimating the probable courses of action of a foreign person or group, we tend to "put ourselves in his place" and then decide what we would do in similar circumstances. We certainly always go through this process in our preliminary thinking. We *inevitably* consider what we would do; even though we may not give much weight to these considerations in our final conclusions about a foreign country.

For some intelligence officers, however, trying to put ourselves in the place of foreigners is anathema. They claim that the areas of knowledge and ignorance, the background, and motives of ourselves are so different from those of the given foreigners, that this point of view leads to all sorts of serious errors—especially as it is such an intriguing way of thinking. It always seems to us quite *natural* for others to decide to do what we would do if we were in their place. So our conclusions from "putting ourselves in their places" are superficially convincing.

Some people regard all men as essentially similar. They consider that the similarities are say, a thousand times as effective as the differences. All people share with the animals physical needs such as hunger and cold, sex, dislike of pain, weariness, etc. As human beings, they share with each other the same motives of pride or vanity, curiosity, combativeness, etc. One can go through the literature of all ages and point out how the same motives have been operative in the Hebrews, the Homeric Greeks, the Romans, the men of the Middle Ages, of Elizabethan England and of the present day. So some people conclude that groups from different countries will react substantially the same under the same circumstances the world over. This is one extreme point of view.

At the other extreme are those who see that an oriental, for example, looks different, talks different and seems different from ourselves. We cannot interpret his facial expression as well as we can those of an American. *We know that his whole culture is different.* For all these reasons we assume that his reactions will be so different from our own that we can never understand them; so we do not try to do so.

In between these extreme points of view are those who, unconsciously perhaps, conclude that an Englishman will react substantially like ourselves, a continental Western European somewhat differently, an Eastern European very differently, and an oriental or Middle Easterner on a basis so different that we can hardly hope to understand it from any comparison with our own.

Whatever point of view we adopt, we should do so only after due consideration. We should be honest with ourselves. We can at least be sure, in regard to General Doriot's statement, that many foreign countries do *not* look at problems from the (enlightened) Anglo-Saxon point of view. In spite of all that Frenchmen might have learned from English and Americans, "it is discouraging to learn that the French are still as French as ever."

Intelligence officers must constantly draw conclusions about foreigners. It should be evident from the brief discussion in this section that each intelligence officer should have a wide knowledge of history and of the area, literature and language with which he deals. The intelligence fabric is made up of the warp and the woof— a knowledge of the pertinent science interwoven with a knowledge of the people concerned. To draw conclusions regarding foreign economics, or foreign chemistry, or foreign politics, one must understand both economics, chemistry or political sciences as the case may be *and also* something of foreigners concerned. This is one of the ways in which an intelligence officer is different from a "mere" economist or other natural or social scientist, however expert.

The foreign point of view then is essential for an intelligence officer to acquire. This is difficult for many. Some resist such understanding. They are like Sir Edward Grey, the British Secretary of State for Foreign Affairs at the outbreak of World War I, who was described as the Foreign Secretary who had little sympathy with foreigners.

We have not answered the question, "How foreign are foreigners?", but we have at least pointed out the desirability for the reader to think out his own answer, if he is to make a satisfying career of foreign intelligence.

Six

PROBABILITY AND CERTAINTY

Use of Probability and Statistical Analysis
On Being Probabiliy Minded
Probability—The No-Man's Land of Intelligence : The Three Part Rule
Application of Probabilities—Carried to Extremes
Expression of Degree of Certainty

Section I *PROBABILITY*

USE OF PROBABILITY AND STATISTICAL ANALYSIS

The understanding and applications of the theory of probability and the closely related methods of statistical analysis are among the most useful accomplishments that an intelligence officer can have. The number of widely different occasions on which this accomplishment can offer positive assistance in intelligence, or can save the worker from a tempting pitfall is large.

Most of us have made no formal study of the theory of probability or statistical analysis. Most of us have little or no facility in higher mathematics. However, many have the erroneous belief that higher mathematics is essential for an understanding of probability. Such people are apt to avoid any consideration of probability as being beyond their capabilities.

To dispel these misconceptions it is worthwhile to remember that a helpful understanding of probability can be acquired at three quite distinct levels. At each of these levels an intelligence officer can make profitable use of the theory.

First, he can become "probability minded" if he understands the meaning of about twenty terms such as probability, normal curve, mean, median, mode, standard deviation, standard error of the mean, probable error, range, correlation, statistical significance, especially significance of differences between means, decile, quartile, sampling errors and confidence limits, etc. From this he will gain understanding, and a healthy perspective, even though he may never learn to carry out any of the calculations of statistical analysis.

Second, he may learn to understand well and to carry out most of the simple calculations connected with the above mentioned basic terms. All of this can be accomplished without any knowledge of mathematics beyond arithmetic and elementary algebra.

Finally, the intelligence officer may already have or may acquire a knowledge of calculus, logic and statistical analysis, so that he is really a master of statistical analysis and can solve many of the problems in the applications of the theory of probability to intelligence production.

Means for reaching each of these three levels are described in the Bibliography.

The general purpose of this chapter is as stated by Moroney (69) for his book *Facts from Figures* (italics added):

> After all, the whole point of a book such as this is that it sets out to *create an interest* in its subject-matter. We shall be well content if some, at least, of our readers, while glad enough to be rid of the present author and his efforts, will at any rate have seen sufficient of the light to wish to go to those better teachers whose names we have placed in the bibliography as if in a roll of honour.

ll of the foregoing pertains equally to the present book and the present author.)

In regard to the general value of statistical analysis to the handling of statistics and to studies in the natural and social sciences I quote the following extracts from Moroney (emphasis added):

> The nearest we get [in school] to anything like statistics is when we learn to work approximations (a dying art, alas!). . . . What I grumble about is the fact that they [teachers] seem positively afraid of doing anything that is not capable of an exact solution. This is indeed a sorry preparation for the life of the real world. Apart from the bank clerk counting someone else's coppers with grimy fingers, it is doubtful whether there is any single case where the full precision of which arithmetic is capable is of the slightest use. What training do we receive even in the basic ideas of handling statistical data, which is the *very life-blood of everyday life?* . . .
>
> A very little consideration shows that there is scarcely a hole or corner of modern life which could not find some application, however simple, for statistical theory and show a profit as a result. . . .
>
> If you are young, then I say: Learn something about statistics as soon as you can. Don't dismiss it through ignorance or because it calls for thought. . . .
>
> Whoever you are, if your work calls for the interpretation of data, you may be able to do without statistics, but YOU WON'T DO SO WELL.

A few examples of the applications of probability-thinking and statistical analysis to specific intelligence problems are given in this chapter.

ON BEING PROBABILITY MINDED

> Knowledge of probabilities is indispensable as a guide to action. The reason people get along without any formal knowledge of probability theory is because they have some intuitive knowledge of it. RAPOPORT (70)

We all have an internal Probability Calculator.

FRIEDMAN

The intelligence officer deals much with probabilities. In fact his most useful contributions are often those in which he makes wise use of probabilities to throw new light on an important situation.

To be "probability minded" and to think of the world from the statistical point of view, helps to bring out the true picture and offers a useful approach to many problems.

Some of the aspects of probability which will automatically come to the attention of one who is probability minded follow.

Probability

The probability minded worker will realize that the various events with which he is concerned as an intelligence officer may have probabilities extending from almost certainty down to almost impossibility. In the theory of probability, certainty is given Probability 1 (for example, that the sun will rise tomorrow which is almost certain); impossibility is given Probability 0 (for example, that he will be hit on the head by a meteor today, which is so highly improbable as to rate as essentially zero).

He will realize that almost anything is theoretically possible and will at the same time realize that for practical purposes one must confine one's attention to events within a certain range of probability. As Churchill said: "You can't fight a war based on certainties." He will realize that those persons who are always interjecting into the argument or into their thinking remote possibilities introduced by the phrase "It is possible that" are wasting time. Considerations based upon the possibility of making a hole-in-one have small place in intelligence.

A person who is probability minded is always critical of

the phrase so often introduced to get agreement: "After all, the difference is only one of degree." He realizes that a difference of degree may be for practical purposes *all the difference between day and night.* For example suppose that as strangers you and I land in New York City. I land with five cents in my pocket. You land with a thousand dollars. Our situation is the same. We both have money in our pockets; so the difference is *only* one of degree.

One who is probability minded makes honest use of the "calculated risk." He does not let the presence of a risk paralyze his action. Neither does he pretend to himself and others that there is no risk. Instead he faces the risk explicitly, and plans what he will do if the risk is realized. If he has any competence, even as an amateur statistician, he may even roughly calculate it, and do so very profitably.

Improbability

The probability minded will realize that the most highly improbable events occur all the time. The chances against your being dealt *any* bridge hand that you actually receive according to Weaver (72), are 635,013,559,600:1. These odds are just the same against any specified completely mediocre hand as against your receiving one that is all trumps.

Scarne (71) expresses the same idea when he says:

> One of the first things we shall discover is that the marvelous run of luck you had yesterday . . . isn't always as astonishing as it seemed. At Bank Craps the gambler who puts his money on two aces and takes 30 to 1 that they will appear on the next roll feels that he is a very lucky egg indeed when the two aces are thrown 4 times in a row and he bets on each roll, especially if he happens to know that the odds against such a thing happening are 1,679,615 to 1 . . . players forget that the statement that the odds are 1,679,615 to 1 against such an event also mean that the

event can be expected to happen on an average once in every 1,679,616 times. They forget that on the night when that succession of double aces appeared there were thousands of other crap games in progress and several millions of throws were made. It would have been even more amazing if someone somewhere had not thrown double aces four times in a row. The fact that it may have happened to you merely means that you happened to be around at the time.

If he is wise the probability minded intelligence officer will read the little article by Weaver (72) entitled "Probability, Rarity, Interest and Surprise." A reading of this whole article makes clearer the meaning of Weaver's statement which emphasizes the difference in the meanings of the words in the title of this article. He says: ". . . all scientists have to be concerned with probability; and it is not altogether rare, although surely surprising, to find scientists who are surprised to find improbable things occurring. They always have a right to be interested, but only seldom do they have a right to be surprised."

Correlation and Coincidences

The above examples have dealt with single events. When the connection of one series of quantities is studied in relation to another series of quantities we can calculate the degree of correlation between the two. Thus in a free market there is usually a high degree of correlation between the size of a crop and the market price of the product. Often such a correlation draws the attention to the fact that there is some cause and effect relationship between the two series under study. In the natural and social sciences a significant correlation often draws attention to the possibility of some connection which would otherwise have been unsuspected. This is markedly true in intelligence.

Closely similar to correlations for intelligence purposes

are several individual events which may be closely synchronized. A guest in a hotel is robbed of five thousand dollars while asleep. Shortly afterwards one of the night watchmen pays off the mortgage on his house and spends cash freely. This is the old principle of: *Post hoc, ergo propter hoc.* What is its significance?

We have described above three kinds of situations each of which may justifiably attract the attention, or even arouse the suspicions of the intelligence officer. These situations are: (1) correlation between two series of events; (2) synchronism of two or more events; (3) occurrence of a given event (like the bridge hand mentioned) having a high degree of a priori improbability.

In each kind of situation absurdities often are naturally encountered, or may be contrived. For example it has been pointed out by Sargent (78) that in the Northern Hemisphere there is a negative correlation between mean monthly temperature compared with the number of letters in the name of the month. December, January, and February, each with many letters, are cold. May, June, and July, with few, are hot. Life is full of amusing but meaningless correlations and coincidences.

Question: What use should the intelligence officer make of these three kinds of situations? Should he ignore them on account of the absurd examples which he may encounter? Or, on the other hand, should he consider that they *prove something,* because such a high correlation, or such a single event, would have occurred by chance only once in a hundred (or a million) times?

Answer: The correct procedure is more difficult than either of the above alternatives. When circumstances seem to warrant the trouble, the intelligence officer should *investigate further.*

A correlation, or a synchronism, or an unusual event *prove nothing* by themselves, but they may properly *draw atten-*

tion, and so lead to further investigation. Intelligence significance occurs only when some *logical connection* can be found between two series of events, or two synchronous events, or when some significant explanation can be found for some unusual single event. The presence of a logical connection or explanation if discovered is the necessary justification for attaching significance.

As Whitehead says: "There is no more common error than to assume that, because prolonged and accurate mathematical calculations have been made, the application of the result to some fact of nature is absolutely certain." (91)

So the probability minded intelligence officer views high correlations, or highly unusual events, in their true perspective. He knows how to get out of them any usefulness that may be in them. If they have *no element of interest except their unusualness,* he may not waste much time in trying to deduce some hidden meaning from the mere fact that they have occurred.

Distribution and Range

In any group of related measurable facts such for example as the height of men, the IQ of students, or the salaries of employees, we find a scattering—some are high and some low. In many cases we find that though some few men are very tall and some few are very short, the great majority of heights are not far from 5 feet 9 inches.

Anyone who is probability minded, even though he may have no knowledge of higher mathematics, is familiar with the "normal curve" as shown in Figure 5 which shows for any given group the relative frequency with which a certain height, or a certain IQ or a certain salary occurs. In a large sample taken from one homogeneous group we expect a curve like the one shown with a clustering around the arithmetic mean.

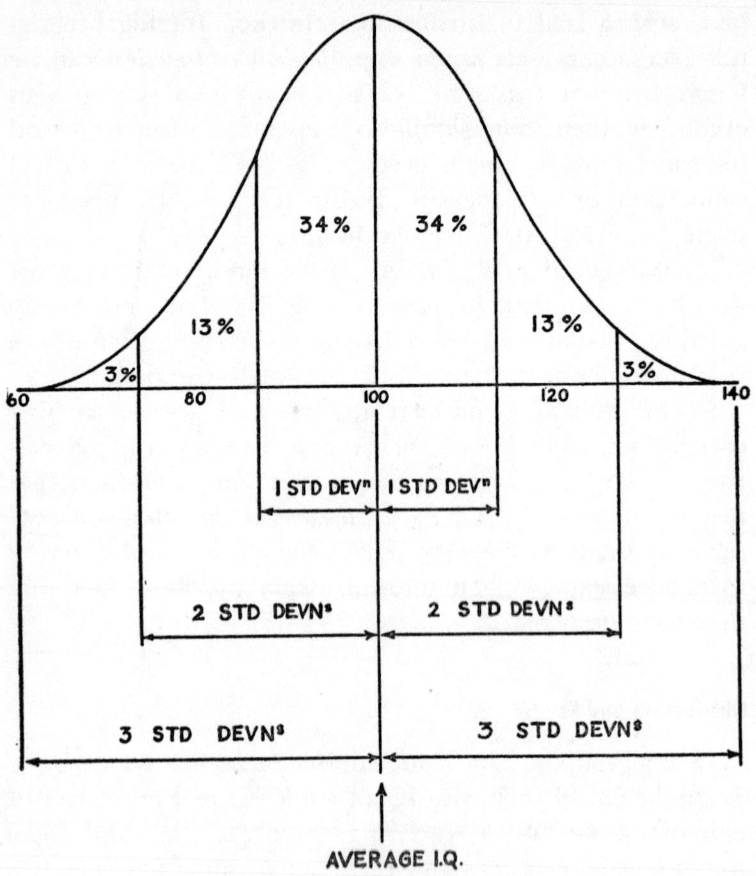

Figure 5 The Normal Curve
Illustrating also Standard Deviation and Average

The amount of dispersion can be indicated in various ways, for example by the range, the standard deviation, the average deviation, the probable error, etc. Definitions and formulae can be found in any book on statistical analysis. (See Bibliography)

On the other hand if an intelligence officer in examining the frequencies of any group should find results like those shown in Figure 6 he would be practically certain that the group that he was studying was in fact two groups of diverse origin.

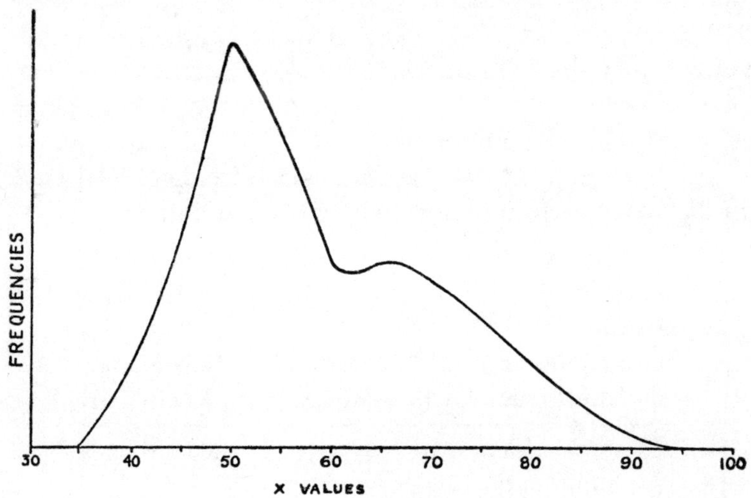

Figure 6 Bimodal Frequency Curve

In studying a body of data he would know that information of intelligence value could be obtained by the use of a "parameter" such as the standard deviation.

He would also know that a great mass of data, say a thousand or so figures, can hardly be made useful without some summarizing parameters. In addition to the parameters indicating the degree of dispersion, there are also others indicating the central tendency. Of these the most important are the arithmetic mean, the median and the mode. These are sometimes all included under the common general term of "average." There is something intriguing about an average. It contains "the best of the worst, and the worst of the best."

From his previous experience however, he never takes at face value glib statements of average. It is common to find in statements of corporations: "The stock of this corporation is widely held. The average holding for each stock holder is 100 shares." Many get an impression from such statements that a very large number of stock holders own approximately 100 shares of stock each. The statement is usually made to convey just that impression. Actually the enormous preponderance of the stock may be held by a very few. Along with this the corporation may have initiated an employee ownership campaign, so that thousands of employees own 5 to 25 shares each. The results might be as follows:

Director A	40,000 shares
Director B	25,000 shares
Director C	20,000 shares
500 employees own 20 shares each	10,000 shares
500 employees own 10 shares each	5,000 shares
1003 stockholders own	100,000 shares

Average holding 99.7 shares.

The probability-conscious officer is aware that the median or the mode often conveys the idea of the central tendency of a mass of figures more helpfully than the arithmetic mean.

The comparison of the mean, median and mode was never better expressed pictorially than in Figure 7 taken from Huff (73).[1]

A probability minded intelligence officer is always aware of the usual grouping around some central point with ever increasing scatter towards the extremes. He knows that the few at either extreme may be quite different from the main body of the group. He makes it clear whether he is most interested in the main body or in the extremes.

[1] Reprinted from *How to Lie with Statistics,* by permission of W. W. Norton & Co., Inc. Copyright 1954 by Darrell Huff & Irving Geis, illustrated by Irving Geis.

The Well-chosen Average
MEAN, MEDIAN or MODE

$45,000

$15,000

$10,000

Figure 7 Mean, Median or Mode

For example in planning a series of lectures for a large number of undergraduates, one must almost completely disregard the extremes. A course which could be followed by dullest of 200 freshmen would be quite unsuited to the middle 90%. Similarly the course which would stimulate the two or three brightest boys would leave most of the others far behind.

By contrast when designing a bridge it is the peak load that concerns us. It is the heaviest and not the average which may break down the bridge.

Sampling

Having in mind the wide scatter in the qualities of any group whether height of men, temperature of days, or accuracy of artillery firing, it is clear to the probability minded that if he takes a completely unbiased sample of ten out of a hundred he may accidentally get most of the highest, or of the lowest, or out of the middle. He seldom draws any firm conclusions from one small sample without further study. He knows that in intelligence many conclusions *must* be drawn from samples. From statistical analysis he learns how to get the most value and the fewest misconceptions from the samples available. He does not have to be versed in higher mathematics to realize these benefits.

He is familiar with the fact that at the extreme of any miscellaneous group you will probably find a few who are very far indeed from the average in both directions. For example in a group of students there may be one or two who are remarkably bright or dull respectively. In a large number of artillery shells fired at the same target one or two will fall quite far over or short without apparent cause. In any political organization or religious or other movement you find the "lunatic fringe," who seem to most of us so extreme as to be unreasonable. We might well say that it is in fact, normal to find at the extremes a certain percentage of the abnormal.

The extent to which the extremes depart from the normal depends in general on three factors: First and evidently upon the degree of selection in the make-up of the group. For example suppose a given county contained 1000 men in their twenties. You would expect to find some with low IQ's. However in 1000 recent Ph.D. graduates in their twenties you would certainly not find any such extremes in mental deficiency.

A second good factor is the size of the sample or group under consideration. Among 4 roommates at college it would be surprising and amusing to find one 6 feet 6 inches tall and one 5 feet tall, but in the whole undergraduate body it is not surprising to find such extremes. In other words as the size of the sample grows larger the *range* to be expected between the tallest and shortest generally increases. Assuming that the groups come from the same population the tallest man in a large group is probably taller than the tallest man in a small group. Similarly for any other extreme. We find that statistical analysis furnishes us with simple and highly useful formulae connecting range (and hence the extremes) with the size of the sample.

The third factor governing the degree of departure from the normal to be expected in the group or "sample" which is of practical importance to us, is simply the nature of the group or "population" from which the sample was taken. Some groups of people, artillery shells, machine parts, or daily temperatures tend to "run uniform" relatively speaking. Other groups tend to be highly variable or even erratic. The standard deviation and other parameters of statistical analysis express in simple and highly useful forms these important differences to be expected in the variation.

We repeat that it is often the extreme that is decisive. This may be the extremely high such as the peak load, or the extremely low such as the weakest link in the chain.

The man who is probability minded is on the look-out for such extremes. By simple calculations he can determine what he can probably expect under given circumstances and can prepare for it. This probability point of view has gained ever increasing applications in industry, in the natural sciences, in some aspects of the social sciences. In military matters "the probable error" has long been utilized in artillery firing. There is opportunity for more wide-spread use of this point of view in intelligence.

Precision of Data, Significance of Differences, Trends

Statistical analysis has much help to offer in regard to all of the above subjects which would help the intelligence officer to get the most meaning out of the data before him and to avoid many common pitfalls. All of this can still be done without any mathematics above elementary algebra.

A Healthy Curiosity

In their excellent chapter on "Selected Quantitative Techniques," written for the *Handbook of Social Psychology*, Mosteller and Bush (77) state in their final remarks: "Formal statistics provides the investigator with tools useful in conducting thoughtful research; these tools are not a substitute for either thinking or working. A major goal for the statistical training of students should be *statistical thinking*[1a] rather than statistical formulas. . . ." In the present section we have followed this advice by trying to encourage statistical thinking as a background for intelligence production, in other words to make the reader probability minded.

[1a] Emphasis added.

An intelligence officer who is not a mathematician but who wishes to increase his understanding of probability and the methods of statistical analysis which will be of greatest use to him, will find most books that he would pick up on this subject *positively detrimental* to his interest or progress. They would leave him with the impression that satistical analysis was a mass of higher mathematics, and that progress therein was far beyond his grasp. This impression is wrong. For the lay reader with a healthy curiosity regarding this subject and an honest desire to improve his competence in intelligence production by some reading we recommend the following in the order given:

Huff (73) *How to Lie with Statistics.* A book which can be read with little mental effort, and which presents in very popular vein some very useful aspects of being probability minded.

Moroney (69) *Facts from Figures.* Simple and easily understandable discussions of the principal concepts, techniques and formulas of statistical analysis. The intelligence officer can profitably select the most elemenary half of this small book. By doing so he can understand the concepts and techniques without difficulty. To learn to carry out the techniques himself with assurance requires time and real industry in reasonable amounts.

Lindquist (74) *A First Course in Statistics,* Revised Ed. and (75) *Study Manual for A First Course in Statistics,* Revised Ed.

Neiswanger (76) *Elementary Statistical Methods, As Applied to Business and Economic Data.* Intended for beginners. Has rather extensive and simple explanations.

Cochran, Mosteller and Tukey (79) *Principles of Sampling.*

An excellent modern example of the necessity for being Probability Minded in tactical situations is given by Jameson (80).

PROBABILITY—THE NO-MAN'S LAND OF INTELLIGENCE

In World War I, No-Man's Land, the area between your own and the enemy trenches, was a very unpopular, but a very fruitful area in which to patrol at night. Though casualties occurred, the side which was willing to patrol aggressively in No-Man's Land gained substantial intelligence and tactical advantages. The side which hesitated to enter this difficult area was definitely handicapped. So with the great area of uncertainty in intelligence production. It is a dangerous but rewarding field of endeavor for the intelligence officer.

Another analogy. John Hays Hammond, the tremendously successful mining engineer of 50 years ago, was one of the first when reporting on a mine to list systematically:

Ore in sight
Probable ore
Possible ore

He made fortunes for his clients from this new point of view, by which he took the probable and the possible into serious consideration in his field studies.

So in intelligence—the field of uncertainty, the probable and possible ore, is a fruitful No-Man's Land—full of pitfalls and casualties, but well worth exploration and exploitation by the bold and experienced intelligence officer.

Many persons hesitate to put an opinion or decision in writing unless they can show what they consider to be an adequate foundation, perhaps with learned documentation.

Those who refuse to make a decision until they have all the facts at hand, are in fact making a decision, namely to delay. Military map problems often present the tactical situation of the Blue and the Red Forces and then state the problem as: "*Required,* the decision of General Blue at 0900 hours on 22 March." In combat a crucial part of the problem before General Blue is *When* should he make his decision? How inadequate may his intelligence be and still justify a decision? Certainly if he waits until his information is complete, he will wait forever.

The elder von Moltke said in military operations—"It is necessary in any particular circumstance, to recognize the situation as it presents itself, enveloped in doubt and unknown factors, then to judge sanely what you see, guess at what you do not see, make a decision rapidly and act in accordance therewith without vacillation." (7)

The point which the above quotation illustrates is very unpalatable to the tender-minded and to the perfectionist. The point is: Our intelligence is *always* imperfect. Government departments constantly make decision based on imperfect data. If a government department says: "We will do nothing about Arkadian imports until we get more information," it is, in fact, making a decision, which presumes that the situation will stand delay.

Some of our conclusions in life are based on objective facts. Many are properly based upon opinion which could not be supported by specific facts. Some conclusions are based upon facts plus opinion. The same thing is true of intelligence and always will be.

It has been said that "mere" opinions should have no place in intelligence conclusions. We prefer demonstrable facts of course, but when these are exhausted we should utilize opinions to the full extent. This means that we must have available persons whose opinions on a given subject are the best obtainable.

The opinion of an intelligence officer—well informed about the country in question and about the natural or social sciences involved, and experienced in intelligence, and of proven judgment and wisdom—is a very solid asset. That part of the paper which is based largely on opinions should be made clear to the reader as opinions. There is no need to apologize for them.

Opinions, like any other important part of intelligence production should be critically examined. The burden of proof is on them.

So with a few changes, we can transform von Moltke's statement into sound practice. Let us say, "After having made every effort to collect in advance the information considered to be necessary, judge sanely what you see, form your best estimate at what you do not see, make a decision rapidly, and get on with the war." (Privately, that is what von Moltke meant in the first place.)

The revision is an improvement in two particulars. First it brings out the necessity for long planned prior preparation for good Strategic Intelligence Production. Second it eliminates "guess"—horrid word—always offensive to the eye.

Seriously speaking an intelligence officer never guesses in the sense that he makes a decision on the basis of *pure chance* without any worthwhile knowledge, as when one guesses that a tossed coin will land heads. On any matter of professional importance an intelligence officer should have at hand the best information available and should have digested this so that he can produce mature intelligence either written or unwritten at short notice.

The point is that intelligence production should not confine itself to fields of near certainty wherein all statements rest directly on a solid foundation of facts. Intelligence should gladly enter the fruitful No-Man's Land of probabilities and should make full use of the great asset known as "Mature Opinion," provided the writer makes clear to the reader when a statement is opinion, and what degree of probability or certainty should be accorded to it.

THE THREE PART RULE

An Example of Statistical Distribution

The Three Part Rule was first described to me by a U. S. Department of Agriculture County Agent who thought he had made a great discovery.

It was the agent's duty to help farmers in his area to improve their agricutural methods, by planting better varieties of wheat, using more fertilizer, etc. He would give a public talk some evening on a new method, distribute literature and use other methods to advertise the improved agricultural practice. He said that with all his efforts he could never get more than the most progresive one third of the farmers to adopt his suggestions when proposed. Later the middle third would follow the lead of their more progressive colleagues. Finally there was the most backward third who were not looking for improvements. It was only a question of time before economics would eliminate them as farm owners.

The same point of view was expressed to me quite independently by a university professor of long experience. He was discussing the gross overcrowding of college courses which occurred in the few years immediately following the end of World War II as a result of the so-called "GI Bill of Rights," and which made good teaching difficult or impossible in many cases. He said to me: "You can't possibly give the needed and customary individual attention to each student. You must plan so as to spend your time to best advantage.

"Find out early who your best students are—the upper quarter of the class. Then never go near these men again. They can learn it by themselves and are sure to pass.

"Next find out as soon as possible who your poor students are—the lowest quarter. Then don't waste any more of your time on them. They will never be any credit to you or to the university. They will probably never get their engineering degrees anyway.

"So to spend your time to best advantage and where you will accomplish the most, spend practically all of it on the middle half. They need your help and are also smart enough to profit by it."

One last example which I have seen somewhere in print.[2] A young doctor in general practice at the beginning of his medical career was somewhat overwhelmed by his responsibility for the lives and health of his patients. An older doctor relieved the tension of the younger one somewhat as follows: "You don't really have to worry about all these patients. One third of them have nothing serious the matter with them. Nature would cure them anyway, with or without your medicines. Then about one third have incurable diseases. You cannot fundamentally affect the course of the disease. So there is only the middle third who need your assistance and for whom you need to worry."

The division of any group of persons or organizations into three categories is useful and helps us to visualize the "dispersion" which is found in any dynamic society and which is such a fundamental part of statistical analysis. It points out the leaders, the central portion who will eventually adopt better methods, and finally those at the tail of the column. It is only a question of time when, due to economic or intellectual competition or to disease, the last group will no longer be with us. This point of view helps us to understand many educational, economic and other situations encountered when attacking strategic intelligence problems, and help us in estimating the probable outcome of present conditions.

It is easy to think of populations divided into three parts.

[2] Probably in the writings of Sir William Osler, Regius Professor of Medicine at Oxford University.

There is of course no sharp dividing line between the three parts. Statistically it is nearer the usual situation to divide into the upper quarter, the middle half and the lowest quarter. A real statistician would make this sound more scientific by speaking of "quartiles." The central half becomes "the inter-quartile range" (Fig. 5) extending over two "probable errors" and so dear to the older statisticians.

The First Law and the Second Law of *Thermo*dynamics have guided thought in the natural sciences for a hundred years. Perhaps this *Three Part Rule* deserves to rank as the First Law of *Homo*dynamics and so is destined to exert a similar influence in the social sciences.

APPLICATION OF PROBABILITIES— CARRIED TO EXTREMES

Consider the following rule 816 from the late Henry G. Weaver's (80A) *Thought Starters* as an application of the theory of probabilities:

Rule No. 816–Relating to New Ideas

WHEN CONFRONTED WITH A NEW IDEA
YOU ARE MORE CERTAIN OF BEING RIGHT
IF YOU VOTE AGAINST IT.

REASONS:–

1st–It may not be a good idea–
they seldom are.

2nd–Even if it is a good idea the
chances are that it will
never be put to the test.

3rd–Even if it is a good idea and
even though it is tried out,
the chances are that it won't
work the first time.

4th—Even if it is a good idea and
even though it is tried out
and even if it succeeds,
there'll be plenty of time
for thinking up alibis.

THEREFORE:

WHEN CONFRONTED WITH A NEW IDEA YOU ARE FAR MORE CERTAIN OF BEING RIGHT (OR AT LEAST SAFE) IF YOU TAKE A VERY DEFINITE AND POSITIVE STAND AGAINST IT.

The theoretical foundations for the above are logical and technically correct.

However, sound argument can be made for the opposite point of view, namely that it is wise to consider new ideas seriously and to investigate those which seem most promising. Such an argument may be just as logical as Rule 816 and much more profitable as a guide for conduct.

Rule 816, as a typical even though humorous example, neglects two important considerations which should always be remembered in making practical applications of the theory of probability. In this example these considerations are:

First. Profits from one successful new idea are often greater than the costs of testing hundreds of unsuccessful ideas. Therefore it *is* desirable to consider new ideas.

Second. Rule 816 is "trying to be more reasonable, than it is reasonable to try to be." In other words it draws its conclusions altogether from probabilities without checking these against the broader outlook of common sense.

Statistical analysis and the theory of probability can never by themselves provide a broad enough base for decisions whether in the applications of this theory to intelligence or to any other practical problems. At some point, judgment and common sense *must* be called in.

In Summary common sense enters as a term in every question of applied statistics. You cannot escape it. This is a matter of constant irritation to many. Again it points to the usefulness of the experienced intelligence officer at every turn where practical decisions are to be made which guide the progress of intelligence production.

Section II *EXPRESSION OF CERTAINTY*

It is frequently impossible to provide an intelligent answer to an intelligence question without attaching a probability factor to it.

EXPRESSION OF DEGREE OF CERTAINTY

In many activities other than intelligence, the natural or social scientist, or other author of a paper feels in general sure of his facts and sure of his conclusions, let us say, "beyond a reasonable doubt"; otherwise he would not publish the paper. In intelligence, on the other hand the mission requires papers to be written and conclusions to be stated having a very wide range of uncertainty.

Some papers containing inadequate facts and doubtful conclusions are highly useful to the Intelligence Community and to the policy-maker, not because they happen to guess right by mere chance; but because they present the best that we have, and because they accurately depict the state of our knowledge and of our ignorance.

The action which any reader of an intelligence paper would take regarding any given statement in the paper, be the reader another member of the Intelligence Community or a policy-maker, will naturally be tremendously influenced by the degree of certainty which can be attached to the statements in it. Some statements can be assumed to be true without further question. Others, though possible, are highly unlikely. Hence it is the duty of the writer of a paper to

The Letter-Figure System

decide the degree of certainty of a given statement and then to make this known to the reader.

A conventional evaluation code, known as the letter-figure system, has been devised for rating both the reliability of sources and the probable accuracy of information. This system consists of a letter from A to F assigned to the source and a figure from 1 to 6 assigned to the information itself. The following is the official meaning of the system:

Reliability of Source

A – Completely reliable
B – Usually reliable
C – Fairly reliable
D – Not usually reliable
E – Unreliable
F – Reliability cannot be judged

Probability of Information

1 – Confirmed by other sources
2 – Probably true
3 – Possibly true
4 – Doubtfully true
5 – Improbable report
6 – Truth cannot be judged

Beyond this simple rating of sources, little has been done to facilitate expressions of certainty and reliability in intelligence papers, or to promote common understanding between writer and reader. In fact, the necessary prevalence of uncertainties in intelligence production has been the excuse for sloppiness of expression in some papers.

As an example one inexcusable phrase is, "It is reported that . . ." without further explanation to enlighten the reader. The writer certainly has *some* knowledge of the nature of the report and its reliability. He should share this information with the reader. Otherwise the reader has nothing to go upon. The writer could usually state at least: "It is reported by defectors who seem to be reliable"—or "in the local press"—or "by travelers," etc.

A second example of an unsatisfactory phrase is: "It is possible that . . ." without any statement of probabilities. The writer who has studied the subject of the paper must have some basis for believing that it is probable or improbable. It is sometimes worthwhile to consider how meaningless an apparently important sentence may be. Consider: "It is possible that at this time an engineer, in Curtania, may be bending over a drawing-board, secretly designing a new weapon which will be capable of wiping out large parts of United States defenses." As a basis for policy or action could anything be more useless?

Phrases like the following are sometimes used in intelligence papers: "It is probable that . . .," or "It is highly probable . . .," etc. Now an event on which the chances are 51-49 is "probable." So is an event on which the chances are 1000:1 in favor. Various other vaguely synonymous phrases, such as "the chances are good that . . .," "the chances are favorable . . .," etc., are used. The writer usually has some more definite idea of the probabilities which he could helpfully convey to the reader without pretending to a precision which does not exist.

Kent's Chart

As a graphic presentation of the spectrum from certainty to impossibility with appropriate words to cover the different ranges, Sherman Kent has prepared the chart shown in Figure 8 which presents the whole situation at a glance. Use of this chart would be a definite step towards giving the reader the full benefit of knowledge possessed by the writer of a paper as to the reliability of the statements made.

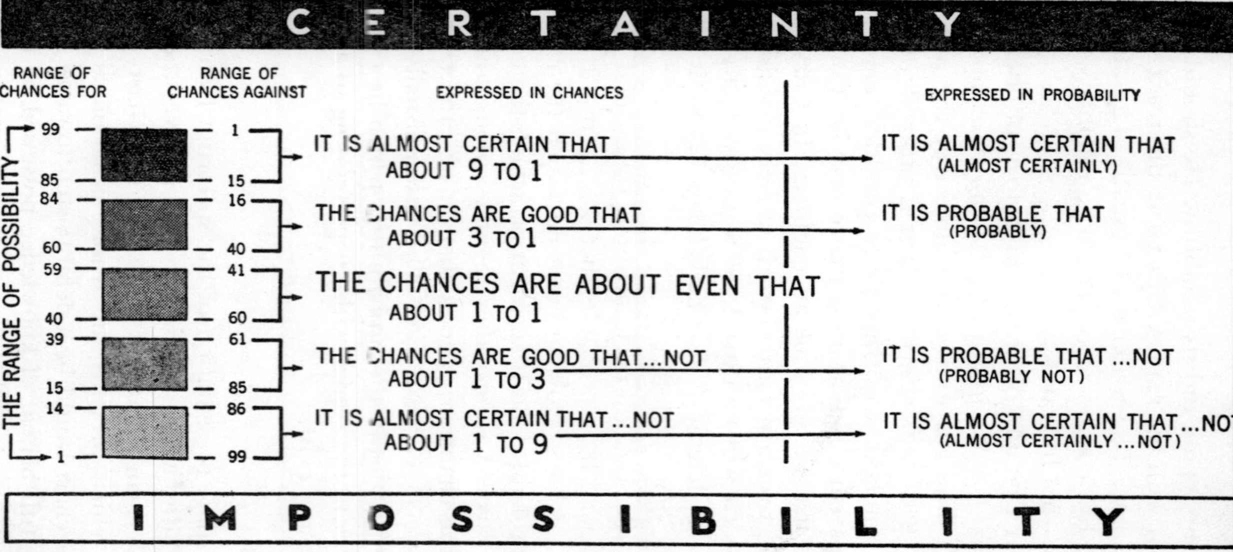

Figure 8 Kent's Chart Showing Degree of Certainty

Nomenclature

Intelligence estimates attempt to indicate the degree of reliability which can be attached to any given statement and its probability of being true. For this purpose exact language, understood in the same way by writer and reader, is essential.

It has been found helpful to divide the degrees of probability into the following classes:

ALMOST CERTAIN
(chances about 9:1 or more in favor)

SYNONYMS:

Note: A flat statement about a situation which evidently cannot be verified is equivalent to saying, "It is almost certain that." Any flat statement regarding the *future* is in this class.

—–indicated that
We believe that
It is evident that (or apparent that)
There is little doubt that (or will undoubtedly)

CHANCES ARE GOOD
(chances about 3:1 in favor)

SYNONYMS

It is probable that (or any other use of "probably")
It is fairly certain that
It is likely that
appears to
should be
is expected (or anticipated)
It is logical to assume
It is reasonable to conclude

CHANCES ABOUT EVEN
(chances about 1:1 or 50-50)

CHANCES GOOD THAT–NOT
(chances about 1:3 in favor or 3:1 *against*)

ALMOST CERTAIN THAT—NOT

(chances about 1:9 or less in favor or 9:1 or more against)

SYNONYMS:

Synonyms are the same as for "Chances are Good" and "Almost Certain" groups respectively, plus the inclusion of NOT or another negative.

INCONCLUSIVE

Only when the writer is unwilling to indicate even approximately the probability of a statement being true will he use the following phrases without further qualification:

It is possible that

may (might should not be used except when followed by a condition)

It could have

Morse and Kimball (81) in speaking of the "Measures of Effectiveness" of operations analysis[3] say: "It is well to emphasize that these constants which measure the operation are useful even though they are extremely approximate. It might almost be said that they are more valuable *because* they are very approximate. This is because useful applications of Operations Research[3] usually result in improvements of 3 or 10 or more . . ."

[These authors go on to characterize thinking in approximate terms, where the differences in results differ from one another by a factor of 3 or more as "hemibel thinking" and to explain this term which has a mathematical origin.]

"Ordinarily in preliminary analysis of an operation, it is sufficient to locate the value of the constant to within a factor of 3."

"Hemibel thinking is extremely useful in any branch of

[3] Operations analysis and operations research pertain to a study of the efficiency of weapons, equipment and military operations with full use of statistical analysis.

science and most successful scientists employ it habitually. It is particularly useful in operations research."

In operations research, probability-thinking and the methods of statistical analysis have proven of outstanding value. Indications are that a systematic application of these methods to intelligence production would be similarly useful. An up-to-date discussion of Operations Research is given by Col. S. I. Gilman. (82) Operations Research consists in the application of mathematical methods to the study of military problems of strategy, tactics, and technique. Full use is made of the knowledge and judgment of military men. The new results are obtained by the *addition* of the mathematical methods which supplement those of the military. Quantification is used wherever possible. The term "operations research" is now used also in industry where it covers many of the methods which have been used profitably for years in industrial engineering.

Seven

FORECASTING

THE FOG OF THE FUTURE

Nor can the wisest wizard guess
What will befall in Lyonesse,
When I set out for Lyonesse
One hundred leagues away.

All forms of intelligence have a lively interest in the future.

In combat intelligence the interest is almost always in the near future, whereas in Strategic Intelligence the emphasis is on a broader band of the future. Realizing the tremendous changes that the future may bring forth whether in weapons, industry or politics, and the necessity to prepare for such changes, there is an increasing need to attempt to peer further and further into the future—even up to 25 or 50 years.

In many cases where the terms of reference refer to the present, it is really the near future in which we are interested rather than in the actual present. All planning is of course for the future. As Schwien (7) says: "The idea of 'what is' would have little importance if it did not contain in embryo the idea of 'what is to be.'" Rapoport (70) expresses this vividly when he says: "The present (with its accumulated past) influences the future."

Much confusion exists in regard to prediction. We find in the same sentence references to predictions in the natural and in the social sciences, whereas in general these two kinds of predictions have little in common and the word prediction has in fact a different meaning.

For our purpose it will be helpful to consider the contrast between a prediction in human affairs and a prediction in the physical sciences.

Few realize how rapidly the oncoming years interject uncertainties at an ever increasing rate into any specific prediction in human affairs. Each uncertainty brings with it a whole flock of secondary uncertainties, so that confusion is worse confounded as we look further ahead.

One way to reach a down-to-earth realization of such uncertainties is to ask yourself at what odds you would be willing to bet on the occurrence of a specific event. Let us take a simple case in a very stable nation and in a relatively stable economy. In August 1955 if I had wished to bet on the favorite to be elected President of the United States in 1956 I might have to give almost even money, and I could hardly hope to get more than 1:2. However if I bet on any definite candidate to be elected in *1960* we all realize that in four short years the uncertainties have *tremendously* increased. The successful 1960 candidate is in 1955 at least 30 years old. He has made his mark in his own community, large numbers of the public have probably heard of him. Yet the odds against *any* given individual to be elected president in 1960 are large.

The reader can do his own estimating. Let us say to bet in 1955 on any individual to be elected in 1960 one would get about 1:50 odds. To extend this to a bet on a specified individual who will be elected president in 1970 the odds would be more than 1:500.

Here is a very simple case dealing with an occurrence with which we are all familiar, namely some native-born American already adult who is to be elected President of the United States. We are not making forecasts about events in Siberia where few of us have ever been; we are not dealing with an alien culture; we are not dealing with a mysterious earth satellite. Yet on a down-to-earth "How much would you bet?" basis, the odds are certainly more than 500:1 against *any* specific person.

Looking backward in other fields of forecasting we realize how sketchy and how faulty our forecasts have sometimes been in the past. It is probable that the forecasts that we make at the present time will be equally faulty, unless we have exerted great efforts to *improve our system of forecasting,* and have some reason to believe that we have made solid progress in this game where the odds are so tremendously against us.

It is worthwhile to repeat that in human affairs, time itself is always introducing unforeseen, and in some cases unforeseeable, factors that change the outcome which we have predicted. These factors may be those that bear directly on a given situation; or may be factors which have an indirect and unexpected bearing such as revolutions, floods, hurricanes, crop failures, development of atomic power, guided missiles, anti-colonialism or inflation. The possible occurrence of unforeseen factors must never be forgotten.

The "Fog of War" has been properly justified as an ever-present factor in combat. Just as real for intelligence is the FOG OF THE FUTURE. It is a rather thin, but all-pervasive fog. We can see near objects quite clearly through it. Further off our vision is definitely impaired. Visibility is better in some directions than in others, and we can see some types of objects better than others, just as in a physical fog. After a certain distance, however, we have to admit that the Fog of the Future makes any clear vision impossible.

In Strategic Intelligence Production we have usually underestimated the tremendous uncertainties which are always introduced by the FOG OF THE FUTURE. We have done surprisingly little to improve our methods for piercing this fog, except in a few isolated cases.

Let us now go to the other extreme from human affairs where no situation can be exactly repeated. Let us look at the physical sciences where the word "prediction" is widely used. It is said for example that the value of a hypothesis is to enable us to "predict" what will happen. We will take the simplest possible example. If I have some pure water which partly fills a closed vessel and heat the whole to any given temperature I can "predict" exactly what the pressure inside the vessel will be.

Please note that "predict" is here used in a different sense from that previously used in this chapter. I do not really mean that I know what *will happen;* I mean that I know what always *does happen,* whether past, present, or future. My knowledge is just as precise and just as certain in regard to any experiment by which such a closed vessel of water is heated 500 years ago, or today, or tomorrow, or 500 years hence respectively. I know what *does* happen in each case. This then is a use of the word *"prediction" where the future is not involved.* The distance of the experiment in the future adds nothing whatever to the uncertainty.[1]

[1] This confusion in the meaning of "prediction" is so important to those seeking to clarify their ideas on intelligence forecasting that some specific

In passing we may note that the contingencies which commonly affect intelligence predictions have no effect whatever on a physical science prediction. It makes no difference whether this physical experiment is carried on by a communist or a capitalist, in England or Siberia, in 500 B. C. or in 2500 A. D. Such predictions involving the physical sciences are sometimes combined in the same sentence or paragraph with human affairs predictions. Predictions of eclipses are mentioned in the same paragraph with predictions of the outcome of elections. The two have *nothing of practical usefulness in common*. Such a combination leads to confusion by lumping together subjects which are superficially similar, but are fundamentally different.

In between the two clear-cut meanings that we have just been discussing there are gradations of the meaning of "prediction," starting with meanings where most of the emphasis is placed on knowing what always *does* happen, as in the case of a general "law" of the social sciences, with little emphasis on what will happen, as in the case of a specific event. We then continue by easy stages to other meanings of prediction where the emphasis is on what will happen, such as in an intelligence prediction.

As examples of a gradation we may be able to predict the mortality rate of a certain disease in a modern civilized community, meaning that we know what *does happen* under modern conditions. This mortality rate did apply to tuberculosis let us say last year and this year. It will be sub-

examples are justified. Smith and Duncan (84) say (page 652): "For one of the objectives of science is, precisely, to forecast. . . . Every scientific law is in a certain sense a forecast. It foretells what will happen under certain conditions. The law of gravitation says, for example, that if a ball is dropped from a tall building it will fall with an acceleration of 32 feet per second." Certainly the "law" of gravitation was equally legal in the past as in the future. Though the quoted sentence, and thousands like it, are given in the future tense they really mean that a falling ball *always does* have a certain acceleration—*without any distinction whatever* between past, present, and future.

stantially the same next year. But it was quite different a hundred years ago, and will be quite different a hundred years hence, due to advances in medical science.

As an example of a second kind of prediction, many faithful workers in the social sciences have striven to understand the "laws" of each social science, so that they can predict what will happen under given conditions (meaning really what *does* happen). As examples: In economics, continual borrowing will bring about inflation; in political sciences, in a democracy hard times will bring about a change of government; these are intended to express general truths, equally applicable five years ago, today and five years hence. But with no change in the wording this form of language may be used in a prediction really involving the future.

An intelligence estimate may say that due to continued hard times, which are expected to continue, the present government of the country under consideration will fall. Here we are talking about a specific real life situation which goes further than the general law and includes many other vital factors. The *future now enters as our active opponent,* interjecting unforeseen contingencies which may affect the outcome. No matter how clear-cut the original situation, the predicted outcome will be less and less certain, depending upon the distance into the future that we attempt to predict. The clear landscape as lit up by the *general laws* of the social sciences in which we can see so clearly and so far, now becomes shrouded in the Fog of the Future, in which visibility is distinctly limited as distances increase.

In intelligence production, predictions refer to the real future of specific situations. For the remainder of this chapter in order to avoid misunderstanding we shall use "forecasting" rather than "prediction" when referring to intelligence estimates of future situations.

In estimating the probability of a future occurrence several different kinds of situations should be distinguished.

One is the situation where the failure of *one* link in the chain makes the occurrence impossible. For example suppose I have reservations to take my wife and three children to a certain seashore hotel for a summer vacation starting August 1. What factors influence the probability of my starting the family vacation there on that date?

There are many factors each one relatively improbable, but any *one* of which would prevent the vacation as planned. For examples: Any one of the five members of the family might be so sick on that date, that the expedition would be called off. Any one might die before that time. We might have a serious automobile accident en route which would prevent our arrival on that date. Furthermore there are hundreds of possibilities which would normally never cross our minds which have happened to others and could easily happen to these vacation plans. The summer hotel might burn down, blow away in a hurricane or go bankrupt. A serious crisis might happen in my own business requiring the cancellation of my vacation at this time. War, or strikes, or an epidemic might prevent. Or my wife or I might simply change our minds.

Many of the forecasts of intelligence are of this pattern. There are hundreds of possible obstacles any one of which would completely prevent the course of action predicted. In this case there is no unexpected occurrence which would make success *more likely*. Every contingency works *against* success.

As an example of this all-or-none situation consider the guided missile. What is the chance for the United States to have an intercontinental guided missile within five years? To simplify the problem we will consider that the elements to be solved are: adequate propulsion, resistance to heating, and guidance. Evidently each of the three must be adequate if results are to be obtained. Averages are meaningless. A brilliant solution of guidance is of no practical value if the propulsion will not work.

An example of a different kind of a situation is that in which there are several alternative methods for accomplishing the objective. For example, to reach a certain city I can travel by train, automobile, or on foot. Only a simultaneous break-down of all three would make the transportation impossible for a determined man.

To sum up, the Fog of the Future[2] acts as a constant threat, tending to becloud the crystal ball of intelligence. It is the purpose of this chapter to seek methods for overcoming this threat at least in part.

THE FIVE FUNDAMENTAL FACTORS IN FORECASTING

We try to make an intelligence forecast as specific and as accurate as possible. We do not expect or require 100%, or a bull's eye every time. In a related field, Marshall (85) says: "Not perfection but utility is the test of planning in a foreign policy," and Moroney (69), "What we seek is not a *perfect* description but an *adequate* one." So we define a successful intelligence forecast as the best forecast available from the data and methods at hand, which is timely and which *substantially benefits the primary user.*

Like all intelligence, usefulness is the criterion. (See Chapter II) If we have done the best possible under the circumstances, and if our forecast has benefited the policy maker, we can feel for the moment satisfied. We hope to do better

[2] One intelligence officer has commented interestingly as follows: "It is thus the 'fog of the present' that bothers me more than the 'fog of the future,' for the first problem is to understand what is happening now. . . . The intelligence officer is charged with a task which no historian, (academic, that is), would tolerate, viz., writing history as it occurs, in that wholeness of the present in which the past and future are blended in the din and confusion of becoming. One may have a foretaste of the *kind* of thing that will happen, but not of the particular form it will take."

next year. For that reason, we try to improve our data, our procedures and our wisdom. We strive especially for a systematic improvement in our methods of forecasting.

As Duff Cooper says: "Counsels of perfection must give way before imminence of war," for which we would have to substitute "the imminence of intelligence production deadlines."

Considering the vital importance of Strategic Intelligence forecasting for national security surprisingly little has been done toward a constructive and critical study of forecasting methodology in the intelligence field. As each problem comes up we use the best methods that we know at the moment, but we have done little in the way of basic research into the improvement of intelligence forecasting methods. At present we have little reason to believe that our methods will be any better next year than they are this year. Sorokin's papers are illuminating and helpful in this field (85A).

At this point a preview of the Fundamental Factors in Forecasting considered as a whole system will be helpful. By reading over the summary of Fundamental Factors given on the following page, the relations of these factors to one another can be seen at a glance. Then after reading the discussion of each factor which follows later in this chapter the full meaning will become clear.

THE FIVE FUNDAMENTAL FACTORS IN FORECASTING

In any successful intelligence forecast the following five factors—widely different in nature—cover the principal aspects.

The author must start with

The Necessary Knowledge

Factor 1. Adequacy, Reliability and Precision of Data and Assumptions

Factor 2. The Spirit of the People Concerned
What Kind of People Are They?
Culture, Progressiveness, the Will to Win

With this nowledge he develops methods for forecasting from the following

General Principles of Forecasting

Factor 3. General Principles:
A. With Overall Applications
Causative, Analogue and Probability Forecasting
B. For Continuing Situations
Persistence, Trajectory and Cyclic Forecasting

Skillful utilization of the Necessary Knowledge, by methods developed from the General Principles, then depends upon

Competence on the Part of the Author

Factor 4. Competence in the Natural and Social Sciences Concerned

Factor 5. Creative Ability and Intelligence Judgment
Education, Experience and Disciplined Imagination
Maturity of Intelligence Judgment and (where possible) Wisdom

A certain minimum achievement in each factor is required for usable results. Beyond this minimum, an improvement in any one factor will in turn improve the final forecast. Only high achievement in **all** factors can lead to an excellent forecast.

THE NECESSARY KNOWLEDGE

Factor 1. Adequacy and Precision of Data and Assumptions

All forecasting starts with the data available. Our estimates of the future of a given situation are founded upon our knowledge of its present, and are influenced by our knowledge of its past.

For intelligence production, the value of data which are sufficient in coverage, in reliability, and in precision needs no further argument. There is no substitute for good data.

In intelligence, data are seldom what we would wish in all these respects. The intelligence officer must form some opinion as to the adequacy of his data in each of these three respects and should make this plain to the reader. Reliability has been discussed in the previous chapter.

For measurable quantities, statistical analysis combined with our common sense, enables us to form a useful estimate of the degree of precision of the figures that we use and of the probable upper and lower limits. From all of this information statistical analysis shows us how to determine the precision of the figures derived by various calculations from the basic data.

Closely related to actual data are the assumptions which we make explicitly or implicitly as a beginning for every forecast. Firestone (89) says: "any forecasting or prediction must be based on a set of assumptions, which if correct, will permit an accurate or reasonably accurate forecast. If premises are false, no matter how accurate are the facts on which the forecast is based, the forecast will be incorrect. . . . Statistics provide an aid for forecasting, but not the means. A better result can be achieved with the aid of statistics, but everything, in this final analysis, depends upon the basic assumptions." Others have also emphasized the importance of the assumptions in addition to the importance of the data.

This is a challenge to clear thinking, and points to the importance of a critical analysis of the forecasts of ourselves and others.

Factor 2. The Spirit of the People

The second factor in a forecast is a knowledge of the spirit of the people in the area involved. In simple language: What kind of people are they?

This is one of the intangibles which cannot be well expressed in figures; so it is apt to be overlooked in favor of tangible facts such as tons of pig iron or rounds of ammunition. Yet this factor plays a vital part in any forecast. Furthermore it is really comprehended only by those who have made a deep study of the area and its culture. It is so different in nature from data on weapons, or pig iron or population that we are treating it separately here.

As a foundation of the study of the spirit of the people we start with the cultural background of the area. This area is usually a nation, but may often be some key group within the nation.

But the spirit of the people has more specific applications than would be implied by the phrase "general cultural background." It includes such decisive questions as: Are they decadent, disillusioned, and disunited;—or are they aggressive, progressive, optimistic and imbued with the Will-to-Win? Do they easily quit, or do they fight to the end? Are they good neighbors or are they quarrelsome and untrustworthy?

It is in the spirit of the people as much as in matters of economics or political science that we can find the explanations to the quick surrenders, as contrasted with the fight-to-the-end attitudes in World War II; the recent rapid technological progress of the U.S.S.R. which was predominantly illiterate in 1917; the industrial recovery of West Germany since 1946; and many other developments which will occur to any reader.

Part of the spirit of the people is to be learned from their recent history and national heroes. Other parts of this subject are discussed more fully, from a different but related point of view, in Chapter V under the heading, Consistency in Character of Groups or Nations.

History shows by many examples of groups with an overpowering will-to-win which, have accomplished the well nigh impossible. On the other hand, other groups equipped with every physical and mental advantage, but imbued with a spirit of disunity, cynicism or lack of public spirit; fail to an extent that is almost unbelievable.

A difference in the spirit of the people can make the difference between achievements which are miraculously high and those which are miraculously low. One need look no farther than the achievements of France in World War I and World War II respectively.

For forecasting, there is no single factor as important as the spirit of the people. It is one of the Nine Principles of Intelligence (Chap. II).

GENERAL PRINCIPLES OF FORECASTING

Factor 3. General Principles

We now come to the third Fundamental Factor, namely, General Principles of Forecasting. As these principles have been little studied, except in a few limited areas of the social sciences, and as they have been studied hardly at all as guides for Strategic Intelligence forecasting, more space is necessary for their discussion.

Efforts at forecasting extend back into the earliest human history starting with magic formulas and divination. More modern examples are the forecasts of enemy activities in combat intelligence, stock market forecasts, employment forecasts, and election forecasts. Every business must constantly forecast its own volume of business. Finally there are the Strategic Intelligence forecasts with which we are here concerned. In the case of various foreign countries, both potential friends and potential enemies, these forecasts may cover such varied problems as:

Industrial production, such as pig iron or oil
Capabilities in various weapons
Economic strength
Scientific capabilities
Maintenance or fall of governments
Probable courses of action—diplomatic, industrial or military
Spread of certain ideas, such as the nationalistic spirit

The basic question arises: Are there any general principles of forecasting which are widely applicable to forecasting in general, and which could profitably be studied, improved and applied to strategic forecasting? If such principles exist, or can be developed, they would justify study by all who are engaged in forecasting.

The general principles applicable to many kinds of forecasting are surprisingly few. These have been covered in part by Bross (57). In general the past is one of the best foundations for judging the future. Even when sudden breaks with the past occur (as in the French and Russian Revolutions for example), a great deal of the past remains and continues to have an influence. So forecasting starts from the past and present situations and shows what changes from the present will probably occur.

The general principles are of two kinds. First are three general forecasting principles which may apply to any kind of a forecast including the one-time situations such as the results of an election, the outbreak of war, or the development of a specific weapon. These are:

Causative Forecasting
Analogue Forecasting
Applications of the Theory of Probability to Forecasting

Next are those which apply only to a continuing situation which can be shown by a graph with time as the independent variable. Examples are prices, employment or population. In these situations plotted from year to year a correct graph shows the situation at a glance. Such principles are:

Persistence Forecasting
Trajectory Forecasting
Cyclic Forecasting

A. Three General Principles with Overall Applications

Causative, Analogue and Probability Forecasting, mentioned above are in no way conflicting. In fact it will be common in a given problem to utilize help from all of these in arriving at the final conclusions.

Causative Forecasting gives first priority when drawing conclusions about the future to the underlying causes of the action we are studying. Such a study includes both positive causes and negative causes or preventatives of the action. It is applicable to *one-time* events such as a revolution, the outbreak of war, the collapse of a dictatorship, etc. It is not based upon a continuous series of events illustrated by a curve. It requires a real understanding of many factors. It requires intelligence officers of broad experience, because it greatly enlarges the areas which must be searched for clues. Events quite remote from the field of interest or remote geographically may have decisive effects. Like other methods it includes an interest in indicators which could act as warnings of the impending action.

One can hardly imagine the study of an intelligence forecasting problem without an attempt to understand the controlling factors or causes of the activities concerned. The study may extend from primary causes, back to secondary causes and so on back. There is no logical place to stop, but there is a very practical place to stop; namely where a further pursuit of remote causes is of no net value when balanced against the time and effort expended.

The word "cause" is much discussed in philosophy including the books on the philosophy of science, such as, *Operational Philosophy,* by Rapoport (70).

As a specific intelligence example consider the problem: Will a given dictator who has seized the power in Arkadia be able to maintain himself in power for the next three years? In attacking this from the causative point of view after acquiring a good background knowledge of the area concerned, its economic, sociological and political problems, and the institutions and personalities concerned we might seek answers to questions such as the following:

What were the causes of the unrest which led to the overthrow of the government preceding that of the present dictator?

What are his present sources of power and support?

Are these sources increasing or decreasing?

What persons or parties would like to oust him?

What are the sources of power and support of this opposition?

Is the opposition growing stronger or weaker and why?

What type of difficulty (such as crop failures, dissolution of a coalition, opposition of a foreign power, etc.) would probably endanger or cause the fall of the regime of the present dictator?

To what extent are these difficulties likely to occur?

Can we find one key factor which will probably be decisive?

and so on.

By an understanding of the actual working of the situation which we are studying, and the causes for success or failure, we have our attention focused on the key factors and can often get a clear picture of the probabilities.

We might decide for example that a drought resulting in serious crop failure would undoubtedly cause a successful revolution under present conditions. We find that such droughts occur about one year in ten.

Analogue Forecasting. Using the principle of Analogy the primary suggestions as to probable action to be expected does not start principally from trends or from causes, but from a study of what has happened in similar situations which are more familiar to us than the given problem, preferably which have occurred in the recent past.

This is in fact going from the known to the unknown. By this principle we draw heavily on the accumulated knowledge of the social sciences. It was discussed as a general tool of the social sciences in Chapter V. Here we consider its application specifically to forecasting. For foreign countries it may be helpful for example to make a comparison with the better known conditions and results which have occurred in the United States, or in some foreign country with which we are familiar. The outcome of a similar situation in history is used to indicate the probable outcome of some present situation. This is so natural that it is used constantly in our everyday thinking and discussions without attaching to it any high sounding name. It is almost universal. For example when Hitler invaded Russia in 1941, many people drew comparisons with Napoleon's invasion of Russia in 1812, and predicted that the outcome might well be similarly disastrous to the 1941 invader.

The danger of this principle is that it is nearly always appealing and convincing, but it is *not* nearly always reliable. Situations superficially similar may be quite different in the *crucial points.* Plausible reasoning by analogy requires no knowledge of anything except a little history. For example anyone, even without a knowledge of economics, can predict a business depression following a national Republican victory and can win many followers.

So Analogue Forecasting is often useful as a start. Hodnett (86) has well said that analogies suggest, but do not prove. The development of this method of forecasting is said to be one of the greatest contributions of intelligence production to social science methodology. It is often used perforce, when other means are unavailable. But it is not by itself reliable. It may be a good way to start, but we should always seek to test these first ideas, by cross checks into causes and general principles.

Probability. The one other general principle applicable to nearly all intelligence forecasts is the great theory of probability. Probability is as fundamental in nature as is mathematics (Chap. VI).

Everything that an intelligence officer can learn about Probability contributes to his understanding of the distribution of events and of qualities in the world in which we live, and so contributes to his competence in forecasting. He may at first merely understand some of the concepts of probability and be probability-minded as described in Chapter VI. He may then bolster this elementary knowledge by the easy outside reading described in the bibliography of that chapter, or he may even master the techniques of statistical analysis. For intelligence production purposes the author agrees with Mosteller and Bush, the distinguished experts in the theory of probability, when they say in the extract already quoted: "A major goal for the statistical training of students should be statistical thinking rather than statistical formulas. . . ."

The extreme case for the importance of pure chance in human affairs, including human knowledge and progress, is given by Brill.[3] To the present author Brill's case is worth reading, thought-provoking but unsound.

B. Three General Principles for Continuing Situations

Persistence Forecasting. In this we start with the assumption that unless there is positive evidence to the contrary, the future within the limit of the forecast will be substantially similar to the present.

This is of course implicitly assumed in regard to the enormous majority of the items with which intelligence forecasts are concerned. For any given nation we usually assume that in general the form of government, industry, culture, boundaries, etc. will remain substantially as at present. If this were not true there would be no stability. Chaos and not order would prevail. So every intelligence forecast includes many implicit important elements of persistence forecasting, even in the difficult task of forecasting an unstable situation. Intelligence forecasts usually concern themselves with a few selected items, some of which may presumably change.

A danger arises where changes are slow and gradual and without overt evidences which attract attention to the changes. Such changes may be quiet but profound. They are likely to be overlooked except by deeper students. The English used to point out with some irritation that just because their progress in social welfare has been gradual and without anything like the French Revolution, some people think they have made no progress at all.

Many situations which seem outwardly stable may include fundamental changes of the greatest importance going on below the surface. Historically there may be a record of apparent stability extended back for many years; yet radical changes may be imminent. One example is the growth of

[3] Brill, John., *The Chance Character of Human Existence,* New York, Philosophical Library, 1956.

the nationalist movement in the countries of North Africa. Another may be considered the decline of the military capabilities of the French in the 1930's.

Such quiet below-the-surface movements are evident to real experts. This is another argument for professional competence in intelligence production.

The natural conservatism of human beings and their resistance to change and refusal to recognize it as long as possible is shown by the remark of an elderly British admiral shortly before World War I who said: "Nobody paid much attention to torpedoes when I first went to sea. I don't see why they talk so much about the damned things now."

So any assumption of "No change" should be critically examined.

In general of course change whether political, economic or technological has become increasingly frequent and rapid in modern times. Few people fully appreciate the *acceleration* of the rate of change, which has become normal in the present as compared with the past. This makes many events which were considered quite extraordinary, according to previous standards, not improbable if we look ahead ten or twenty-five years.

Trajectory Forecasting is used where there is a definite trend upwards or downwards and we assume that the curve will continue in the same direction for the period of the forecast unless we have evidence to the contrary.

With the modern prevalence of graphic aids and curves on charts this sort of forecasting is common—perhaps too common. We see such curves with time as the independent variable for population, numbers of college graduates, pig iron production, imports, expenditures, and almost every conceivable item that is measurable or pseudomeasurable.

There is a natural tendency to assume that a curve which has continued in one direction for a number of years will continue in the same direction for a number of years more.

The trend can of course be indicated as well by figures as by a curve, but its effect is not so easy to grasp at a glance. If the curve is upwards we in America, with our general optimistic philosophy of "Bigger and Better," are particularly apt to follow the trend upward into the future further than is justified.

Suppose Curtania's capabilities in some measurable respect are considerably below those of the United States. Suppose that for the last several years Curtania's capabilities have been increasing at a greater rate than those of the United States, but are still considerably below us. Suppose finally that you wish "to point with alarm" to this condition and to imply that this situation "perils"[4] the U. S. national security, then all you have to do is to make a public statement: "If this trend continues" the condition will be almost anything you wish.

You are mathematically correct *if the trend continues at the present rate* over the period necessary for the peril to materialize. The practical point here is the condition: *"If this trend continues."* Everything that follows depends upon this condition.

The public, hearing such a statement, nearly always assumes that the author believes that this trend is likely to continue and hence that the peril will occur in the foreseeable future. No author should make such a statement without including his own belief as to whether the trend will continue or not. No reader should swallow such a statement whole.

An amusing example of carrying a trend to its logical conclusion in both directions is the following, which may help the reader to remember this point. It is taken from

[4] "Peril" is widely used in modern newspaper headlines. It is useful for headlines because it contains only five letters. It is unfortunate because the newspapers have now overstocked us with perils. A good old English word —like a number of others—has largely lost its value through inflation. What have we left when we really mean "peril"?

S. L. Clemens' *Life on the Mississippi* written in 1883:

"In the space of one hundred and seventy-six years the Lower Mississippi has shortened itself two hundred and forty-two miles. That is an average of a trifle over one mile and a third per year. Therefore, any calm person, who is not blind or idiotic, can see that in the Old Oolitic Silurian Period, just a million years ago next November, the Lower Mississippi River was upward of one million three hundred thousand miles long, and stuck out over the Gulf of Mexico like a fishing-rod. And by the same token any person can see that seven hundred and forty-two years from now the Lower Mississippi will be only a mile and three-quarters long, and Cairo and New Orleans will have joined their streets together, and be plodding comfortably along under a single mayor and a mutual board of aldermen. There is something fascinating about science. One gets such wholesale returns of conjecture out of such a trifling investment of fact."

Examples of Trajectory Forecasting in the field of intelligence are population growth, Soviet production based upon a Five Year Plan, progress in research and development in a given field, decreasing world reserves of oil or copper. Every bull market exemplifies trajectory forecasting (until the tide turns).

As is well known from a study of the natural or social sciences or from practical experiences, few trends or curves do continue in substantially the same direction for very long.

There are some general conditions which may cause a rising curve to continue to rise at an ever increasing rate for a time (the so called exponential or logarithmic curve). The best known is the compound interest curve or the rate-of-growth curve.

This same tendency to grow ever faster and faster based upon a rate of growth is seen dramatically in a forest fire which spreads out in all directions, or in the case where every ten customers (or converts to Communism) get one new customer every week. This sort of rapid and pyramiding growth is common in the early stages of an expansion. The simple mathematics of it are covered usefully and interestingly in books on elementary mathematics such as Sawyer (87) or on methods of graphical presentation such as Schmid (88).

But we all know that there are also influences which tend to hold such growth in check. As a matter of fact no investment has ever grown to infinite proportions in spite of the compound interest curve of ever-increasing growth. No forest fire has ever wiped out all the forests on the earth. There is the well-known and fundamentally important *Principle of Le Chatelier* by which growth tends to check itself. This was first developed in the natural sciences and later extended to the social sciences. For example: (1) In population, unrestricted growth when confined to a given area produces over-crowding, starvation and disease which acts as a deterrent to a further increase in population. (2) A continual rise in prices restricts buying, increases production and so slows up the rise. The effect of the Principle of Le Chatelier in causing a rising curve to flatten out and perhaps even to turn downward is noticeable especially in the later stages of any upward movement.

The intelligence officer who looks behind the curve to the underlying causes and conditions will always be on the look-out for influences which will cause the trajectory to change direction significantly, so that the pure trajectory will no longer be correct. This is in fact precisely his responsibility.

This tendency of any rising curve to flatten out is widespread and so of fundamental importance in intelligence forecasting. One should always suspect such a tendency and look for evidences thereof.

In general the momentum of any aggressive human movements tends to die down. Nations which rise do not continue to expand until they encompass the globe. However neither the principle of Le Chatelier nor Toynbee can tell us whether the downward turn will occur in a few years or a few centuries. So this principle is one which the forecaster should always have in mind, but he usually cannot make specific use of it without much additional evidence from other sources.

Cyclic Forecasting. Many movements, besides tides, ebb and flow. Prices rise and fall, business goes up and down in irregular cycles, so do the fortunes of political parties. Cyclic forecasting is in part based upon the assumption that history to some extent repeats itself, i.e., activities which have gone in cycles will continue to do so.

Evidently the cyclic movement when it occurs, spells the ruin of those who pin their fate to the trajectory method of forecasting over a long period. Such people are those who believe that a bull market will continue to advance and who invest on the basis of this belief.

Cycles in human affairs are in general caused by the built-in correctives to extremes of human action as described under trajectory forecasting. Thus an aggressive, militant, political party becomes soft and corrupt with continual success, and so opens the way to its own downfall. In forecasting any movement suspected of being cyclic, it is essential to have reliable data going well back. Two full cycles is the minimum on which any judgment at all can be based. Many more than two cycles are necessary for a worth-while opinion as to the usual duration of either booms or depressions.

In the physical, geophysical and astronomical sciences many cycles whether tides, seasons, or wave lengths occur with almost perfect regularity, so that reliable predictions can be made. Cycles of wild animal population occur with considerable regularity. The cyclic method has been extensively studied in economics.

This author knows of no cycles of human activity which proceed with sufficient regularity to make possible even rough predictions *purely* on the basis of the cyclic period, although a knowledge of this period is useful when combined with many other factors. Furthermore political, economic and social conditions change rapidly, so that the cyclic pattern which existed over the past 50 years in any field of intelligence interest will almost certainly be seriously modified in the next 50 years.

The most useful lead for intelligence forecasting that can be obtained from a study of cyclic phenomena is the knowledge that certain activities *can be expected to go in cycles,* rather than to remain substantially constant, or to retain a consistent trend. This puts us on our guard.

Next in value would come a chart of the past cycles as far back as available with notations on the chart of events such as war, political action, etc., which could be expected to influence the cycle of prices or employment, or of politics in the past or future. Backing this chart of past cycles we could use a verbal description that the period between peaks was of this, this and this length.

Finally in the study of any given activity such as stock market prices, a statement of advance indications of a change in the cycle (like the Dow-Jones Index) would be helpful. Beyond this the cyclic method provides no reliable assistance to the intelligence officer.

In a given period any subject of interest to intelligence which continues to exist and which can be quantified to any extent so that it can be represented as a curve with time as the independent variable, must either remain substantially the same, or it must increase or decrease, or it must move in cycles (or there could conceivably be combinations of these). So the persistence, trajectory and cyclic systems of forecasting cover all of the basic possibilities for forecasting based on this "graphic" approach.

COMPETENCE ON THE PART OF THE AUTHOR

Factor 4. Competence in the Natural and Social Sciences Concerned

Competence in the disciplines concerned is the fourth of the fundamental factors for forecasting. In all types of forecasting there are of course the general principles mentioned earlier in this section to keep in mind. However to take a specific example, if we are forecasting prices, or industrial production, or employment, we are dealing with economic operations. If we have competence in economics, we handle the questions involved with a sure hand. If not, we are merely beginners and cannot expect the full success which is the due of the expert.

Similarly in forecasts of population, after considering the few general principles of all forecasting we find ourselves in the well-worked field of the demographer. If we have competence in this field we at once use the right tools in the right way. If not, we flounder.

In a similar way intelligence forecasts may demand professional competence in meteorology, physics, epidemiology or other natural science. Similarly in the social sciences which have recently devoted their best brains to a real understanding of the underlying causes and mechanisms which explain the phenomena of political science, sociology, and cultural anthropology. A professional in any one of these fields feels at home. He is familiar with somewhat similar situations which have occurred in this field. Certainly a professional is a better guide and can see the probable outcome more reliably than a stranger to the field or a dabbler therein.

So as an important component for successful forecasts, we list the services of professionals in the natural or social sciences primarily concerned, who are also familiar with the methods and points of view of intelligence production.

Factor 5. Creative Ability and Intelligence Judgment

The fifth and final fundamental factor in a successful forecast is the creative ability and good judgment of the author in putting this mass of data, this understanding of the spirit of the people, these principles of forecasting, and the knowledge of the natural and social sciences, all into a meaningful whole, showing the causative relations between the parts. His good judgment selects the key factors for emphasis. Such a person must have knowledge, judgment and wisdom.

The *overall professional competence,* essential for first rate forecasting is of three quite different kinds, achieved at different times and places: First, knowledge of the natural or social sciences which are principally involved in the forecast. This is the kind of knowledge derived from education and higher study. Second, knowledge of intelligence methods and of the area concerned derived principally in the course of intelligence work. Third, the judgment and wisdom which come to some from many years of experience, mature thought, and discussion. In all of these respects the requirements for producing a strictly first class professional intelligence officer are essentially the same as the requirements for producing a strictly first class professional in the fields of law, medicine, or military art, namely a first class education, experience in his profession, and natural ability.

Many have stressed the need for competence and have shown that it cannot be picked up ready-made. Kent (5) says for example:

"Speculative knowledge is not common and it is not to be had for the gathering. It is the rarest ingredient in the output of intelligence and is produced only by the most competent students this country possesses. It requires of its producers that they be masters of the subject matter, impartial in the presence of new evidence, ingenious in the development of research techniques, imaginative in their hypotheses, sharp in the analysis of their own predilections or prejudices, and skillful in the presentation of their conclusions. It requires of its producers the best in professional training, the highest intellectual integrity, and a very large amount of worldly wisdom. In this case, what I am speaking of is not the important but gross substance which can be called recorded fact; it is that subtle form of knowledge which comes from a set of well-stocked and well-ordered brain cells."

FORECASTING BY TEAMWORK

To some extent the necessary competence for forecasting, if it cannot be found in one individual, may be obtained from several differently trained people working as an informal committee, each making a contribution in his own field, and joining in a free discussion. By this means we get the great advantage of a larger body of knowledge and broader points of view being contributed to the solution of any given problem.

In a forecast of some phase of economic progress in Curtania for example, we might have an expert in economics who was preferably also an intelligence officer, working with a Curtanian area specialist who should be making a career in intelligence and should have been working at Curtanian intelligence for several years. One of these men could be in charge of the project with the other as his assistant for that project; or they might well have some quite senior intelligence officer in charge, specializing in national intelligence forecasts, who would supply a large part of the judgment and wisdom. Such a man might come into the picture only after the first draft of the paper was completed. If he were not to play an active part at the working level, it would be much better if he could take part in the project at the *very beginning,* discussing the problems with the other two members, coming to an understanding as to purpose, scope, and terms of reference. Then when he rejoined the committee after the first draft was completed for the final critique and review of methods and conclusions he would find less to undo.

With the proper organization and leadership the number of individuals who helpfully contribute to a given forecast may be large.

THE KEY SITUATION IN FORECASTING

One of the sound and fruitful services of the social sciences has been their contribution to an understanding of how and why social changes *really take place.* Where are political decisions really made, who makes them and what happens then?

As a few examples we may take the life history of an important bill in Congress with the parts played by committees, party leaders, pressure groups, speeches on the floor, etc.; or the organization of primitive communities, showing what mankind can really put up with; or the recent changes in the life of rural communities; or the causes, (after the event), of election results. Such contributions can be made with little or no quantification; but where quantification of important factors can be carried out satisfactorily, so much the better.

Many social scientists now glory in saying that their strong point is to tell the *kinds of results* which usually follow from certain kinds of situations. For example inflation usually follows from long-continued increase in the national debt. But many social scientists are loath to risk their professional reputation on a specific forecast even in their own fields; for examples, forecasts of *when and to what degree* inflation will occur after a given increase in the national debt; or the results of a specific coming election; or the maintenance of peace between two rival nations over a period of five years.

It is easy to see that for national policy-making, for national securtiy and hence for many intelligence papers, the intelligence production officer *must* make such a forecast before a given deadline whether he likes it or not,—often on the basis of scanty evidence. Certainly *someone* must make a forecast. The intelligence officer is certainly cast for the part of Rusher-in where angels fear to tread—if social scientists may be described as angels.

The social scientist can often render crucial service, even when he shrinks from the necessary final prediction, by pointing out the key situation in an election, or in a battle, or in the progress of an idea, on which the final result hinges.

For example, in the presidential campaign of Charles E. Hughes vs. Woodrow Wilson, Hughes was the favorite. It was said that he lost the campaign because, when he was electioneering in California, he failed to walk across the room to shake hands with Johnson, the Republican leader in California. Johnson's feelings were hurt. He gave lukewarm support to Hughes. As a direct result of this, Hughes lost the electoral votes of California, and as a further result he lost the national election.

It is said that political scientists could have pointed out with confidence that the election would hinge on California, and that the California results would depend upon the personal support of Mr. Johnson, even if they were unwilling to predict what action Mr. Johnson would take. It is fair to assume that if political scientists had pointed this out to Hughes in such a way as to convince him, his actions would have been different.

Similarly in a battle, or in any other situation covered by intelligence forecasts, if anyone can soundly and convincingly point to the *key situation,* he makes it possible to concentrate attention at that point, and so assists in the forecasting. Evidently a statement of the key situation on which the election, or battle, or social effort hinges requires a knowledge of the other parts of the picture also, and assumes that the other election units, or the other parts of the battle line, will perform as expected and not fail us.

STANDARD FORMS FOR FORECASTING

For a long time the U.S. Army has made wide use of standard forms for many important documents. They include the Commander's Estimate of the Situation, Combat Orders, and many documents of Combat Intelligence such as the Periodic Intelligence Report and the Intelligence Estimate.

In US Army FM 101-5 Staff Officers' Field Manual—Staff Organization and Procedure 1954 these forms are described at length and actual examples are given fully filled out.[5] See "Military Problem Solving." (86A)

When used intelligently as a guide and not followed slavishly those standard forms as revised from time to time have proven their value over a long period of years. They are highly useful in training at nearly all levels. They make sure that all important headings are remembered. They are economical of time and effort.

It is highly probable that some of these benefits could be obtained by the same means for some aspects of Strategic Intelligence. Standard outlines could certainly be useful in intelligence training, in cultivating systematic thinking, and in developing unity of understanding and doctrine throughout the Intelligence Community.

As a start towards the development of standard forms for Strategic Intelligence, a form for a *Forecast of the Capabil-*

[5] An article in *Punch* (88A) presents the working out of such a systematic form following "the intellectual process known as appreciation," taught at the British Naval Staff College. Even though the procedure is humorously described, it is presented in full detail, clearly, and very readably.

ities of a nation in a given direction is outlined below. A table for making a systematic *Estimate of Probable Courses of Action* of a given foreign country can also be constructed.[6]

The form herein described shows the desirability of considering both sides of a problem so as to bring out the strong and weak points of the argument. This is as advocated by Conant (31) and is discussed more at length in Chapter IV.

FORM PERTAINING TO FOREIGN CAPABILITIES

Purpose of the form:

To improve our methods of attack on capability forecasts by special emphasis on the following features:

(a) Systematic written discussion of favorable[7] and unfavorable factors with an estimate of the net result, somewhat like the Commander's Estimate of the Situation as set forth in Army FM 101-5, Staff Officers' Field Manual.

(b) Comparing the foreign situation with a known situation where applicable.

(c) Explicit statement of reasonable assumptions, upper and lower limits to be expected, and probabilities; so that the estimate would be provided with some over-all limiting factors and an indication of the reliability of the forecast.

Discussion of the Form:

A systematic written statement of favorable factors followed by a similar statement of difficulties helps to smoke

6 This latter is a modification of a table proposed by Colonel Walter E. Sewell, "Calculating the Risk," *Military Review,* Command and General Staff College, Ft. Leavenworth, Kansas, Aug. 1953.

7 By "favorable" is meant favorable to the proposition under discussion. For example, if the five year estimates concern "Progress in Soviet Higher Education" or the "Development of a Chinese Communist Air Force" then favorable factors are those which will assist such progress or development, not those necessarily favorable to the United States. The main point is that arguments both pro and con are represented.

out all the important factors in the situation and to face their probable effect, pro or con. This will improve the *systematic coverage* and the clarity of some of our present methods, and will help to bring out the crucial features on which the estimate rests.

A specific comparison with an analogous situation where the effects of the factors can be known and studied will throw some light into foreign situations which would otherwise be dark.

Specific reasonable assumptions will provide upper and lower limits as to what may be expected and will sharpen our understanding of quantity and precision in the estimates given.

All of this will merely do a little better for intelligence estimates in general what is already being done to some extent and what has been done to a notable degree in some other fields such as econometrics. It will help cultivate systematic habits of thinking and will make more clear the basis for the conclusions reached.

The Form in Outline:

Regard this form as a guide only. Use where applicable. Omit entirely sections which do not apply.

The Problem.

Assumptions.

Scope & Definitions.

General Discussion. Indicating importance of the problem, background, brief listing of general controlling factors. Most of the discussion under this heading is concerned with the factors which must *always* be considered whereever *this kind of problem* is studied, rather than those which pertain to the particular country and situation presented by the present problem. All the rest of the present form pertains to the given country and the conditions of the specific problem where applicable, unless otherwise stated.

History. Development and trends. Graphs where possible. Causes for changes in direction of the trends. Does the history indicate that this is a case of Persistence, Trajectory or Cyclic forecasting?

Present Situation. Considering the present as the starting point for a sudy of the future. Extent of our knowledge of facts and methods.

Favorable Factors. Each major factor favorable to development of the situation discussed in this estimate is considered separately with estimates of the maximum and minimum effects that it might have. The probability that each factor will continue at a given level of effectiveness for certain periods is stated.

Unfavorable Factors. Treatment similar to that of favorable factors.

Analogous Situations. Comparisons with analogous situations, about which more is known; for example, a comparison with past situations in the same foreign country, or with known situations in U. S. or some friendly country.

Underlying Causes, Controlling Factors, and Critical Points. A special study in depth of any of these which are of outstanding importance, or may even be decisive.

Final Discussion. Considering the interrelations of all of the foregoing.

Conclusions. Including an indication of the degree of certainty, and where possible, of the precision of figures used.

[illegible] [illegible] [illegible] Prognosis [illegible]

PART III

Intelligence as a profession

Eight

CHARACTERISTICS OF THE INTELLIGENCE PROFESSION

Characteristics of the Learned Professions : Formal Education
Informal Graduate Courses in Intelligence : Professional Inspiration
Intelligence—A Profession with One Client : A British Parallel
Peculiarities — Security Restrictions and Rigid Barriers
Why Be an Intelligence Officer?

In the preceding chapters we have been discussing the inner workings of Strategic Intelligence Production as these appear to the intelligence officer. Now in this chapter we consider intelligence as a profession.[1] We look at intelligence from the broader point of view in comparison with other professions such as law, medicine, the military service or the diplomatic service. In making such a study we find there is much that intelligence officers can learn from other professions.

1 Whitehead (91) explains the word as follows: "Here the term profession means an avocation* whose activities are subjected to theoretical analysis, and are modified by theoretical conclusions derived from that analysis. . . .

"The antithesis of a profession is an avocation* based upon customary activities and modified by the trial and error of individual practice. Such an avocation* is a Craft, . . . The ancient civilizations were dominated by craft. Modern life ever to a greater extent is grouping itself into professions." (* In current usage, "vocation" would be the word.)

Intelligence has been called a highly skilled and honorable profession. This is certainly in large part true. However, intelligence is still so different from other professions that it will be worth while to explore some of these differences rather carefully.

Perhaps it would be more correct to say that as at present practiced *intelligence has the makings of a profession*, rather than that it *is* a profession. In the mission, type of operations, level of ability required of personnel, and possibilities for progress in fundamental principles and methods, intelligence fills the specifications of a learned profession. The qualities which intelligence now lacks as demonstrated later in this chapter can be developed in a few years if some of the leaders of thought in this activity care enough about professional development to bring about the unity of understanding and accepted doctrine which have not yet been developed.

The present exploration of intelligence deficiencies is not undertaken as an academic exercise. The purpose is entirely practical. Intelligence has certain serious shortcomings as a profession *which can be remedied*. The author hopes that the present discussion may be one step towards correction.

The present discussion of intelligence as a profession is concerned with Strategic Intelligence as at present carried out in the U. S. Intelligence Community. It includes all of those who must make decisions as to the intelligence value of information that comes to their attention. It, therefore, includes everyone who is making a career of intelligence.

The remarks pertain most directly to those intelligence activities concerned with evaluation, selection, interpretation and presentation of intelligence. In the broad purpose of extracting significance from a mass of information, and using insight and wisdom to draw correct and helpful conclusions, the intelligence profession compares closely with some others, especially law, the sciences and journalism.

CHARACTERISTICS OF THE LEARNED PROFESSIONS

A look at some of the other professions will help us better to appraise our own, using the point of view that, "He knows not England, who only England knows."

Certain organized activities such as law, medicine, engineering, journalism, accounting and many others lay claim to being recognized professions. We realize at once that some like law or medicine are fully developed professions, and some like journalism are only partly developed.

Some activities possess a sense of unity, a vigorous progressive spirit and an urge to develop a full professional status. Others are not going ahead professionally.

We shall first see what the characteristics of a learned profession are, and how each of these characteristics contributes to professional competence. We shall then see what the Intelligence Community has to learn from other and better established professions.

In regard to each outstanding profession which seems to have useful similarities to intelligence, we ask ourselves: How does the system for building professional competence and esprit de corps actually work in this other profession? To what extent would a similar system be beneficial in the intelligence profession? What stands in the way of introducing some of these promising improvements into intelligence activities?

As Metcalf and Urwick (92) point out in their interesting discussion: "The word profession connotes for most people . . . a motive of *service*." Certainly the emphasis on service is much greater than in business. A professional man is much prouder of his professional achievements than of the money he has made. This emphasis on service and on the systematic scholarly foundations as mentioned by Whitehead are distinguishing marks of all professions.

The other characteristics usually associated with a learned profession are shown in the Table.

These characteristics may be arranged for convenience of systematic discussion as follows:

1. Education
   - a. Formal Education
     - Basic disciplines
     - Graduate courses and degrees
   - b. Continuation of Education by Home-study
     - Professional journals
2. Factors of Stimulus and Inspiration
   - a. Professional societies
   - b. Opportunity to establish professional reputation by publications
3. Esprit de Corps
   - a. Professional traditions, ethics and heroes
   - b. Professional Unity
     - fostered by professional societies, requirements for admission, legal recognition, etc.

The table following shows the present status of each profession. The status of any profession in regard to any characteristic may of course change. The status will change for the better or for the worse in any given case depending largely upon the efforts of the members of the profession.

TABLE SHOWING CHARACTERISTICS OF SEVERAL LEARNED PROFESSIONS

*** indicates that the quality named is possessed to a very high degree
** indicates that the quality named is possessed to a sufficient degree
* indicates that the quality named is possessed to a slight degree
\- indicates that the quality named is not possessed to any degree worth mentioning

	Law and Medicine	*Accounting*	*Journalism*	*Engineering*	*Practice of any one Natural or Social Science*	*Military Science*	*Diplomatic Service*	*Intelligence*
EDUCATION								
A. Possession of a special body of higher knowledge common to the whole profession, distinctly greater than that which would be possessed by many well educated men not members of the profession	***	***	*	***	**	***	**	**
B. Graduate degrees in the *professional* subject commonly found among members	***	***	*	*	**	-	*	-
C. High class professional journals and literature, providing at home a continuation of one's professional education	***	**	-	***	***	**	**	-
FACTORS OF STIMULUS AND INSPIRATION								
D. Strong professional associations covering the whole profession	***	***	**	-	**	-	*	-
E. Strong professional associations covering sections of the profession	***	**	-	***	***	*	-	-
ESPRIT DE CORPS								
F. Sense of Professional Unity	***	**	***	**	**	***	***	-
G. Traditions and Professional Heroes	***	*	**	**	**	***	**	*
H. Progressive Spirit as a Profession	***	**	***	**	**	**	*	-
I. Special privileges and responsibilities recognized by law	***	***	-	*	-	***	***	-

The Spirit of a Profession

We learn much about a profession from the above table. We learn it in usable form, so that we can put our fingers on the strong and weak spots.

We feel that we also miss something in this table, and that it is something important, even if intangible and difficult to express. For each profession it is the *spirit,* the point of view, to some extent the ideal, which is really at the heart of the matter. We shall now try to present the spirits of some of the professions. Then with the spirits and ideals of several other professions as a background, we shall see what can be said of the intelligence ideal, and point of view. This effort will certainly make a contribution to our understanding of the intelligence profession at its present stage of development.

The ideals as here given are evidently closely related to the *mission* of each profession.

In a mature profession each member is conscious of the professional ideal and of the professional point of view. This common consciousness is one factor in the sense of professional unity.

Some of the contrasts in the professions shown in the foregoing and following tables are illuminating.

As examples: In journalism, thoroughness and depth are often willingly sacrificed to promptness and vigor of reporting. For the sciences, thoroughness and depth come first. In the profession of arms, physical courage and violence have a natural place, while these have no place in the law.

Looking now at intelligence, we find that it certainly shares with arms the honor of including patriotism among its ideals. It shares with journalism its appreciation of timeliness. It offers a contrast to much of the scholarly production in the social sciences. In history, for example, many excellent papers are without practical usefulness; whereas

THE SPIRIT OF A PROFESSION
as illustrated by its
Ideal and Point of View

Ideals	*Characteristic Point of View* Shown by emphasis on:
	LAW
Impartial Justice	Hearing for both sides. Due process of law, Legal precedents
	MEDICINE
Medical Service to Humanity	Value of human life and health, Constant warfare against disease, Resistance to commercialism
	JOURNALISM
Prompt and vivid Reporting to Public	Sense of newsvalue, Timeliness, Aggressiveness, a Conviction that only a well informed people can preserve its liberties
	ENGINEERING
Efficient Service to Physical Needs of Mankind	Application of Science and Experience, Efficiency and Economy, Physical Achievements
	NATURAL AND SOCIAL SCIENCES
Thoroughness and Truth	Hypothesis, Experiment, Observation, Logical Interpretation, Objectivity
	ARMS
Patriotism, Courage, Sacrifice	Mission, Unity of Command, Discipline, Offensive Spirit
	INTELLIGENCE
Patriotic Service Through "Timely Truth Well Told"	Usefulness, Significance, Depth of Understanding, Forecasting, Importance of Spirit of the people

an intelligence paper without some hope of usefulness has no excuse for existence. The intelligence ideal and point of view could be fairly well concocted by selecting in proper proportions from the ideals and points of view of the professions of arms, journalism, and the social sciences. In making such a composite, the rejections are as important as the selections.

Perhaps all of this brings us a little closer to a full comprehension of the learned professions which are certainly among the proudest achievements of the human race. We see from this table something more of the present place of intelligence in relation to the other professions.

FORMAL EDUCATION

Much has been said in praise of on-the-job training. It is certainly one way to learn many skills and it is the *only* way to learn some others, such as horseback riding. However most of the professions are adopting an *ever-increasing proportion* of their education as formal education. The best combination in general is formal education followed by practical experience.

We study in a law school which is the best possible way to learn the fundamental principles. We then practice law where we learn aspects of legal practice which cannot possibly be learned out of books. The old custom of studying law by "reading law" in some law office and learning by doing has been found quite inferior to formal education in a law school.

The professional instruction of many intelligence officers in Strategic Intelligence is certainly scanty when measured in hours or level of effort required. The present instruction is closely similar to the old practice of "reading law" and has all of its shortcomings. In the great field of Intelligence

Production, there is a need for more advanced courses, comparable to graduate courses in other professions.

For professional competence the best system is one by which formal education at ever higher levels *alternates* with practice. For example an undergraduate course majoring in chemistry may be followed by several years' practice of chemistry. Then formal education in a graduate school leading to a Ph.D. in chemistry. This system is found in other learned professions. It is well exemplified by a career in the Armed Services, with a sequence somewhat as follows: (1) Formal education at the Military Academy on an undergraduate level; (2) Command of troops as a junior officer; (3) Basic course at The Infantry School; (4) Command or Staff duties with troops; (5) Advanced course at the Infantry School; (6) Staff duties; (7) Command and General Staff College; (8) Higher command and staff assignments as a senior officer; (9) Perhaps the service or National War College. See *Military Review,* "Command and General Staff College Number" (94).

In each assignment above the Military Academy the formal education mentioned is *in the profession itself,* e.g. in this case in military science. This is a quite separate kind of effort from that of an army officer being detailed to a civilian university for advanced study of some non-military subject such as meteorology, or civil engineering, or the Russian language. This latter may be highly useful, but is not a substitute for advanced training in his own profession.

The alternation of formal education with practice, even at high levels is in strict accord with the educational program recently adopted by the U. S. State Department as a result of the recommendations of the Wriston Committee. The purpose of their new educational program is to fill certain needs within the State Department closely similar to needs evident in the Intelligence Community.

The State Department plan provides for three periods of full time formal courses in the general career training program. These are known as: Junior Foreign Service Officers' Course, Mid-Career Course in Foreign Affairs, and Senior Course in Foreign Affairs. They normally occur respectively: before assignment to the first post abroad; at mid-career when the officer has served from five to eight years; and as a senior officer who has served 15 or more years. Secretary Dulles in a memo to the President expresses the hope that this program "may provide an example which other career services of the government will be disposed to emulate." This new State Department general career training program is separate from and in addition to a large program of training in substantive matters including language, area studies, and university courses in the social sciences.

As a preparation for true professional education each profession has many basic subjects which are taken on an undergraduate level. Medicine rests among other things on chemistry and biology; engineering on mathematics, physics and graphics; military science on mathematics, history, geography, psychology, etc.

The present language and area courses given within the government or by outside educational institutions, provide some of the basic prerequisites for the intelligence profession. Those who enter a profession start with a somewhat miscellaneous background of undergraduate courses, but some prerequisites are now widely understood as desirable in each of the other professions. This is helpful. It would be correspondingly helpful if a similar list of undergraduate prerequisites to the profession of intelligence were made known to prospects. This list would include perhaps modern history, geography, economics, political science, social psychology, research methods in the social sciences, and report writing.

For the intelligence profession the only official statements of a desirable educational foundation known to the present author are the U. S. Civil Service Commission's announcements for the positions of intelligence research specialist and military intelligence research specialist. These were not compiled as prerequisites for the intelligence production officer, and are in fact inadequate for this purpose.

So every student preparing for any of the professions must cover in his secondary school and undergraduate education a large number of prerequisite subjects preparatory to real professional work. However, it is in the professional school that these basic subjects are all focused on the chosen profession and that the professional ideals are formed.

A young would-be lawyer may go twelve years to primary and secondary schools plus four years to an undergraduate college, yet it is the following three years at law school that shape his professional thinking. It is the final three years out of his total of 19 years in formal education that make him a true professional lawyer.

Similarly an engineer who uses mathematics, physics and graphics every day of his life in his engineering work does not regard himself as a mathematician or a physicist. It is the engineering courses that set the professional standards.

We shall see later that the professional schools do much more than teach professional subjects. In some professions like law, medicine, theology, journalism and engineering there are schools or colleges bearing the name of the profession, e.g. law school, school of journalism, etc., usually and preferably as parts of a university. In others there are in a university departments of chemistry, or economics, or history, etc. Each has its own traditions as part of the profession of chemistry, economics or history, etc. Each offers graduate courses leading to masters' and doctors' degrees in those disciplines. Professional traditions and esprit de corps are soaked up in schools of law, medicine or engineering, and in graduate departments of chemistry, economics, etc.

Graduate Study in Intelligence

In every profession other than intelligence, it is accepted that advanced studies on a graduate level, *specifically in that profession,* are highly desirable. It is accepted that in general, those who have the advanced degrees in their own profession accomplish more that is worth-while than those who do not.

The intelligence production profession is, with the partial exception of combat intelligence, the only profession which has no professional opportunities or schools of its own for formal *advanced* professional study.

The many Army, Navy, and Air Force courses in intelligence are properly focused on combat intelligence and military intelligence techniques such as photo interpretation and prisoner of war interrogation. The Strategic Intelligence School presents in a few weeks much useful information. Each fulfills its immediate mission. As far as this author can learn, however, none of these schools presents intelligence courses on a level comparable to graduate courses in law, economics, political science or engineering for example. At none of these schools, as far as the present author knows, are members of the school faculties regularly engaged in research, as an important part of their duties, into the underlying philosophy and improved methodology of intelligence, comparable to the research into first principles carried out by institutions of higher learning in other professions.

There are no university departments of intelligence, and only one advanced course in the field of Strategic Intelligence. Nor is there anyone specifically assigned to do systematic research into intelligence production methods, or to explore the *basic principles* of this great field of human activity. Yet to cary on such research or to give such courses one does not need the expensive equipment associated with chemical, medical or engineering research. Nothing beyond a few tables, chairs and typewriters plus existing files and library facilities is needed.

The total faculty, student body and administrative officers for a professional school of Strategic Intelligence Production need not be more than half a dozen (plus clerical assistance). But these few pioneers must be professional intelligence officers of learning, experience, vision, originality, and enthusiasm for their profession, who would have at least half of their time available for such study and research over a period of at least one year.

An ideal solution might be a graduate department added to one of the present government intelligence activities serving the whole Intelligence Community. The essentials would be: (1) Members of the faculty competent to give graduate instruction and interested in so doing. These members of the faculty should be actively engaged in research projects in the field of intelligence. (2) Selected graduate students relieved temporarily from other duties. Each one carrying out his own research under appropriate guidance and with a minimum of classes and seminars. (3) Opportunities to publish the results of the research in classified or unclassified form. (4) An opportunity for the graduates to carry some of the inspiration and the light of learning so acquired through discussion groups into their new assignments after leaving the school.

Conclusion: Compared on the basis of the higher education provided, research, and literature available on principles and methods, intelligence at present ranks below other professions.

INFORMAL GRADUATE COURSES IN INTELLIGENCE

As a digression, it may be noted that the peculiarities of intelligence, and its present lack of graduate courses, need not be an impossible barrier to a determined man.

In the absence of any graduate school for intelligence, or any graduate courses dealing with intelligence production problems, each intelligence officer can lay out a course of advanced study for himself, starting with the references here given.

If he can get together informally even two or three other intelligence officers with similar ideals for improving their professional standards, all could gain by weekly discussions in order to exchange ideas and benefit from criticism. It is always surprising how a discussion of a definite subject among well informed persons clarifies the ideas of almost all of them (see Chapter IV.).

A word of warning is necessary. When taking a prescribed "course" in any subject, whether by physical attendance at a class, or by correspondence, the subjects to be covered and their scope are laid down by the school. Within a given course the student has little responsibility for deciding what is and is not *worth-while* for him. However, when an otherwise employed student is doing some informal voluntary studying on his own time, the question as to what to study is of the first importance. The student himself must decide.

For a man doing informal studying, without specific credit, there is a natural temptation to reduce, rather than to extend, the new material which he decides to master and to apply to his work. This is especially true of intelligence production where there are few precedents, or subjects required by general consent, which would set a standard.

The dilemma which faces the student is the typical Scylla and Charybdis situation.

On the one hand, what he reads may seem so simple as to be self-evident. It does not arrest his attention because it seems obvious. Sometimes more thought by the student would show that the ideas presented in the course seemed simple only because the author had had the skill to single out the key factors of a complicated situation and to present them simply and clearly.

The well-known correspondence between Briggs and Napier regarding the discovery of logarithms is a case in point: (94A)

> My lord, I have undertaken this long journey purposely to see your person, and to know by what engine of wit or ingenuity you came first to think of this most excellent help in astronomy, viz., the logarithms; but, my lord, being by you so found out, I wonder nobody found it out before, *when now known it is so easy.*[2]
>
> HENRY BRIGGS
> to JOHN NAPIER, inventor of logarithms

On the exactly opposite, or Charybdis, side, a subject may be avoided by the lone student because it seems so complicated that it would not be worth the trouble of mastering.

The problems of the selection of subjects for study, resisting the excuses that a course is too self-evident or too difficult, and maintaining standards of achievements, are all made easier if the intelligence officer who starts out informally as a "lone student" will consult some senior as an advisor; or will join several colleagues in a small informal, study group. Either of these expedients has, also, a powerful effect in stimulating mental activity, and in maintaining morale and direction.

Here endeth the digression on a highly important subject.

The purpose of most formal professional education is certainly not to teach a student everything he will ever need to know about his profession. It is rather to provide a reliable and useful *foundation upon which the student can and must continue to build* after graduation.

So the home or office study after the student leaves an educational institution is an essential part of his professional

[2] Emphasis added.

development. One of the characteristics of a professional man is his keen interest in his profession and his custom of doing professional reading at home or after hours.

One of the principal means for keeping abreast of one's profession after graduation is the high grade journal devoted to progress in that profession. By reading such journals, the professional knows that he is aware of the new developments in his own field. Furthermore, there are also a considerable number of new books published each year in any field and these are reviewed in the journals. Those pertaining to a given profession are usually easily identified as such by the title of the book. Such books and journals help to keep alive a professional interest, and provide a constant supply of new methods and ideas.

Unfortunately there are few journals of intelligence which present general principles or discuss improvements in methods, or where intelligence activities are subjected to that "theoretical analysis" which Whitehead says is the characteristic of a profession in contrast to a craft.

PROFESSIONAL INSPIRATION

Another characteristic of most professions is a strong progressive professional society. We think of the American Bar Association, the American Chemical Society, the American Statistical Association, etc. Each numbers thousands of members in its national organization, and usually has local chapters which hold stimulating professional meetings at many places throughout the country.

Each society has a national convention which it is a privilege to attend. Members of the profession submit papers bearing the names of the authors, and so each member of the profession has an opportunity to present his ideas before interested and informed colleagues, to enter into free discussions formally or informally, and to establish his reputation in his profession. This opportunity continues *throughout* the professional man's career.

The leading men of the profession in the country, or in the world, attend these meetings and discuss new ideas freely. This is an inspiring experience for all members of the profesion. Furthermore, professional recognition is available at many levels. Anyone may try for the prizes associated with recognized achievement. This acts as a tremendous stimulus. Such recognition does not depend upon one's supervisors, but upon one's professional colleagues.

On the level of the author and analyst with original ideas, the intelligence profession misses this great incentive and source of inspiration. Nothing has been substituted for it.

Esprit de Corps

Many professions have pride of profession. This starts with the traditional heroes of the profession. For example the spirit of Hippocrates is still a living presence at medical graduations. Medical men glory in the achievements of Harvey, Jenner, Koch, and Osler. In the military profession, a pride in the great men is marked. Every officer is proud to be a humble member of the same profession as Caesar, Hannibal, Marlborough, Napoleon, and Lee. A scientist will often have in his office pictures of Pasteur, Faraday, Newton, etc., as the case may be.

It is very, very common to see on the office walls autographed photographs of some of the distinguished modern scientists. It is common for members of the profession to read the biographies of their predecessors. Some of these biographies, notably those in military affairs, medicine, and natural science, have had a powerful influence on professional policy and ethics.

Esprit de corps and acceptance of great professional traditions start naturally from pride in professional heroes. It is easy and natural to be interested in fellow human beings who have struggled with the same problems as oneself. The great names in the sciences and in diplomacy demonstrate that it is not necessary to command an army or to carry out spectacular operations in order to become a professional hero.

This is an opportunity which the intelligence profession, except in covert operations, has overlooked. Much excellent intelligence work was done in World War II, for example, in both Combat and Strategic Intelligence. There is still time to obtain and to display officially at some intelligence headquarters autographed photographs of some of the recent outstanding figures. In any advanced study of Strategic Intelligence Production, some inclusion of the history and heroes of the profession is useful and inspirational just as it is in studying military science, law, engineering or any other profession.

Summary

In summary of this part of this study it is apparent that intelligence as a highly skilled and honorable profession is deficient in that it still lacks many attributes which other professions have found useful in building up both the skill and the honor. With effort on the part of members of the intelligence profession these deficiencies can be overcome.

We can at least describe this profession in the words which Sir Edward Bridges (94B) used to describe the upper levels of the British Civil Service as: "a calling essential in any state of affairs which I can foresee, and one of the most worthwhile, if also perhaps one of the least understood, of professions."

INTELLIGENCE—A PROFESSION WITH ONE CLIENT

One serious peculiarity of the intelligence profession in the United States is that there is only one possible client, namely the U. S. Government.

As a contrast, suppose I am an assistant professor of mechanical engineering at Cornell University. I put all my efforts into acquiring a high level of competence in this difficult profession. Suppose, for some reason, the dean of engineering has little confidence in my ability. In that case, with moderate effort, I can transfer to a position as assistant professor of mechanical engineering at Columbia, or at some other university, or as a mechanical engineer in any one of a thousand positions in industry.

In moving I need not discard any of the professional competence which I have acquired at Cornell. If I have some professional reputation arising from articles published, inventions, or engineering achievements, *all of this reputation* goes with me as an asset in my new position.

There is small excuse for a person feeling frozen or frustrated in other professions. If he has real ability he should lose little and may gain much by moving to a position where his abilities will be better appreciated.

How different is the situation of the intelligence officer! Suppose I have put all my efforts into obtaining a high degree of competence in intelligence production. Suppose I have prepared the first drafts of various high grade intelligence papers in my own field for many years. Suppose that for personal or other reasons my supervisor takes a different view of intelligence from mine. Suppose he does not like me personally. In contrast to those in almost any other profession, I cannot change employers and still remain in my profession. I have built up no outside professional reputation. I cannot exhibit to prospective new employers Top Secret examples of my work.

If I change to some occupation other than intelligence, I jettison the professional intelligence competence which I have built up with so much effort and pride for so many years.

A BRITISH PARALLEL

During part of World War II, the British statesman, Duff Cooper, was the head of the British Ministry of Information. His illuminating description of this ministry (98) covers some of the peculiarities just mentioned for intelligence activities. I quote only a few sentences. Describing the make-up of his ministry, which might be taken as a description of some U. S. intelligence organization, he says:

> Ex-ambassadors . . . abounded, the brightest ornaments of the Bar were employed on minor duties . . . and all were prepared to work at any hour . . . in their enthusiasm for the cause.
>
> . . . The main defect was that there were too few ordinary civil servants in it, and too many brilliant amateurs. The word I got most used to hearing and most to dislike was "frustration." Day after day admirable, although temporary, officials would come to me to offer their resignation. And in every case they wanted to leave because their work was being frustrated. They had conceived some brilliant idea and put it forward to their official superior, who had either turned it down flat or else altered it in such a way as to destroy its usefulness. Had they been regular civil servants they would have been neither surprised nor aggrieved, but not being accustomed to such treatment they were astonished and indignant.

As a practical matter I do not agree with Cooper's implied remedy. He *almost* says that things would have been better if the ministry had had fewer workers who really cared whether they accomplished anything or not. Saying that the ministry would have profited by more regular civil servants who "would have been neither surprised nor aggrieved" to have their ideas turned down is reminiscent of the so-called Tenth Beatitude: "Blessed are they who expect little, for they shall get what they expect."

Perhaps a better remedy for the Ministry of Information and for intelligence organizations is to retain the originality and enthusiasm of the workers, but to temper this by a more *wide-spread understanding of the intelligence process as a whole,* and of the part which each individual must play in his organization. Such general understanding starts preferably with intellectual leadership at the top. It can be fostered by discussions at many levels. The present book may facilitate such discussions and promote the necessary understanding. Such an understanding clears away many irritations and promotes esprit de corps.

PECULIARITIES—SECURITY RESTRICTIONS AND RIGID BARRIERS

Much about intelligence methods and intelligence production must always be more or less secret. This will necessarily offer some restrictions on activities. Some of these restrictions are a necessary nuisance. It is important that the intelligence officer should understand this and accept it.

Publications with Authors' Names Attached

Some of the security restrictions are difficult to justify, however. Some of them have a seriously detrimental effect upon vital intelligence activities. Such restrictions could apparently be modified so that we would be .01% less secure, but 50% less handicapped in some vital activities.

One example is the matter of attaching to an intelligence paper the names of the principal authors. Attaching the name of the author to a paper has acted as a stimulus to good work in the case of scholarly and popular books and magazine articles. It is becoming ever more common in the case of feature newspaper articles, and has had an important effect in raising standards of journalism. Names are attached to State Department dispatches. Attaching the names to classified papers, as published within the Intelligence Community, would have a similar beneficial effect upon intelligence officers.

In case the names of authors appear on a paper, it would still go out, as at present, as an official publication bearing the authority of the office, agency or other organization which issued it. The name of the principal author (and of junior authors, if any) would be attached as a matter of information.

Ignorance of Reader Reaction and of Ultimate Use of Intelligence Papers

In all other professions the author has some means for gauging reader reaction. This may be from total sales of a book, from requests for reprints of an article, or from letters received favorable or unfavorable—often offering valuable comments. In Strategic Intelligence papers with the author's name removed, all of this guidance and inspiration is denied to the author. (Incidentally, helpful correspondence with the author is denied to the reader also.)

Here the contrast with combat intelligence is marked. In combat you are in constant personal contact with your primary users, namely the commanding general and staff of the unit to which you are assigned. You have frequent contacts with your secondary users, namely the higher, lower and adjacent units to which your intelligence papers go. You hear promptly, and in no uncertain terms—sometimes in a matter of minutes—whether your oral presentation is satisfactory. You see your written estimates specifically confirmed or disproved in a matter of days. If according to your estimate "light resistance is to be expected" for the coming attack by your unit, everyone soon knows whether you were right or wrong. The score may be expressed in human lives.

In Strategic Intelligence this stimulus to good work, and this healthy and prompt criticism of work which is unsatisfactory (or even which is as good as possible, but is *considered* unsatisfactory), is lacking. Strategic Intelligence analysts almost never see the primary users of their papers.

Finally a thoughtful student of intelligence has said that the greatest stimulus to an intelligence officer is the satisfaction of seeing his intelligence paper *used,* either directly or indirectly as the basis of policy or action.

In combat intelligence this satisfaction occurs regularly. Artillery shells are poured onto targets where *your* reports indicate enemy concentrations. Tactics are directly influenced by *your* estimates of the enemy capabilities. On the other hand, a Strategic Intelligence paper usually has many echelons of review through which it must pass after it leaves the original author or analyst before it reaches its primary user; namely the "ultimate consumer" in the National Security Council. The upper echelons of edit and review have probably never even heard the name of the original author.

WHY BE AN INTELLIGENCE OFFICER?

We have discussed in this book the duties of an officer engaged in Strategic Intelligence Production. The advantages and disadvantages of intelligence *as a profession* have been covered in the present chapter. In the light of all that has been said, why should anyone spend his time as an intelligence officer?

Perhaps the answer to the whole question can best be summed up by the following:

Some years ago, I was talking with a mechanical engineer who had been a railroad employee for 40 years. I asked him what he thought of a railroad career as he looked back upon it. He said with great conviction: "Well, there's nothing in it, *unless you love railroading.*" (which he obviously did).

A similar statement may be made about a career in Strategic Intelligence (or in many other professions). For the best men, for those who have their hearts in their work: *There's nothing in it, unless you love intelligence.*

EPILOGUE

SOME CLOSING CONCLUSIONS ON STRATEGIC INTELLIGENCE PRODUCTION

What general conclusions about Strategic Intelligence Production may be drawn from this book as a whole?

First, *General Principles:* Intelligence, like other professions, has its own general principles and its own point of view. For the intelligence officer, these are worth learning.

Usefulness is the governing principle. To this principle timeliness is always a corollary. The Search for Significance is vital.

The other general principles, as summed up in the Nine Principles of Intelligence, afford a useful background for all intelligence production. (Chapter II)

Second, *The Intellectual Process:* Intelligence production is essentially an intellectual process. Systematic study and research into fundamental principles and methods and into conditions most favorable to productive intellectual activity is rewarding. (Chapters III and IV)

Third, *Social Sciences:* Much can be learned from the social sciences which is directly helpful in intelligence. (Chapter V)

Fourth, *Intelligence Tools:* From the above mentioned general principles and background studies, definite methods and intelligence tools can be constructed which are specifically helpful in intelligence problems. Of all such problems, none is of more importance than piercing the Fog of the Future by improved methods of forecasting. (Chapter VII)

Fifth, *Questions:* Some insistent questions are raised to which each intelligence officer must find his own answers. Is the standard scientific method helpful in intelligence? Is there a "national character"? How foreign are foreigners?

Sixth, *Graduate Study:* Intelligence Production is an immature profession. Progress so far has been more by trial and error, rather than by systematic study. There are no graduate courses in the profession, and almost no research into methods. However, each intelligence officer, by using the leads here given, can lay out graduate studies for himself at home. If several officers can work together, there is no limit to the progress they can make. (Chapter VIII)

Finally, *Warning:* Intelligence is a profession full of peculiarities and difficulties. (Chapter VIII) It has only one client. Those who enter it face all of the hardships and handicaps of the pioneer in any field.

Be warned, there is nothing in it,

unless you love Intelligence.

APPENDIX A

THE PETER-THE-GREAT APPROACH

All human activities have their roots in the past. The past is indeed a part of the present. Students of current affairs who have a vivid sense of the historical background of current situations possess a valuable asset for correct understanding.

Consideration for the past can be carried to extremes. An example is that of Admiral King of the U. S. Navy, who played such a distinguished part in the naval operations of World War II. He was asked to write a book on those naval battles in which he participated, and to show the *basis for the decisions* which he made so successfully in combat. The resulting book, however, was in effect a complete life of Admiral King describing at length his training at the Naval Academy, and his various assignments throughout his whole career. Naval combat operations occupy only a limited part of the book and not the predominant position originally intended. (99)

On being asked why he gave so much space to the early years instead of emphasizing the factors which influenced his decisions in battle, the Admiral, according to the reviewer of his book, replied that everything in his life—all his Academy training and all his former naval experience—had an influence on his final decisions in battle.

Theoretically the Admiral was correct. His statement, in fact, raises some interesting questions in psychology. Practically, however, he was wrong. He has included so much background that he has weakened the interest of his book.

So, in intelligence production. It is desirable for the intelligence officer personally to have an understanding of the history of countries under discussion, and a knowledge of the history of the specific situations with which he is concerned. However, he does not necessarily have to include the details of all of this in an intelligence paper. Or he may do so in two or three sentences and then plunge into the existing situation.

When the writer's time is short, it is seldom wise to devote much space in an intelligence paper to details of historical development. When the reader's time is limited, which it always is, it is nearly always unwise to ask him to read much history, however interesting. A sentence or two to sum up the general historical background, a statement that the traditions upon which present activities are founded run back to such a person and date, and a reference to a good source of further historical information are usually all that are justified.

Yet there are many authors who find it almost impossible to begin any reference to Russian science, for example, without starting with Peter the Great, and tracing Russian scientific activities all the way through from Czar Peter to the present.[1] For most current situations in Russian science, the influence of Peter the Great is one of the factors, but Peter and all of his successors do not have to appear in person in the paper. There is no logical place to stop when tracing back the historical background or the theoretical foundations for a paper. No intelligence paper can ever be "complete" in this respect. No author of an intelligence paper should ever even try to make it so. The stopping point for background and for foundations is set by common sense and not by logic.

Due to shortages of time, the objective of the writer should usually be to see in how few words he can present the high spots of the historical background. Some analysts are so haunted by the ghost of Peter and other worthy historic persons that they have to skimp on the present.

[1] I find that Carl Becker (100) outdoes me in giving to William the Conqueror the position as a starting point which I here accord to Peter the Great. He even mentions students who, in describing the fall of a current administration in France, begin the paper with the fall of the Roman Empire.

APPENDIX B

VARIED STATEMENTS OF AMERICAN NATIONAL CHARACTER

It is suggested that the reader interested in understanding the limits of national character statements and studies, read a dozen or so of them on a single national group. A list of works on the American mind, national character, or spirit is appended to facilitate this research. The list is not exhaustive, nor is it particularly selective; equally valid listings could be made of other authors. It is hoped, however, that a sampling among these titles will give the reader a real feeling for the variety, achievements, and inadequacies of these works and the necessity of using his critical judgment when reading them.

Adams, James Truslow. *The American.* 1943.

Baldwin, James Mark. *French and American Ideals.* 1913.

Breckinridge, Robert J. *A Discourse on the Formation and Development of the American Mind.* 1837.

Brogan, Denis William. *The American Character.* 1944.

Brooks, Van Wyck. *Three Essays on America.* 1934.

Brown, Elijah. *The Real America.* 1913.

Brownell, William Crary. *Democratic Distinction in America.* 1927.

Butler, Nicholas Murray. *The American As He is.* 1908

Canby, Henry Seidel. *Everyday Americans.* 1920.

Collier, Price. *America and the Americans from a French Point of View.* 1897.

Commager, Henry Steele, ed. *America in Perspective. The United States Through Foreign Eyes.* 1947.

Commager, Henry Steele. *The American Mind. An Interpretation of American Thought and Character since the 1880's.* 1950.

Dowd, Jerome. *Democracy in America.* 1921.

Fay, Bernard, and Claflin, Avery. *The American Experiment.* 1929.

Francis, Alexander. *Americans, an Impression.* 1909.

Gorer, Geoffrey. *The American People. A Study in National Character.* 1948.

Mead, Margaret. *And Keep Your Powder Dry.* 1942.

Munsterberg, Hugo. *American Traits from the Point of View of a German.* 1902.

Nathan, George Jean, and Mencken, H. L. *The American Credo. A Contribution toward the Interpretation of the National Mind.* 1921.

Perry, Bliss. *The American Mind.* 1912.

de Tocqueville, Alexis. *Democracy in America.* 1835.

Turner, Frederick J. *The Frontier in American History.* 1920.

West, James. *Plainville, U. S. A.* 1945.

BIBLIOGRAPHY

General comments regarding our approach to the preparation of the bibliography appear in Chapter I. The bibliography is divided by chapters.

All publications listed have been numbered in order to facilitate cross reference. However, not all publications have been quoted or specifically mentioned in the text.

For completeness, we repeated here the titles of the three books and articles suggested for general reading, and mentioned in our comments on bibliography in Chapter I:

(1) WHITEHEAD, ALFRED NORTH, *The Aims of Education,* New York, Macmillan, 1929. Published also as a Mentor Book by New American Library of World Literature, 1949.

(2) GOTTSCHALK, LOUIS, *Understanding History, A Primer of Historical Method,* New York, Knopf, 1954. Specific principles of intelligence production can be gained by substituting "intelligence" for "history" in this text. One of the most helpful and readable books.

(3) DRISCOLL, J. M. AND HYNEMAN, C. S., *Methodology for Political Scientists: Perspective for Study*. Amer. Political Science Review 49 (1955), pp. 192-217.

A major difficulty arises from the following situation. Each newcomer to the field of intelligence production arrives with whatever knowledge of philosophy, logic, mathematics, or social and natural sciences he happens to have. He would be a better Strategic Intelligence officer if he had greater competence in *all* of these subjects.

Now it is evident that he can seldom take a formal advanced course in any of the above subjects at this stage in his career, although he *can* improve himself in any of them by home study. It is *not* so evident, however, that most of the advanced books which he would find on philosophy, logic, mathematics, etc., would be found "spitefully formidable," and so would discourage him before he started.

Hence the peculiar need for a bibliography like the present one. In contrast to the bibliography of a book on chemistry for chemists, this is the bibliography of books on Strategic Intelligence for those who are certainly not experts in philosophy *and* mathematics *and* economics, for example. The aim of the bibliography is to assist and not to repel the ambitious and busy intelligence officer. So the object here is to point out books and articles sufficiently advanced to be worth-while, but chosen from that selected few which are readable, interesting and within the grasp of the ambitious amateur in each field.

BIBLIOGRAPHY FOR CHAPTER I

One of the writers of history whose ideas are often applicable to intelligence is Trevelyan who is quoted several times in this volume.

(4) TREVELYAN, G. M., *Clio a Muse, and Other Essays,* London, Longmans, Green, 1913, p. 173.

(5) KENT, SHERMAN, *Strategic Intelligence,* Princeton, Princeton Univ. Press, 1949.

This book is essential for any worker in this field. It contains many thoughtful discussions and many cogent phrases. It bears reading and rereading.

(6) PETTEE, GEORGE S., *Future of American Secret Intelligence,* Washington, Infantry Journal Press, 1946, contains many useful concepts for Strategic Intelligence. In spite of the title, it is not focused on the secret aspects.

The principles of combat intelligence are simpler and better understood than any others. They make easy reading because they are so clear cut. Many of the combat intelligence principles are equally applicable to all forms of intelligence.

One of the first books in this field after World War I by an American officer and one of the best worth reading for general principles is:

(7) SCHWIEN, E. E., *Combat Intelligence,* Washington, Infantry Journal Press, 1936. Gives case histories from W. W. I. Opposes any attempted statement of enemy intentions or probable courses

of action. Well worth reading by any student of intelligence principles.

The Army has a whole series of Field Manuals touching on combat intelligence of which the basic one is:

(8) FM-30-5, *Combat Intelligence.*

(9) GLASS, R. R., and DAVIDSON, P. B., *Intelligence Is for Commanders,* Harrisburg, Military Service Pub. Co., 1948.

An elementary, readable and well-presented statement of combat intelligence, with examples, maps and forms. Excellent within these limits. Many of the clear and simple principles of combat intelligence make firm starting points for an understanding of Strategic Intelligence.

(10) GIBSON, R. E., *Some Implications of Scientific Research,* Johns Hopkins Magazine, 6 (April 1955) 8.

BIBLIOGRAPHY FOR CHAPTER II

(11) MORISON, S. E., *Admiral of the Ocean Sea: A Life of Christopher Columbus,* Boston, Litle, Brown, 1942.

(12) HIGHET, GILBERT, *Juvenal the Satirist,* New York, Oxford Univ. Press, 1955.

(13) TOWNLEY, K. A., *Clarity in Geological Writing,* Science 121 (1955) 537, 2 April 1955.

(13A) LORD STRANG, *Home and Abroad,* London, André Deutsch, 1956.

BIBLIOGRAPHY FOR CHAPTER III

This is the first chapter in Part II. This part covers intelligence production as an intellectual process. If one wished to look into the fundamental philosophy upon which knowledge and constructive intellectual efforts rests, Chapters III and IV would be a good place to start. For this purpose the bibliography on "Methodology for Political Scientists" already referred to will be found particularly useful. (3)

For consideration we suggest:

(14) BENJAMIN, HAROLD, *An Introduction to Human Problems,* Boston, Houghton-Mifflin, 1930.

(15) Cohen, Morris R., *Reason and Nature: An Essay on the Meaning of Scientific Method,* New York, Harcourt, Brace, 2nd ed., 1953.

A good introductory text in sematics is:

(16) Lee, Irving, *Language Habits in Human Affairs,* New York, Harper, 1941.

A good theoretical discussion of some of the problems connected with getting the meaning out of facts is:

(17) Furfey, P. H., *The Scope and Method of Sociology,* New York, Harper, 1953.

Contains valuable chapters on logic, heuristic and productive thinking which are not confined to sociology.

Underlying the present book is a firm conviction that in the social sciences (of which we consider intelligence production to be one) "by taking time out to examine questions of methodology, the period of fumbling and stumbling can be appreciably shortened." This is a hope quoted by Driscoll and Hyneman (loc. cit.).

A good modern book is:

(18) Goode, Wm. J. and Hatt, P. K., *Methods in Social Research,* New York, McGraw-Hill, 1952.

References to many publications which might be considered at this place have been reserved for other chapters of Part II, especially Chapter IV.

(19) Meade, Margaret and Metraux, Rhoda, Editors, *The Study of Culture at a Distance,* Chicago, University of Chicago Press, 1953.

(20) Thomson, Sir J. A., *Introduction to Science,* New York, Holt, 1911, and *The Outline of Science,* New York, Putnam, 1922.

(21) Gee, Wilson, *Social Science Research Methods,* New York, Appleton-Century-Crofts, Inc., 1950.

(22) Conant, J. B., *Modern Science and Modern Man,* New York, Columbia University Press, 1952.

(10) Gibson, R. E., loc. cit.

(23) Ruby, Lionel, *The Art of Making Sense,* Philadelphia, Lippincott, 1954.

For ideas connected with the interpretation and writing of history which are useful also in intelligence production see, besides Gottschalk (2) already quoted:

(24) Kent, Sherman, *Writing History,* New York, Appleton-Century-Crofts, Inc., 1947.

(25) *Harvard Guide to American History,* Cambridge, Harvard Univ. Press, 1954, especially the general introductory sections on the Nature of History, Theory of Historical Interpretations and even Methods of Note Taking.

BIBLIOGRAPHY FOR CHAPTER IV

(26) Poincare', Henri, *Science et Methode,* Paris, 1920.

(27) Bancroft, W. D., *The Methods of Research,* Rice Institute Pamphlet, 15, 1928, 167-286.

(28) Platt, W., and Baker, R. A., *The Relation of the Scientific Hunch to Research,* Jour. Chem. Education, 8 (1931), 1969-2002.

(29) Rossman, J., *The Psychology of the Inventor,* Washington, Washington Inventors' Publishing Co., 1931.

(30) Polya, G., *How to Solve It,* Princeton, Princeton Univ. Press, 1945. Full of stimulating ideas.

(31) Conant, J. B., *On Understanding Science,* New Haven, Yale Univ. Press, 1947.

(32) Beveridge, W. I. B., *The Art of Scientific Investigation,* New York, Norton, 1951.

(33) James, Wm., *Pragmatism,* New York, Longmans, 1907. The pragmatic point of view makes a sound start for the intelligence officer.

(34) Dewey, John, *How We Think,* Boston, Heath, 1910.

(35) Humphrey, Geo., *Directed Thinking,* New York, Dodd, Mead, 1948. Excellent but elementary.

(36) Wallas, Graham, *The Art of Thought,* New York, Harcourt, Brace, 1926. Readable and useful.

(37) Lowes, J. L., *Road to Xanadu; A Study in the Ways of the Imagination,* Boston, Houghton Mifflin, 1927.

(38) Osborn, A. F., *Applied Imagination, Principles and Procedures of Creative Thinking,* New York, Scribners, 1953.

(39) Holmes, O. W., *Mechanism in Thought and Morals,* Boston, Osgood, 1871.

(39A) Ruger, H. A., *Psychology of Efficiency,* New York, Science Press, 1910.

(39B) Bentley, I. M., *The Field of Psychology,* New York, Appleton-Century-Crofts, Inc., 1924.

(39C) Poffenberger, A. T., *Applied Psychology; Its Principles and Methods,* New York, Appleton-Century-Crofts, Inc., 1927.

(39D) Woodward, R. S., *Psychology,* New York, Holt, 1929.

(39E) Benger, E. D., *The Organization of Industrial Research,* Ind. Eng. Chem. 22 (1930) 572.

(40) Charteris, J., *Field Marshall Earl Haig,* New York, Scribners, 1929.

For an excellent brief statement of creative thinking which presents the same factors differently classified see:

(40A) Kent, Allen, *Literature Research as a Tool for Creative Thinking,* a paper presented before the Special Libraries Assn., 4 June 1956. Obtainable from School of Library Science, Western Reserve Univ., Cleveland, Ohio.

(41) Robinson, J. H., *Mind in the Making,* New York, Harper, 1921. Contains many stimulating passages.

(42) Cros, Pierre, et al, *Imagination—Undeveloped Resource.* New York, Creative Thinking Associates, Box 913, Grand Central Station, New York 17, N. Y., 1955.

(43) Platt, Washington, *Organization of Industrial Research,* Ind. Eng. Chem. 21 (1929) 655.

Some other good readable references containing ideas on the logical and intellectual problems of research which can be applied to intelligence research are:

(44) Wilson, E. B. Jr., *An Introduction to Scientific Research,* New York, McGraw-Hill, 1952.

(45) Burtt, E. A., *Right Thinking,* New York, Harper, 1946. Discusses formal reasoning, probability, end-judgments, the criteria of evidence, etc. Good critical bibliography.

(46) Smith, H. B., *How the Mind Falls into Error.* From First Book in Logic, New York, Appleton-Century-Crofts, 2nd ed., 1938. Many original examples.

(47) Holmes, R. W., *The Rhyme of Reason,* New York, Appleton-Century-Crofts, 1939. An unusually readable statement.

Some references on the value of conferences and discussions in the development of ideas are:

(48) COOPER, A. M., *How to Conduct Conferences,* New York, McGraw-Hill, 1946.

(49) STRAUSS, B. and F., *New Ways to Better Meetings,* New York, Viking Press, 1951.

On the general subject of creative thinking there is nothing better than:

(49A) CURTIS, CHAS. P. JR., and GREENSLET, F., *The Practical Cogitator,* Boston, Houghton, Mifflin, 1950.

BIBLIOGRAPHY FOR CHAPTER V

(21) GEE, WILSON, op. cit.

(50) CHASE, STUART, *The Proper Study of Mankind: An Inquiry into the Science of Human Relations,* New York, Harper, 1948 (Quoted by Gee).

(51) COHEN, MORRIS R., *The Social Sciences and the Natural Sciences* in Ogburn and Goldenweiser, The Social Sciences and their Interrelationships. Boston, Houghton, Mifflin, 1927. (Quoted by Gee.)

(6) PETTEE, G. S., op. cit.

(52) YOUNG, KIMBALL, *An Introductory Sociology,* New York, Amer. Book Co., 1934.

(52A) BROWN, L. G., *Social Psychology,* New York, McGraw-Hill, 1934.

(53) DAMINOS, PIERRE, *The Notebooks of Major Thompson,* New York, Knopf, 1955.

(54) MUNRO, WM. B., *Political Science,* in Edgar Dawson, Teaching Social Studies, New York, Macmillan, 1928. (Quoted by Gee.)

(54A) FRANKEL, CHARLES, *The Case for Modern Man,* New York, Harper, 1956.

(54B) FARAGO, LADISLAS, *War of Wits,* New York, Funk and Wagnalls, 1954.

The question "Does History Repeat Itself?" is still being debated specifically or by implication. See for example:

(4) Trevelyan, op. cit. From his article first published somewhat differently in Independent Review, 1904.

(55) BEARD, C. A., *Political Science* in Gee, Wilson, Editor, Research in the Social Sciences, New York, Macmillan, 1929.

(56) MULLER, H. J., *Uses of the Past, Profiles of Former Societies,* New York, Oxford Univ. Press, 1952. A most stimulating study of the meaning of history. His chapters 2 and 11 have much meaning for the intelligence officer.

(57) BROSS, I. D. J., *Design for Decision,* New York, Macmillan, 1953.

Only when the original question is clarified does the answer become clear and useful in intelligence.

(58) LAZARSFELD, P. F. and ROSENBERG, MORRIS, Editors, *The Language of Social Research, a Reader in Methodology,* Glencoe, Ill., Free Press, 1955.

(59) FRYE, A. M. and LEVI, A. W., *Rational Belief,* New York, Harcourt Brace, 1941. (Quoted by Gee.)

See also stimulating remarks by Gottschalk, loc. cit., for example pages 264-5.

Two additional highly rewarding articles are:

(59A) STERN, ALFRED, *Science and the Philosopher,* Amer. Scientist, 44 (1956) 281.

(59B) KARTMAN, LEO, *Metaphorical Appeals in Biological Thought,* Amer. Scientist 44 (1956) 296.

(60) BERNARD, L. L., quoted in *Research Methods and Procedure in Agricultural Economics,* Social Sci. Research Council, New York, 1928.

(60A) JEROME, JEROME K., *Three Men on a Bummel,* London, Arrowsmith, 1900.

(61) KLINEBERG, OTTO, *A Science of National Character,* Jour. Social Psychology 19 (1944) p. 147-62.

(62) VALENTIN, VEIT, *The German People, Their History and Civilization from the Holy Roman Empire to the Third Reich,* New York, Knopf, 1946.

(63) COMMAGER, H. S., *The American Mind, Thought and Character Since the 1880's,* New Haven, Yale Univ. Press, 1950.

(64) SANTAYANA, GEO. *The Best in English Character* from *Soliquies in England,* quoted in Gentry, Summer Issue, 1953.

(65) BOUCHER, MAJ. GEN. C. H., *Infantry Tactics,* The Army Quarterly (Great Britain) July 1948, quoted in Military Review 29 (1949) p. 97.

(66) NICOLSON, HAROLD, *The Evolution of Diplomatic Method,* New York, Macmillan, 1954.

See also:

(67) BARKER, SIR ERNEST, *National Character,* London, Methuen, 1948.

(68) POTTER, D. M., *People of Plenty,* Chicago Univ. Press, 1954, and Appendix B.

BIBLIOGRAPHY FOR CHAPTER VI

The general principles of the theory of probability or what may be called the probability point of view are useful for any one concerned with understanding the world around us whether physical or social. These principles do not require a knowledge of higher mathematics.

Unfortunately there is no one book that presents these principles adequately for the large non-mathematical audience which could use it. Each reader must pick up these basic principles here and there for himself from books and articles. The quest is interesting and worth the effort. Much of general interest helpful to the layman can be found in the introductions to books on probability and statistics—even those which are highly mathematical. Much as to point of view can be gained from such miscellaneous articles as those of Weaver and Cochran et al quoted below.

The remarks in the body of this chapter under "A Healthy Curiosity" are pertinent at this point.

The most helpful book on the elements of statistical analysis and the arithmetic of its basic calculations is:

(69) MORONEY, M. J. *Facts from Figures,* A Pelican Book, Baltimore, Penguin Books, 1953.

As a book which contains much on an advanced level which is applicable to the philosophy of intelligence see:

(70) RAPOPORT, ANATOL, *Operational Philosophy, Integrating Knowledge and Action,* New York, Harper, 1953.

Γhe two books named below help to eradicate the impression ıeld by many, that because an event is highly improbable, it is therefore interesting or significant.

(71) SCARNE, JOHN, and RAWSON, CLAYTON, *Scarne on Dice,* Copyright by John Scarne and Clayton Rawson, 1945.

(72) WEAVER, WARREN, *Probability, Rarity, Interest and Surprise,* Sci. Monthly 67 (1948) 390.

Other useful references are:

(73) HUFF, DARRELL, *How to Lie with Statistics,* New York, Norton, 1954.

(74) LINDQUIST, E. F., *A First Course in Statistics,* Boston, Houghton, Mifflin, 1942. Useful as a book for home study.

(75) ——, *Study Manual for a First Course in Statistics,* Boston, Houghton, Mifflin, revised edition, 1942.

(76) NEISWANGER, W. A., *Elementary Statistical Methods, As Applied to Business and Economic Data,* New York, Macmillan, 1943.

(77) MOSTELLER, F. and BUSH, R. R., *Selected Quantitative Techniques,* from Lindzey, Handbook of Social Psychology, Reading, Cambridge, Mass., Addison-Wesley Pub. Co., 1954.

(78) SARGENT, F., *An Application of Statistics,* Science 121 (18 Mar '55) 402.

(79) COCHRAN, WM. G., MOSTELLER, FRED., TUKEY, J. W., *Principles of Sampling,* Jour. Amer. Statisitcal Ass'n. 49 (1954) pp. 13-35.

(80) JAMESON, LT. COL. M. M., *Probability and Atomic Support,* Military Review, Aug. 1955, p. 13.

(80A) WEAVER, H. G., *Thought Starter #31,* General Motors Corp., 1935.

(81) MORSE, P. M. and KIMBALL, G. E., *Methods of Operations Research,* New York and Boston, Wiley and Massachusetts Institute of Technology Press, 1951. Reprinted with their permission.

(82) GILMAN, S. I., COL., *Operations Research in the Army,* Military Review 36 (1956) 54.

For a more advanced discussion of Probability and for some excellent references see:

(83) NAGEL, ERNEST, *Principles of the Theory of Probability,* Chicago, Chicago Univ. Press, 1939.

BIBLIOGRAPHY FOR CHAPTER VII

(84) Smith, J. G., and Duncan, A J., *Elementary Statistics and Applications, Fundamentals of the Theory of Statistics,* New York, McGraw-Hill, 1944.

(85) Marshall, C. B., *The Limits of Foreign Policy,* New York, Holt, 1954.

A healthy criticism of many current methods of the social sciences, including methods for prediction, is given in:

(85A) Sorokin, P. A., *Fads and Foibles in Modern Sociology and Related Sciences,* Chicago, Regnery, 1956.

In his chapter on "Predictability and Scientific Theory" Sorokin summarizes his earlier writings on this subject. To summarize his summary, Sorokin believes that predictions in "Socio-cultural Phenomena" should be made by what he calls the "meaningful-causal principle." This recognizes three channels for cognition, "sensory, rational and supersensory–super-rational." He says: "A roughly adequate knowledge of psychosocial reality requires a concerted use of all three channels. . . . In the integrated utilization of all three channels, the knowledge obtained through one channel is supplemented and checked by the knowledge from the other two channels. This mutual checking is an additional insurance against the errors of one-channel knowledge, and an important guarantee of fuller validity for our cognition."

". . . So conceived, the integral study of the psychosocial world contains in itself all the main methods of investigating and understanding psychosocial reality: the empirical, the logic-mathematical and the intuitional. . . ."

Returning now to the application of all of the above to intelligence production, the key position of forecasting in this activity justifies the reader in consulting Sorokin's original papers, which illuminate and extend the meaning and usefulness of much of what is presented in the present book, especially Chapters IV, V, and VII.

(57) Bross, I. D. J., op. cit.

(86) Hodnett, Edward, *The Art of Problem Solving,* New York, Harper, 1955.

(86A) Schremp, Lt. Col. John E., *Military Problem Solving,* Military Review, Aug. 1956, p. 28.

(87) Sawyer, W. W., *Mathematician's Delight,* A Pelican Book, Baltimore, Penguin Books, 1943.

(88) Schmid, C. F., *Handbook of Graphic Presentation,* New York, Ronald Press, 1954.

(88A) Barton, A. H., *Think First,* Punch. 231 (1956) 105.

(89) Firestone, J. M., as summarized by L. L. Snyder in *Meaning of Nationalism,* New Brunswick, Rutgers University Press, 1954.

BIBLIOGRAPHY FOR CHAPTER VIII

In describing the vitality contributed to any intellectual effort by *active research into fundamentals,* no one is more eloquent than Whitehead already referenced and below. As an introduction to the Principles of Intelligence Production, no book could be better than Whitehead's, because of his constant encouragement of initiative, originality and imagination.

President Reed of Johns Hopkins University shows that many institutes "do not continue to thrive and keep their vitality unless provision is made within them for continuing graduate work." All of this only emphasizes the handicap experienced by the intelligence profession, as compared with other professions through the absence of lively, imaginative research into fundamentals and methods. See:

(90) Reed, L. J., *A Modern University in a Modern World,* Baltimore, Johns Hopkins University Press, 1954.

(91) Whitehead, A. N., *Adventures of Ideas,* New York, Macmillan, 1933, pp. 72-3.

(92) Metcalf, H. C. and Urwick, L., Editors, *Dynamic Administration, the Collected Papers of Mary Parker Follett,* New York, Harper, 1940.

Some additional light on professions in general is thrown at an elementary level by:

(93) Blanch, L. E. *Education for the Professions,* Washington, U.S. Department of Health, Education and Welfare, Sup't. of Documents, 1955.

(94) Military Review, *Diamond Jubilee of the Command and General Staff College Number,* May 1956, Fort Leavenworth, Kansas.

(94A) Quoted by Sawyer, W. W., op. cit.

(94B) Bridges, Sir Edward, *Portrait of a Profession, The Civil Service Tradition,* London, Cambridge Univ. Press, 1953.

The literature on education itself is of course limitless. Two references to the importance of research in stimulating good teaching on the higher level are:

(90) Reed, L. J., loc. cit.

(95) Holme, T. T., *Industrial Administration Looks to the Future,* Yale Scientific Magazine, Jan. 1956, page 15.

(96) Nicolson, Harold, *Evolution of Diplomatic Method,* London, Constable, 1954.

(87) Other references are quoted in Sawyer, W. W., op. cit.

(97) Swisher, Carl B., *Needed a Rededicated Supreme Court,* Johns Hopkins Magazine (April 1953). Well worth reading by anyone concerned with watering down statements to obtain concurrence.

(98) From the Book: Cooper, Duff, *Old Men Forget, An Autobiography,* New York, E. P. Dutton and Co., Inc., 1954.

BIBLIOGRAPHY FOR APPENDIX A

(99) King, Fleet Admiral E. J., and Whitehill, W. M., *Fleet Admiral King. A Naval Record,* New York, Norton, 1952.

(100) Becker, Carl, *Everyman His Own Historian,* New York, Appleton-Century-Crofts, Inc., 1935.

INDEX

Note: Numerals in parentheses refer to Bibliography listings.

DEPRECIATION IN VAL

A TACTICAL COMBAT INTELLIGE

B STRATEGIC INTELLIGENCE IN

C STRATEGIC INTELLIGENCE IN

D SEMIPERMANENT FEATURES
(roads, bridges, natural reso

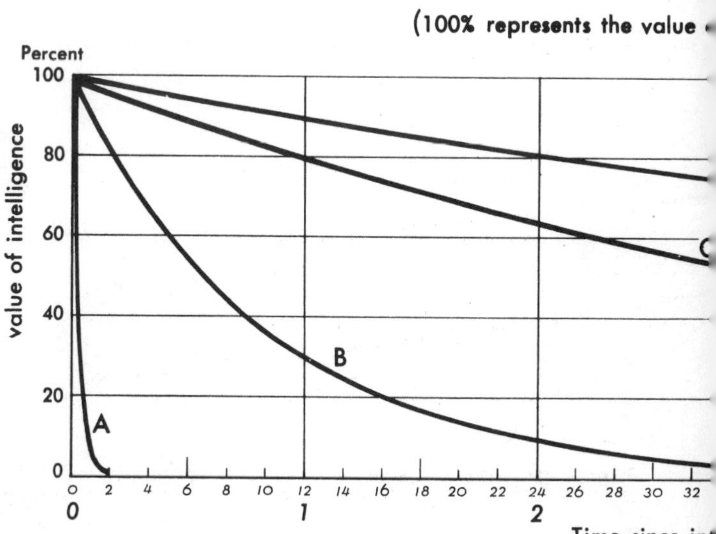